Worry

Worry

Controlling It and Using It Wisely

Edward M. Hallowell, M.D.

Pantheon Books • New York

Grateful acknowledgment is made to Harcourt Brace & Company for permission to reprint
excerpts from *Samuel Johnson* by Walter Jackson Bate. Copyright © 1977 by Walter Jackson
Bate. Reprinted by permission of Harcourt Brace & Company.

Library of Congress Cataloging-in-Publication Data
Hallowell, Edward M.
  Worry : controlling it and using it wisely / Edward M. Hallowell.
    p.   cm.
  Includes index.
  ISBN 0-679-44237-5
  1. Anxiety.   2. Worry.   I. Title.
  RC531.H263   1997
  616.85'223—dc21   97-8609
                                                 CIP

Random House Web Address: http://www.randomhouse.com/

Book design by Debbie Glasserman

Printed in the United States of America
First Edition
9 8 7 6 5 4 3 2 1

To Josselyn Bliss,
my cousin, but also sister, mother, friend, manager, agent,
editor, confidante, baby-sitter, problem solver, advisor,
and all-around improver of my life

Worry: *to strangle, throttle, kill by violence ... to seize by the throat and tear or lacerate, e.g., dogs or wolves attacking sheep*
Oxford English Dictionary

Contents

Preface

Excessive worry is an exhausting and dangerous problem for millions of Americans. People who worry a lot *suffer,* as do the people close to them. Some people worry so intensely that worry becomes much more than an annoyance: it hinders their work, their personal lives, or both. A recent survey of primary care physicians in the United States reported that at least *one-third* of office visits were prompted by some form of anxiety. Furthermore, over the course of a lifetime at least one in four people—25 percent of the population or some 65 million individuals—will meet the criteria for one or more of the medical conditions called "anxiety disorders," treatable disorders defined by the presence of debilitating worry.

Like high blood pressure, excessive worry can make you physically sick; it can even kill you. As Dr. Charles Mayo of the Mayo Clinic said years ago, "Worry affects circulation, the glands, the whole nervous system, and profoundly affects the heart. I have never known a man who died from overwork, but many who died from doubt."

Worry is a core component of numerous medical disorders and is central in many solvable, if not medically diagnosable, problems in life, such as excessive pessimism, timidity, procrastination, and under-achievement. The key to dealing with it is to acquire the knowledge that will allow you to approach worry as a problem you can *manage,* as opposed to suffering worry as if it were a miserable, immutable given.

The fact is that tens of millions of Americans suffer from some treatable kind of worry without knowing either that there is a medical name for what they are suffering from, or that there are affordable, practical treatments that can help them get over what they've got.

Worry is like blood pressure: you need a certain level to live, but too high a level can hurt you. Most people don't realize that worry, like blood pressure, can be regulated. In fact, we can use some of the same treatments we use for high blood pressure to reduce excessive worry, treatments such as meditation, exercise, stress reduction, dietary modi-fication, and certain medications. In addition, we now have various new treatments specifically designed for worry that are highly effective. Most of these do not involve medication, but even the medications we use now are safer and more effective than ever.

Each generation needs to update itself to keep abreast of new meth-ods for dealing with a problem as ubiquitous as worry. The best-selling book about worry in the last generation was Dale Carnegie's *How to Stop Worrying and Start Living: Time-Tested Methods for Conquering Worry.* The book originally had great appeal, but today's audiences might find its tone and suggestions somewhat naïve, and of course its scientific content is a bit out of date. While in some ways Carnegie's advice is timeless, a tremendous amount of new information has be-come available since 1944, the year the book was published.

Most people today are not aware of all that we have learned about worry in the last fifty-odd years. Although we have new knowledge, it spreads slowly, even in this age of instant access. People need to know how much we now understand about the treatable conditions that in-volve worry—such as depression, panic disorder, obsessive-compulsive disorder, generalized anxiety disorder, post-traumatic stress disorder, and attention deficit disorder, and they also have to learn about what we know concerning the ordinary worry of everyday life. The good news is that we know much more today than we did in Carnegie's time and we have practical methods of treatment that our parents' generation never heard of.

When worry becomes toxic it ceases to serve as the useful built-in alarm system nature meant it to be and becomes instead a painful problem in itself. As a car alarm system that won't shut off, our human alarm system can drive its owner crazy—and get him into trouble—when it won't silence itself.

Sufferers of excessive worry know they worry more than they need to, but they don't know how to stop. They suffer with worry as if it were inescapable. Although reassurance can help temporarily, people who worry too much require more than simple reassurance or some hearty exhortation to "buck up." They already know they should "buck up" and worry less; what they yearn to know is *how.* They need practical methods of extinguishing excessive worry, remedies that actually work, to reduce both the pain of worry and the tremendous damage worry can do at work and at home. At its worst, worry can be a relentless scavenger, roaming the corners of your mind, feeding on anything, never leaving you alone.

On the other hand, not *all* worry is bad. Effective planning depends on anticipating danger. This is worry at its best. Obliterating worry entirely, as, say, by using a drug, can be even more dangerous than worrying too much. The trick is to learn to *worry well,* at the right time, to the right degree.

Toxic worry is a disease of the imagination. It is insidious and invisible, like a virus. It sets upon you unwanted and unbidden, subtly stealing its way into your consciousness until it dominates your life. As worry infiltrates your mind, it diminishes your ability to enjoy your family, your friends, your physical being, and your achievements because you live in fear of what might go wrong. It undermines your ability to work, to love, and to play. It interferes with your starting a new task or even enjoying the completion of an old one.

There are many ways to field your worries with skill, and this book will describe a wide array of them. Some of the most dramatic involve medications. The advent of inhibitors of the reuptake of serotonin, such as Prozac and Zoloft, coupled with the development of new antianxiety medications, such as Buspar, Klonopin, and various beta-blockers, have given millions of people better lives. However, medication is not usually necessary in dealing with worry. This book will explore many of the highly effective nonmedication approaches now available. Some of these are ancient and time-tested, such as exercise, rest, reassurance, and humor. Some are old yet not in widespread use in this country, such as meditation and yoga. Some are in fact quite new and proving to be highly effective, such as cognitive-behavioral therapy and eye-movement desensitization and reprocessing. These—and many more—will be explained throughout the book.

These remedies build upon what we underestimated as recently as fifteen years ago: the biological, genetic underpinnings of various kinds of excessive worry. From the habitual worrier who torments himself by incessantly searching for what can go wrong in life, to the survivor of a traumatic past who is unable to let go of the pain, to the self-castigating perfectionist who lives in major fear of even minor failures, excessive worriers abound in all stations of life. We are only now, in the 1990s, which has been called "the decade of the brain," beginning to pinpoint what is happening in the nerve cells of the worrier, instead of just in his soul—what neurotransmitters might be to blame and what remedies might quiet the storm inside.

Indeed, the discovery of a gene implicated in producing chronic worriers made front-page news in the *New York Times* in November 1996. The paper reported on a study published in the prestigious journal *Science* linking a certain gene to individuals who are prone to anxiety, pessimism, and negative thinking. The gene involved was isolated and found to be a short version of what in other people is a longer gene—specifically, the SLC6A4 gene on chromosome 17q12. What does this mean? Put simply, you might be born a worrier! Of course, such studies mark just a beginning, small pieces of the very large puzzle of worry, but all the pieces help answer the age-old question of how to worry wisely.

The new research explores not only the biology of the brain and the physical nature of worry. It also looks into the psychology of worry.

For too many centuries we have been sidetracked by debates about nature versus nurture, genetics versus life experience. The approach that makes sense is to embrace what we know about both body and mind, nature and nurture.

I originally became interested in the subject of worry from my work with people suffering from attention deficit disorder (ADD), a neurological condition that involves a wandering of attention, which is often accompanied by excessive worrying. However, more and more I began to hear from patients who did not have ADD that they, too, were plagued by one form or another of excessive worry, to such a degree that it hurt and compromised their daily activities.

On the other end of the spectrum, I treated some high-risk takers who didn't worry enough! *Some* worry is necessary. After all, the refusal to worry constitutes a serious problem in its own right, commonly called denial.

It is essential to distinguish among the different kinds of worry, and this book points out ways of recognizing each of them. Broadly speaking, there is, on the one hand, adaptive worry—wise worry that alerts you to real danger and, on the other hand, there is maladaptive worry—unwise worry that serves no useful purpose and can hamper your life. Further, among the toxic forms of worry we can identify different types. First, there is the toxic worry that accompanies certain underlying treatable conditions that are often genetically transmitted, such as depression or generalized anxiety disorder or hyperthyroidism. Then there is the worry that life may inflict through some tragedy or trauma. Finally, there is the toxic worry of the habitual worrier, who seems to have learned from the air he breathes to worry always and everywhere no matter what. He doesn't meet the diagnostic criteria of any actual medical or psychiatric disorder but he suffers nonetheless. We need to help not only those who suffer from severe worry but also those people who are doing fine in life but still know that they worry too much for their own good. No one should be beset by legions of worries night and day trooping in out of the dark recesses of their imaginations like carpenter ants, eager to eat away the foundations of their lives.

. . .

This book is filled with stories. All of the examples and anecdotes are drawn from real life. Some of them are presented without any changes in identifying details, and these are noted as such in the text. However, I have changed the names and identifying details of most of the individuals described. My heartfelt thanks go to all those people who generously gave of themselves so that the examples in this book would be both vivid and helpful.

—Edward M. Hallowell

Part I

The World of Worry

1 When Life Feels More Threatening Than It Should

Worry gives a small thing a big shadow.

Swedish proverb

How much worry is "excessive"? Let me give an example from my own life. Not long ago I was giving a lecture at Cambridge Hospital, a teaching hospital affiliated with Harvard Medical School. The people who come to these lectures can be quite critical, so the presenter tries to be on his or her toes.

I was "on" that day and gave a good talk. When it was over and the applause died down, my old teacher, Dr. Leston Havens, shook my hand and told me the talk was "superb." He told me I should feel proud. And I did . . . for about as long as it takes a light bulb to fade after you flick off the switch.

Why was it that at the very moment Dr. Havens was shaking my hand, I picked out the face of a woman at the back of the room who was scowling at me? My eyes connected with hers, and her scowling face stuck in my mind as if it were a poisonous dart. As I left the lecture hall, that face overwhelmed my mind. Rather than feeling the gentle warmth of a job well done, I felt a chill rising within me instead.

3

What was the meaning of that scowl, I wondered to myself. *Why had that woman looked so disapprovingly at me? What had I done wrong? And what bad thing would happen to me as a result?*

This kind of worry surfaces fast, like a diver coming up too quickly from the deep, and, like the bends, it puts the mind and body into a toxic state. As my heart pounded, my mind raced to identify the woman and to catalogue all the possible causes of my having upset her. For the life of me I couldn't place her face . . . although perhaps it rang a distant bell? I couldn't say. As to how I might have upset her, who knew? It is all but impossible to give a lecture and not offend someone. I understood this and yet still I picked at my brain, trying to remember every anecdote, illustration, joke, and exclamation I had used in the lecture. How might I have misspoken? What could I have said wrong? As I reconstructed my lecture, I could recall no offensive word or phrase, even by the most picayune standard. *But why did I care?*

This is stupid, I told myself, trying to shut me up. You can't please everyone in any audience. That woman probably wasn't scowling at you. Maybe she had thought of some odious chore she had to do later that day, and it had made her scowl to think of it. Or maybe she was having a hard day or was just one of those people who scowls all the time. And even if she was scowling at you, *so what?* You didn't do anything wrong. If she was upset with you, which is unlikely, that's her problem. With that spry thought I drove on, happily putting her out of my mind.

For about three minutes. At the next stoplight she burst back into my mind like a summons-server breaking down my back door. *What had I done wrong,* I asked myself again desperately. *Was she going to try to attack me in some way, maybe sue me?*

The face haunted me for the rest of the day, darting in and out of my mind uncontrollably. This worry had become totally irrational and out of proportion to any viable reality. It made no sense. I should have been able to put it out of my mind and focus my energy on real issues. But I could not do it. As it turned out, of course, I never did hear from the woman with the scowl again, or even ever see her. By taking a little drop of reality and turning it into an ocean of worry, I had created the danger she represented to me. My problem is that I can find a scowl like that anywhere. I could probably find such a face at the entrance to paradise if I looked hard enough.

This is excessive worry. It happens to otherwise normal people, like me and many millions of others. Is there any way to stop it? Rational admonitions, however well-meaning, usually don't work. For example, such often-heard phrases as: "Gee, you don't need to worry, you look great!" "Honey, everything will be fine. We are not about to go broke." "There really is no reason to obsess about your boss. He just told you that you were doing a great job!" "Truly, that mole on your back is *not* malignant melanoma. How many times does Dr. Jones have to tell you that?" "Your presentation is going to go great. Just don't worry so much about it!" get no farther into the psyche of the worrier than if they were spoken in Martian.

These heartfelt exhortations don't penetrate because the mind of the worrier, in an effort to anticipate danger or stave off some bad outcome, has gone into a spasm, a lock that can't relax and accept good news. The mind can't let go of the matter at hand and can't see it in any but a negative way. Hours, whole days, weeks, or even years can be poisoned by ruminating on a single fear, one predominating worry.

We now have good evidence that there is actually a physical basis for this kind of worrying—that the caudate nucleus or another one of the brain's "switching stations" gets stuck, as a muscle in a cramp, and does not physically allow a particular worry to subside.

It does not take a disastrous event to create such a "cramp." Although my worry that day would not let up and my brain's switching stations had got stuck, the event that set off the spasm was trivial. Even I knew that it should not have mattered. But what happens when the event is not minor, when it is in fact traumatic? Then an additional biological process kicks in and it can make worry horrific. The body sends out various hormones, neurotransmitters, and other substances in response to trauma, which make the worry "burn" itself into the brain, and the brain's physical state actually changes. The combination of trauma and worry can in fact permanently alter one's brain chemistry. An individual can change from a confident risk-taker to a skittish, guarded, melancholy person over the course of a few months. Some pain can last forever. But the good news is that we have effective treatments. The brain can always change back.

Most excessive worriers need new methods of handling perceived danger. Some of these methods can benefit all of us. Some are specifically formulated for particular forms of worry. People worry in a wide variety of ways. I have learned there is not one kind of worry, but many. A look at some of the worriers I have worked with in my office illustrates this point.

Ben Miller was afraid of life. That was how his daughter, Sally, put it when she came to see me for help, saying she was tired of watching her father suffer. "He's such a talented man," she told me, "but he's not nearly as successful or happy as he should be. I want him to get help before it's too late. A friend told me I should give you a call. Can you see him?"

"Does your dad want to come in?" I asked.

"I haven't asked him, but probably not," Sally replied. "Since we moved to Cape Cod when I was five, he hasn't been off the Cape more than two or three times. And I'm twenty-one."

"It'll be hard for me to help him if I can't see him," I said.

"I know, but I thought maybe you'd be willing to speak to him on the telephone?" Sally suggested.

"Could you prepare him for that? I mean, I can't just call up and say, 'Hi, I'm a psychiatrist. Your daughter wants you to talk to me.' "

That made Sally laugh. "Yes, I can see your point. Dad does know I'm concerned about him. I'll see if I can talk him into it. He usually tries to please me."

Sally must have been very persuasive because her dad agreed not only to talk to me, but to come and see me in person. Sally couldn't believe it. We made the appointment, seizing the moment before he could change his mind.

When Ben Miller walked into my office he did not give the impression of a man who was afraid of anything. Standing tall at about 6'2", he strode right in, shook my hand, sat down, and opened the conversation before I could even speak. "Sally says we should talk," he said.

"Yes, I'm glad you could come in."

"And I'm glad to have the chance to meet you," Ben responded. "I've always wanted to talk to a psychiatrist."

I got the feeling he meant it more like, "I've always wanted to try rattlesnake," rather than as though he'd always wanted to seek help.

"Well, I am a psychiatrist," I said.

"Yes, you are," Ben replied. "And I'm me, and here we are." He looked very fit. I imagined him to be about fifty, but I wasn't sure. He then began what sounded almost like a rehearsed dialogue.

"This isn't easy for me to say. I'm sure Sally told you I'm not always the happiest man on earth. The fact is, I'm not where I should be in life's food chain. I'm pretty much what you could call a failure. I know it but I don't seem to be able to do anything about it."

"I'm impressed," I replied, "at your being able to be so straightforward and honest right now."

"It's because I planned what to say before I came. It's the only way I could get here—by making a plan. The fact is, if I stop and think about anything, I start to worry. I become a nervous wreck. My father was the same way. He was afraid of being buried alive. I'm afraid of being buried alive, too. I'm not stupid. I graduated from Dartmouth *summa cum laude* in economics *and* Romance languages. I wanted to become a high financier in Boston, like my uncle Dash, and make business deals at The Country Club in Brookline, and look out at the world with confidence all the time. What a dream! All I'm doing now is running a clothing store in Chatham. I'm fifty-three years old, and I've missed the boat."

"What do you think has held you back?" I asked.

"My nerves," he immediately replied. "I'm afraid of any situation where I'm expected to appear competent. Actually, I can be competent. I'm quite skilled and intelligent if I do say so myself, but what trips me up is that I worry I can't do anything right, so I don't let myself ever try. Worry stops me before I get started. Just making a telephone call makes me jittery. Even something simple, like calling someone up and asking him to go fishing, makes me nervous," he said.

"But if that's the way you are, how can you run the store?" I asked.

"My wife does a lot of it. I have good help. And, as I said, I do have some skills myself. I can hide out in the back office, do the numbers, place the orders, and keep track of the inventory. When the boss in Hyannis asks me to come up for a meeting, though, I put myself through a wringer. It's murder."

"May I ask how you got here today?" I inquired. "I mean, you didn't hesitate when you called. We were on the telephone yesterday, and you're here in my office today."

"To tell you the truth, if I had thought about it much longer I wouldn't have come. I just took Sally's word for it that I should see you, and I acted on the impulse. I said to myself, 'Walk into his office, tell him your name, tell him your problem, and see what happens.' That was my plan. I knew if I gave it any more thought than that I wouldn't do it. Also it helped that my wife was willing to drive me."

"Is driving difficult for you?" I asked.

He nodded. "Not the mechanics of it, of course. But the emotions are hell. I'm afraid at every turn. All the cars pass me. Doesn't this sound like I'm a major wimp? Actually, I was Ivy League heavyweight boxing champion and I could probably knock you out today with one punch," he announced with some pride.

"Wow," I said, a little taken aback and duly impressed.

"If Sally were sitting here right now she'd tell me to shut up and stop being so macho," Ben went on, "but it's just the way I grew up. Dad wanted me to be able to stand up for myself. I'm glad he did. Too bad he didn't get me brain lessons to go along with boxing lessons."

Ben Miller went on to tell me the life history of a worried man. We have learned over the past few decades that problems with intense anxiety or chronic worry have a strong genetic component, so Ben's comparison of himself to his father was apt. Sally also, as she told me later, struggled with an anxious temperament.

Ben had assumed all his life that his worrying was unstoppable, moreover that it was a moral weakness rather than a treatable condition. But there are more treatable causes of worry than people imagine, and there are more effective remedies available today than most people know about.

Worry is a special form of fear. To create worry, humans elongate fear with anticipation and memory, expand it in imagination, and fuel it with emotion. The uniquely human mental process called worrying depends upon having a brain that can reason, remember, reflect, feel, and imagine. Only humans have a brain big enough to do all this simultaneously and do it well. Worry is what humans do with simple fear once it reaches their cerebral cortex. They make it complex.

Not all worry is the same. Just as thunder-and-lightning storms strike in different ways, so does worry attack its victims variously. Some forms of worry are signs of diagnosable conditions such as depression, or generalized anxiety disorder, or post-traumatic stress disorder. Other kinds of worry, such as the worry that accompanies shyness, are built in from birth, part of one's genetic temperament. Still other kinds of worry ebb and flow in everyday life like hunger and thirst.

We used to think of worry purely in terms of life experience. When a person became anxious the immediate question was, "What is going on in the world outside to make me feel this way?" Now, however, we are adding another question, one that we are discovering is equally relevant: "What is happening in my brain to make me worry?" Our natural reaction to anxiety is to look *outside* ourselves for the cause. If we do actually look within, we tend to ignore our physiology and focus only on our psychological makeup, and, until recently, overlook the physical basis of worry.

New life sciences research, such as the discovery of a gene implicated in excessive worrying, has triggered humankind's old fears of being "reduced" by science. When the *New York Times* ran its story on the worry gene, the discovery was played down by the scientific community, which knew that while interesting it did not fully account for worry, nor indeed even come close. However, such is the concern (worry?) on the part of the rest of humanity that somehow science is going to rob of us free will and reduce us to predetermined genetic machines that some of our most influential intellectuals began to rumble. The op-ed page of the *New York Times,* for example, ran a lucid piece by the British psychoanalyst and writer Adam Phillips, who wrote, "We have genes, but we also have lives." He went on to point out some of the many formative uses of worry, noting,

> Whether or not there is a gene for worrying—or indeed a gene for being a geneticist—a psychoanalytic story about worrying would try to persuade people to see that by worrying they are doing a number of interesting things . . . worry is an ironic form of hope. . . . Worries, like secrets, are part of the essential currency of intimacy. Last, but not least, worrying is a form of thinking. . . . If worrying can persecute us, it can also work for us, as self-preparation. No stage fright, no performance.

Phillips was absolutely right. Some worry is good, indeed essential.

However, in the case of Ben Miller, and many millions of others like him, worry was not good. It was disabling. The key he had been missing in his lifelong struggle with worry was the knowledge that there was a physical basis for it. If Ben Miller's genetic makeup had been different, he would not have been *such* an anxious man. He would not have had to worry and fret before every business meeting *so intensely*. He would not have become so afraid of life that he needed to withdraw to Cape Cod. Perhaps he could have functioned in the competitive world of high finance as he had hoped.

Instead, he inherited a nervous system that was high-strung. He lived at the mercy of a built-in fear system that was set to go off at the drop of a pin. It usually took some external event to set it off, but once set off the internal alarm system skyrocketed like fireworks on the Fourth of July. Rather than embarrass himself with his nervous and flustered behavior at business meeting after business meeting, Ben settled for something less competitive and stressful. He did what millions of excessive worriers do: he used avoidance as his chief means of coping.

One way to understand his fear would be purely psychological, but it is only half the story. The other half is Ben's nervous system and the genetically determined vulnerability he inherited. This man was scared of life because, at least in part, such fear was hard-wired into him. His nervous system was rigged to sense danger at the slightest provocation.

Ben had what we would diagnose today as a generalized anxiety disorder (GAD). "Nonsense!" a skeptic might retort, "That's just psychobabble. All that man needed to do was toughen up." And the skeptic would be right! Ben *did* need to toughen up. *But why didn't he?* It was not because he didn't want to. The skeptic doesn't understand that Ben's incessant fretting and worrying was not voluntary. Telling a person with GAD that all he needs to do is toughen up is like telling a person who has coronary artery disease that all he needs to do is unclog his coronary arteries. *Yes, but how?* In telling the individual to toughen up, a key part of the problem is being overlooked—the physical, uncontrollable part. Ben did not want to fail any more than the individual with coronary artery disease wants to have a heart attack. He did not want to sabotage his dream of becoming a major financier. Nor was he led to such sabotage by unconscious forces or by moral weakness or by laziness. He went to Cape Cod, to a place of less stress, because he knew, intuitively, that that was the only way he could survive. Just as the man with untreated coronary artery disease might avoid stairs or other kinds of physical exertion as self-protective measures, so Ben knew that he needed to avoid life's heavy action if he wanted to be OK.

How does the biological perspective influence treatment? First of all, it takes the monkey off Ben's back. I could give Ben the liberating news that what he had was a treatable, medical condition, like coronary artery disease, to replace a guilt-laden self-diagnosis such as "loser" or "wimp." The tens of millions of people in the country right now who suffer from worry in one of its toxic forms, such as GAD, may think they are morally weak and that their pain represents a shortcoming in themselves. If they feel ashamed, they cover up their symptoms as best they can and deny themselves the very help they need, help that could change their lives.

With Ben, my work was to convince him that he was not just a "royal loser," as he put it. "Are you sure you're not just offering me a big excuse?" he asked me.

"If I told you that you had coronary artery disease and that was why you couldn't climb stairs without pain, would you think that was just a big excuse for being lazy and taking the elevator?"

"No," he said. "I guess I wouldn't. It's just that I have carried around this guilt for so long it's hard to unload it all at once."

It does take time for someone such as Ben to move from what I call the "moral diagnosis" (e.g., wimp, loser) to the medical diagnosis (e.g., GAD, or whatever the correct diagnosis might happen to be). It takes time because one has to switch one's perspective in a major way. It is like going from thinking the world is flat to knowing it is round.

Knowledge is the key. Ben had to learn something about his own nervous system.

"You mean my life could be different?" Ben asked.

I could hear in his voice the tone of tentative hope I have come to recognize very well in people who have long ago given up on themselves when they begin to see the first glimmer of a possibility that there is a chance their lives could change. "Yes," I replied. "I think there is a good chance."

"So, if I have this sensitive nervous system," Ben asked, "what do I do about it?"

"First, learn about it. I want you to do some reading, so you can manage your own treatment and understand it. I think medication could help you, but that is not the whole story and it certainly is not a cure. You're going to have to learn some new ways of talking to yourself, and then you'll be ready to start challenging yourself in ways you haven't dared to in quite a while."

"What do you mean, 'talking to myself'?" Ben asked. "I thought only crazy people did that."

"Oh, no," I replied. "It's very important to learn how to talk to yourself in a positive, helpful way. Not necessarily talk out loud, but talk to yourself in your mind. Reassure yourself and offer yourself perspective and encouragement. Stop listening to all the negative thoughts that follow you around."

"All I do when I talk to myself in my mind is worry about all the things that can go wrong," Ben said.

"Exactly," I replied. "That's why you need to learn a better way of talking to yourself. You'd be amazed what a difference talking to yourself in the right way can make."

His treatment was based upon a comprehensive approach. There is no "magic bullet" for GAD or for worry in general. The most effective treatments involve a range of modalities. Education was the starting point. Ben needed to learn about his brain and his genetic makeup. This laid the foundation for his seeing his anxiety as a natural phenomenon he needed to *manage,* as opposed to some curse or moral failing he could not change. I gave him some articles to read and summarized for him in my own words much of what we have learned lately about GAD.

Once we had established GAD as a medical (as opposed to a moral) diagnosis, it became much easier to move into the specifics of treatment. Many people never get far in treatment because their underlying suspicion that they are simply morally "weak" never gets addressed. Until this bias is dealt with, the success of the treatment is in jeopardy.

The next steps included starting Ben on a low dose of Klonopin, an antianxiety medication. While medication does not cure GAD, it can provide short-term relief while the rest of treatment is starting.

The medication helped right away. Ben felt a reduction in his general level of vigilance and concern. Then we began introducing some relaxation techniques. I always approach this in terms of what the person is comfortable with. Some people feel strange meditating, as if it were too trendy or "New Age." This was the case with Ben. However, he had been brought up going to church and felt not uncomfortable (although out of practice) with praying. Prayer and meditation are closely related from a neurological point of view. So I put Ben on a program of twice-a-day praying. As people usually do, once he got over his initial self-consciousness, he found his praying to be relaxing and quite helpful. After a short period of time he started to look forward to his prayer time, as runners do to their daily run.

Along those lines, I also advised Ben to start an exercise program. He loved this idea, reminding me that he used to box. Pretty soon he was on a daily training program and trying to convince his sedentary friends of the tonic effects of exercise!

In addition to these physical steps and the medication, we also had our therapy sessions, which focused both on helping him learn a new way of talking to himself as well as discussing issues from his past and current life that bothered him. Again, Ben balked at this at first, declaring that he didn't want to have his head "shrunk," but with a little prodding he discovered that it was indeed relaxing and helpful to learn some new approaches to his inner mental life as well as to talk about painful issues he had been carrying around for a long time.

This process requires some time. Ben and I met regularly. We talked for several months, as he told his tale, going back over his life, retelling the various moral fables he had been raised on: "Where there's a will, there's a way." "The little train that could." "I can and I will." The message—and a good one—was that hard work conquers all. The problem is that it conquers a lot but it does not conquer *all.* Hard work does not conquer diabetes, nor does it change your height, nor will it remove a predisposition to anxiety. It can certainly help in the treatment—hard work is good for most problems—but it is not the cure.

As Ben began to understand this, he began to forgive himself, slowly, like a pavement cracking. We began to unearth and look at a whole host of feelings and hopes and sadnesses that he had buried. With this came new energy, new optimism, and new thoughts about what he might do.

Once Ben understood that he was not in the grip of a moral infirmity, he was able to put a lot of the energy he had been using to feel ashamed of himself into finding a better way of managing his emotions. Once he understood that there was a physical basis to his problem, he felt freed up.

We continued to develop practical strategies for dealing with his anxieties. This is really the most creative part of the treatment process because different strategies work for different people. In Part III of this book, I outline a number of practical tips. The reader might want to turn to the chapter entitled "Fifty Tips on the Management of Worry Without Using Medication" to get a sampling right now. I went over these tips with Ben to see which ones would be helpful for him.

I also worked with him more on how to talk to himself, a technique based on the wonderful work of Dr. Aaron Beck and many others in the field of cognitive therapy. The fundamental idea is to learn how to direct your mind away from harmful anxiety by means of what you say to yourself. By changing how you talk to yourself, you can change how you feel. You need to redirect or move past your anxiety, if you possibly can. Just as Ben had learned how to feel inadequate and ashamed by hearing punitive refrains in his head such as, "Where there's a will there's a way, and your problem is that you just don't try hard enough," so he could learn how to soothe himself with new phrases, such as, "You're doing your best," or "Give it a shot," or "Cut yourself some slack," or "Rome wasn't built in a day." These are not excuses, nor are they hokey rationalizations for being mediocre. Rather they are honest words of encouragement, words to prevent one from losing heart. These little sayings and stock phrases cue emotional responses. If a person can learn how to talk to himself effectively, he can often learn how to avoid the emotional pitfalls of depression and anxiety.

Furthermore, if he can learn to recognize anxiety as it begins to build, he can apply the physical treatments I recommended for Ben as well, such as prayer, meditation, exercise, slow breathing, and relaxation.

The key is to approach anxiety as a manageable state rather than as a beast from which one must flee. More of the specific techniques of management will be presented in Part III.

Ben and I worked together for about a year. The medication made him feel better after only a few days, but there were many issues in his life to talk about and the new techniques he was learning needed to be reinforced, so we continued to meet over an extended period of time. He stopped the medication after six weeks, but continued with the prayer and exercise. And he did very well. Although he never became a high financier in Boston, he did on Cape Cod!

Although Ben Miller's tendency to worry was handed down genetically, not all treatable states of worry are genetic in origin. Consider the case of Allison Barnes. Allison came to see me at a crisis point in her life. As soon as she sat down I could see that she was full of fear.

"Thank you for giving me an appointment so promptly," she said. "I don't know what to do with myself. I'm upset and worried almost all of the time."

Allison—Dr. Allison Barnes—had called me from her office the day before. She had told me on the phone that she was a specialist in internal medicine, and that she was growing increasingly unhappy in her work because of her constant fear of getting sued. She said she was having thoughts every day of leaving medicine altogether. I suggested she come in and talk about it right away.

"Medicine is not what it used to be," she said. "When I finished my residency in 1974, there was still some trust between patient and doctor. You could pretty much assume that if problems came up, you could talk them out. Now, my God, everyone who walks in the door I have to see as a potential adversary. Every note I write I have to imagine reading aloud in court. It's horrible. I can't stand it."

"Have you ever been sued?" I asked.

"Yes," she said. "Once. Five years ago. I don't think I've gotten over it yet."

"What was the complaint?" I asked.

She took a deep breath, then answered as if saying it for the millionth time. "The patient said," Allison paused, "I didn't spend," and she paused again, "enough *time*," pausing once more at the word "time," then concluding, "with him."

"He sued you for *that*?" I asked, incredulously.

"Yes. Basically. He and his lawyer made it sound a lot worse, of course. They made it sound as if I had exercised poor judgment because of my haste. The case actually went to trial. Do you know how miserable that was? We won, easily, as my attorney had told me we would. But, we lost, too. Or at least I did. It was *the* single most devastating experience of my life."

"I can hear it in your voice," I said. "I can hear how much it hurts."

"It hurts too much," Allison replied. "It shouldn't hurt this much. I know it, and all my friends tell me so, but it hurts anyway. Ever since the suit, I just can't look at my work in the same way. I can't get past

the pain. You have no idea how hard I try. You have no idea how conscientious I am, always taking the extra minute, the extra few phrases
on the way out the door, trying to do everything I can to feel safe, but
the fun has gone out of my work, because I know I'm being defensive.
Everything I do is defensive. And there's no time to talk, to enjoy my
patients. You know how it is these days in medicine. Well, maybe you
don't because you run your own practice, but for me, where I work,
they want us to get the patients in and out as fast as possible."

"This suit happened five years ago," I said, almost to myself.

"Five years," she answered.

"And you still think about it," I repeated.

"Every day. Often many times a day. I go over it and over it, what I
should have done differently, even though I know there was nothing I
could have done any better. This was just one angry man who decided
to take his frustrations in the world out on me. He said I didn't give
him enough time. The worst part of it was I thought we had a great relationship. His name was Jim Tracker. It makes me wince just to say his
name out loud. He'd been a patient of mine for a long time, and he
was someone who I thought of as a friend. We exchanged family pictures. When his son Simon had leukemia I gave blood and so did my
husband, and our children gave blood too. Then Simon died. I was
with Jim through that and it was just about the saddest thing I've ever
seen. Then one day, a year or so after Simon's death, Jim came in for a
headache workup. I spent an hour with him, then I sent him off for
some tests. He said I 'dismissed' him without giving him the time he
needed, so he went to another doctor, who diagnosed a benign menin-
gioma after doing the same tests I had originally ordered. But Jim said
I missed the diagnosis, even though he never followed through on the
tests I had told him to get."

"Did anyone take his complaint against you seriously?" I asked. "It
sounds patently frivolous."

"Just me," Allison replied. "I took it seriously. I still do. Even the
bureaucrats at work told me not to worry about it. But it sure has
stayed on my mind. Like a voice that just won't go away. I'm fright-

ened. What if he comes back? What if he sends some other patient in to see me, to set me up? Look, I know that is paranoid and crazy, but these are the kinds of thoughts I'm having."

"Have you ever talked to anyone about this?"

"Not at length. I feel ashamed. Even my husband doesn't know how much I'm bothered by it and how frightened I am. I used to love my work, but now I'm terrified of it. I worry every day about someone trying to go after me, to sue me, or make me look bad, or embarrass my children and my husband."

"The world of medicine has changed," I said. "Most doctors worry a lot more than they used to."

"I know. I hear my colleagues talk. But I can't shake it the way most of them can. It's ruining my life as a doctor. The moments I used to look forward to, the tender moments with patients, they're all gone. Now it's purely a technical business. I just try to get through the day without any glitches."

Allison's feeling of heightened insecurity is common these days, indeed maybe epidemic. Not only do people feel insecure at work, but they also feel their social bonds loosening. They fear being overlooked ("I'm just so busy") by a friend, betrayed out of the blue, or, like Allison, sandbagged by someone they had trusted.

"Tell me more," I said to Allison.

She had a lot more to tell. She told of sleepless nights, of distracted thoughts as she was driving, and of happy times spoiled by sudden jolts of worry in the pit of her stomach. "All related to the lawsuit?" I asked. "No," she replied. "That was just the starting point. Now I can find worry in a cigarette butt on the sidewalk. I can turn anything into worry. I'll give you a good example. There was a time when I looked forward to getting my mail. I loved the mail. It was a high point of my day. Now I dread it. I flip through all the mail quickly, looking at the return addresses, scanning for anything scary, such as a lawyer's return address. I have an automatic fear response to the mail now."

I took a deep breath and let it out slowly, shaking my head. "What you've gone through is awful," I said.

"I'm at the end of my rope," Allison went on. "We could get by on my husband's income alone, but it would be tight. Or I could take a totally different job, like work in a bookstore or a florist."

"Is that what you want to do?"

"I wouldn't mind. If times were different, definitely not. I love medicine. Or at least I used to. What has happened just makes me so mad. What do you think?"

"I think we can work together on this and come up with a better solution than what you're living with right now," I replied.

Allison's problem, as the problems of most of the patients I see these days, was rooted both in the reality of today's world and in how she processed that reality. Life *is* scary and insecure. But many people are suffering excessively because they do not know how to keep the dangers of life in any kind of realistic perspective. They do not know how or where to get support. They do not know how to bolster themselves so that they won't feel as helpless and vulnerable as Allison did.

Many people who worry too much do so out of some kind of broken trust or loss of faith. They may tell you they worry because of all the problems of the world, the many dangers that really do swarm around us all. But if these people open up to you and share what they really feel in their hearts, they will tell you a story that will give you the deeper reason for their worry. The story will be like Allison's, one of lost faith, a broken heart, or trust gone bad.

They will tell you a story in which their basic faith in human nature was destroyed and their basic trust in the safety of life was forever shaken. The story may be as huge as the Holocaust or as small as getting beaten up on the playground by a close friend, but whatever it is, it still flashes through their minds as a continuing signal of danger and alarm.

I could tell many stories besides Allison's to illustrate what broken trust can do. We all know someone who has endured betrayal. We have all seen injustice. In fact, most of us have experienced it and we ourselves have probably wreaked it on others. So what's the big deal?

The big deal is that if you suffer injustice in a major way at the wrong time you may never be the same. You may worry forever after. It does not seem fair. There should be some court, some place of last appeal, where injustice can be redressed. But there is no such place, at least not on this Earth. We have no Court of Ultimate Appeal, no place for Job to take his grievance.

There are many Allison Barneses out there. People feeling as if they are living on the edge of doom. *Who is going to sue me? When will I get fired? What did that memo really mean? Will I be able to make it this year? And next? Will it ever get easy?*

These are the refrains I hear every day. People who feel in danger, even if they're not. "Allison, you didn't do anything wrong," I said to her.

"That doesn't matter," she said. "Being right is not enough any more. You can still get dragged through the mud. The gossips don't care about the verdict. All they remember is the accusation. The taint lasts. The fear doesn't go away. Being right is the least of my worries. I know I'm a good doctor. I know I do good work. It's how people will react that I can't control. The lawsuit taught me that. You can be totally right, and know you're dealing with people the way you should, and still have five years of your life turned to shit." She was red in the face. "I'm sorry," she said. "I don't usually talk like that."

"It's quite all right," I said. "I think you put it very well."

"I think the world has lost its sense of decency," she went on, wiping away tears. "That man who sued me was working out his own problems on my back. He didn't care about what was right, and the lawyer who took his case sure as hell didn't care. Each one got what he wanted. My old patient found someone to blame for his misery, and the lawyer got a fee. The only person who lost totally was the person who won the suit—me. Everyone else thought the suit was no big deal, just a nuisance. And I guess, as a lawsuit, that's what it was, no big deal. But for me it was a betrayal. I couldn't believe Jim Tracker was taking me to court! Can you imagine, my whole family gave blood to help try to save his son, and he turns around a year later and sues me? How could he do that?" she asked, her voice shaking.

"Did you ever ask him?" I inquired.

"Yes. I did ask him. It was a horribly awkward moment when we both found ourselves standing at the same water fountain in the court-house. I just blurted out, 'How could you have done this to me?' "

"And what did he say?" I asked.

"I'll never forget what he said. He said, 'Sometimes innocent peo-ple have to get hurt in any great cause.' "

" 'What's the *great cause* here?' I asked him in disbelief. And he replied, full of righteous indignation, 'The cause is making you doc-tors responsible for the lives of the people you treat.' There it was, plain as day. He was taking out his anger about the death of his son on me."

"Had doctors made mistakes with his son?" I asked.

"Not as far as I know," Allison answered. "But that didn't matter. He wanted someone to blame. He wanted an excuse to sue a doctor, so he found one with me, his old friend. My theory, and I've only thought about it a million times, is that he picked someone close to him to sue to make it hurt all the more. If he could drag me into his pain, then that would be more satisfying than suing just any old doc-tor, someone who maybe could shrug it off."

"You're thinking along the lines of misery loving company?" I asked.

"Yes," Allison said, "but worse than that. Because his life was ruined he wanted to ruin the life of someone he liked or at least used to like. I became the innocent person who had to get hurt in his 'great cause.' It's sick but I think that's what happened."

"What an ordeal," I said, "to be attacked like that by someone you'd cared for. And yet, do you think it might have cut too deep?" I asked. "I mean, don't you think you've taken it too hard? Maybe what we need for you is a better system of barriers, so the bad stuff from people like Jim Tracker doesn't go in so deep."

"Yes," Allison said. "That would be nice. Do you have those barri-ers for sale today?"

"Sort of," I replied. Allison and I then planned out a course of treatment. Over the next few months we talked about her feelings of fear and hurt. Just getting the pain out helped. Her constant worry stemmed from her feelings of vulnerability and powerlessness in the wake of the betrayal, so as we talked of her hurt we simultaneously tried to build up a feeling of strength to reduce her vulnerability.

In a way, the kind of injury Allison had suffered was like a prolonged fever. She was still febrile when she came to see me. My job was to apply metaphorical cold towels to her forehead and to strengthen her with hot chicken soup and herbal tea. My cold towels, soup, and tea consisted of listening, encouraging, and offering a different perspective. Just as the body can get sick with a virus, so can the mind get sick with worry. Over time, the old-fashioned remedy of being nursed back to health helped Allison a great deal. Sometimes the simplest cure is the best.

But Allison did not get *all* better. People rarely do from that kind of injury. The treatments we have are palliative, not radical. Often the improvement is dramatic, but we rarely see total recovery.

Beyond the basic treatment of listening and offering encouragement and perspective, I also needed to help Allison retrain her brain, so to speak, to reduce the chances of this kind of thing happening again.

What do I mean by "retraining the brain"? It is a key concept in the treatment of worry because in adults toxic worry is usually a deeply ingrained habit and not a sudden spasm that can, equally suddenly, be reversed. While severe worrying may be precipitated by a sudden event, the habit of worry itself is usually long-standing. Often it serves as a positive aid in an individual's profession; indeed, one may have trained hard to *become* a strong worrier! Certainly in medicine, learning to worry a lot is part of every doctor's induction. The habit of considering every possible outcome of a particular treatment as well as initially weighing a number of alternative diagnoses—in other words what could be called worrying about the accuracy of your initial conclusions—is essential in arriving at the best possible treatment plan for each individual patient.

It is ironic that a skill that one has worked to acquire can turn into such a demon. But it often does. Most of the worriers I treat are inveterate, not novice, and they have often worried intentionally, not against their wishes. As inveterate worriers, they need to take their minds back to school for retraining and learn new mental skills. These skills will be described throughout this book, but I begin here by introducing the basic idea of "brain training." Just as you can train your muscles to learn certain patterns, say the pattern of a golf or a tennis swing, and then train those muscles to develop what we call "muscle memory" so that the correct swing becomes automatic, so you can train your brain to learn certain patterns, certain ways of dealing with situations that arise again and again, such as financial worries, or fears of failure. You can train your brain to learn a certain approach, a certain "swing," so that you can deal with these worries automatically without having to spend a day or a week obsessing over the same issue you have already dealt with dozens of times before.

When people develop bad mental habits—such as persistent negative thinking and destructive worrying—they need to be given new methods of dealing with conflict and uncertainty, methods they can use in everyday life to replace the aching, toxic method of frenzied worrying.

In Allison's case I urged her to learn to recognize a period of irrational worry the moment it began and to intercept it before it could get started. For example, I suggested that when she went to pick up her mail, she consciously and deliberately remind herself before she opens the box that any bad news could be dealt with effectively, that she is a powerful enough woman to do this, and that she is supported by other powerful people as well. I also suggested that she give a name to her fear. We decided to call it Hugo and we decided it looked like a toad. Before opening her mailbox she would shoo Hugo away. This may sound childish, but it helped Allison in opening her mail. The idea behind it was for Allison to consciously push away the feelings of powerlessness and vulnerability she had been left with after the lawsuit.

In other situations, whenever Allison felt the familiar surge of fear in her stomach—for example, when a patient became annoyed with her and questioned her aggressively—I coached her to say to herself firmly, "Get lost, Hugo. I'm a good doctor and I can handle this situation just fine." Such conscious redirecting of the mind can help calm you in many anxious and fearful situations. It helps to put your fear and anxiety outside of yourself, where it can be seen and put into realistic perspective. Giving your worry a name can help in this effort.

Allison became creative in finding ways of putting her worry outside herself. She would blow into the palms of her hands sometimes before going into a meeting and say she had just "blown off" her worries. She bought a ugly-looking toad figurine, which she kept in her purse ready to deposit on a shelf whenever she needed a reminder that her worries could be put aside.

You have to be willing to play along and suspend your disbelief for this method to work, but if you are willing it can work very well. You are enlisting the aid of your imagination, allowing your imagination to work on your behalf instead of on behalf of your worry factory, as it too often does. (The theoretical basis for this method derives from the work of Dr. Michael White, an Australian family therapist who coaches families to "externalize" their problems in the form of stories and fables.)

There were a few other "brain training" tips I gave to Allison, tips that I give to nearly all my patients. Chief among them is to get exercise at least every other day. Although we have been aware for some time of the benefits of exercise for the cardiovascular system, we are just beginning to appreciate the physiological benefits of exercise for the brain. Exercise is probably the best natural antianxiety, antiworry agent we have. Exercise is great for the brain in many other ways: It is an antidepressant, it reduces tension, it drains off excess aggression and frustration, it enhances a sense of well-being, it improves sleep, it curbs the tendency to eat absentmindedly, it aids in concentration, and it reduces distractibility. The benefits of exercise for the rest of the body are well-known: it is good for your heart, your circulation, your bones, your respiratory system, your skin, your kidneys, and just about every other part of your body as well. It helps to reduce weight and blood pressure and regulate blood sugar.

Allison and I also worked on her learning how to disengage from worry the second it appeared. She learned to distinguish instantly between good worry (The plane might be late. I'd better call the airport) and toxic worry (The plane may have crashed. I'd better sit here and be miserable until I meet the plane). The way to distinguish between the two is simply to learn that there *are* two kinds of worry, one helpful and the other toxic. Once you know this, the kind of worry you are dealing with is usually self-evident. Allison learned to disengage the instant toxic worry tried to fill her mind.

There is a window of opportunity—it lasts perhaps as long as a minute—during which you can sever the tentacle of a toxic worry before it grips you totally. For most people, once it gets a tight grip, it lasts for hours, even days or weeks. To cut it off immediately, you must take decisive action. Run up and down stairs. Talk to your spouse or a friend about something totally unrelated to the worry. Sing some old camp song loudly. Write a letter to the newspaper about some topic you know a lot about. If you are religious, get down on your knees and pray. Splash water on your face or, even better, take a cold shower. The old-fashioned remedy of a cold shower and a run around the block is probably one of the best, even though we may make fun of its puritanical overtones.

I coached Allison regularly on these methods of managing her worry and over time she learned to use them well.

But what was perhaps the most important part of her treatment did not depend upon me at all. What Allison needed to do was increase the amount of support she had in her life. She needed to develop deeper, more active connections to other people, places, ideas, and institutions. She had a good marriage and she had wonderful children. This was the basis of her connections in life. But she, like millions of other people, needed more. One of the reasons the lawsuit rocked her so badly was that she did not have a solid enough sense of being connected to something larger than herself, an entity that could look out for her when she was in trouble.

What sort of entity can do this? It is one made up of the sum of all our connections: connections to our immediate family and extended family; connections to our past and our traditions; connections to our friends, neighbors, and colleagues; connections to institutions, organizations, and country; connections to information and ideas; and connections to whatever is transcendent, whether we call it Nature or God or some other name. This entity, the sum of all our meaningful connections, I call *connectedness,* and it is, in my opinion, the key to emotional health and the surest protection we have against the psychological ravages of worry.

I urged Allison to work consciously and deliberately on developing her sphere of connectedness in all its different domains. It took time but she did it. She made dates with friends. She made regular telephone calls to members of her extended family. She sought out colleagues and developed a supper group with five other physicians once a month. She went back to church, not without doubts. She got a consultation with a lawyer who specialized in malpractice prevention, so she could develop a more realistic, less catastrophic sense of what risks she was dealing with day in and day out as well as what protections were available. She scheduled a night out with her husband once a week. Setting up all these steps took time, but she found it was the most valuable time she had ever spent.

After several months Allison began to notice her baseline level of worry dropping significantly. She began to realize that she was not a helpless victim, ready to be shanghaied at any moment by anybody, anywhere. In one of our last sessions she talked philosophically of how medicine had changed but how she was loving it once again. She handed me an article published in the *New England Journal of Medicine* by Dr. David Loxterkamp, a family physician in Maine, in which she had highlighted the following passage:

> What has become of our calling? The answer depends on whom we listen to. We are obliged to listen to licensing boards, credentialing committees, peer-review organizations, and insurance carriers. But they do not define us. We have listened to the general practitioners who laid the moral foundation for family medicine, the humanists who reformed it, the market analysts who will repackage it for the twenty-first century. But these voices tell only part of the story. The one person who will challenge us the most, who will deliver us to our finest hours, who will talk us through every moral conundrum, is the patient who we thought needed us.

"I've come back to my patients," Allison said to me. "These days I actually look forward to going to work."

The basic program Allison and I developed for her would in fact help most people with their worrying. Aside from the psychotherapy, Allison's program could have been conducted without the aid of a professional, once a professional had helped get it started.

The key to dealing with worry is to start learning how to *manage* worry instead of letting it manage you.

Jacob Sheldon came to see me because he was tired of not getting what he wanted out of life. "Potential. I have so much *potential*. If I hear that word one more time I think I'll strangle whoever says it."

"What's getting in your way?" I asked.

"My nerves," he replied. "I have a case of the nerves, just like my father. He was scared of his own shadow and so am I." Jacob was twenty-nine years old and worked as a reference librarian at Harvard, but what he really wanted to do was write.

"What do you want to write?" I asked him.

"Oh, you know, anything that will win me the Nobel Prize," he replied casually.

I smiled. "Well, at least you don't set your sights too low. Have you published anything?"

"Not since I published a story in the Harvard *Advocate* when I was an undergraduate. Since then it's been all po and no show."

"Hmm?" I asked.

"All po. All potential. No results," he replied, impatiently.

"Do you have a specific time for your writing?" I asked.

"No. I don't dare sit down at the keyboard because I'm afraid of what invariably happens. It's horrible. I have all these stories I want to write in my head, but the minute I sit down and look at the keys, the stories vanish. They are replaced by a gray, granite wall. Nothing comes out. I pound my head, but it's like kicking a broken vending machine. There is no payoff. I hate myself for it."

"Does this mean that you have given up trying?" I asked.

"Almost," Jacob answered. "I still jot down notes for plots and characters, I still imagine scenes when I'm driving along, I still hear a piece of dialog and imagine putting it somewhere in a novel, but I can't write a sentence if I think it might become part of a larger piece of work."

"How long has it been this way?" I asked.

"Well, I graduated from college when I was twenty-two, and embarked upon my career as a writer. I wrote a novel that was rejected by seventeen publishers before I quit sending it out. I found an agent who liked it, and she sent it out ten more times. Ten more rejections. Meanwhile, I wrote another novel. More rejections. But many of them told me I had talent and to keep at it. This is an old story, familiar to thousands of my nameless, unpublished fellow writers. We get enough encouragement to go on but we don't get that one break we need. In my case, I responded to all the rejections by freezing up. I started to worry more and more and write less and less. Over the past year it has been impossible for me to write anything of substance."

"Do you have any idea of what gets in your way?" I asked.

"Bees," he replied without missing a beat.

"Bees?" I asked, nonplussed.

"It's my metaphor for how I get stung in my head. These mental bees swarm in and tell me all the things that can go wrong. I can either stay there and get stung or leave the room. When I think of my career as a writer, the bees fly in right away. Now I don't even tell people that I write. Not only am I ashamed that I have nothing to show for it, but I don't want to deal with the fucking bees."

The Greeks called them Furies and Harpies, Jacob called them bees, and this book calls them worries. Whatever their name, these infernal creatures of the mind blight the lives of many people. For Jacob they stifled his writing. But they can also undercut a person who wants to start a business or sabotage someone who wants to go to medical school, or discourage someone who wants to run a marathon, or undermine anyone who wants to achieve anything at all.

These creatures are the worries of self-doubt and perfectionism.

You can reach a state of paralysis from this kind of worrying, particularly if you have suffered rejection as often as Jacob had.

The treatment for such worry, and for most worry, is to build up your feeling of power while at the same time reducing your sense of vulnerability. You need to feel safe enough to fail. Jacob was so hurt by the letters of rejection that he couldn't write a word without imagining some editor's nasty, critical comment. He came to feel that unless each sentence was perfect, it could not be tried. Since nothing is perfect at first, Jacob could not begin. Instead he was trapped in a swarm of worries.

The paralysis of perfectionism is just another form of toxic worry. Built on a desire to do right, paradoxically it causes the individual to do nothing.

"Can you help me?" Jacob asked.

The fact is that I have treated many people like Jacob, some of whom I've been able to help and others not. I never know in advance. So I had to tell Jacob that I didn't know, but that I'd try.

Our treatment plan approached Jacob's problem from several different angles. The field of mental health has developed a large arsenal of new techniques over the past twenty-five years. In Jacob's case, we needed several of these so that we could sneak up on his problem and catch it unawares. "We can't come at your problem head on or with just one gun," I said, "or it will be waiting for us, ready to beat us back or run away. Instead we have to circle it, so that it can't pay attention to everything we are doing simultaneously. You see, your mind is very quick and the minute it senses what we are up to, it will close its doors. The minute your mind understands our game, it will beat us."

"But doesn't my mind want me to win?" Jacob asked, incredulously. "I mean, I am my mind, and I want to write, so I must want us to win!"

"Not totally," I replied. "That's the damn thing about human nature. Everywhere you look there is ambivalence. There're always two sides to every feeling. Even the desire for success has two sides."

"But why?" Jacob demanded, almost as if I were lying.

"I don't know. People have theories but all I can tell you is what I see in my office every day—and that is that nobody is ever unambivalent. In your case, one part of you wants to write and create, but another part of you is afraid that it won't be good enough and you'll get rejected again, so that part of you sends in the bees, as you call them, to prevent you from getting started."

"But if that's the case, if I don't want to succeed, why would I be here, paying you to help me?" Jacob protested.

"The part of you that wants to write is here. But the part of you that is afraid is practicing up right now to try to defeat our efforts. After all, those bees are your creation, too. They do not exist outside your mind, so there must be a part of you that wants *not* to write. This is the part of you that sends in the bees, and that's why we need to circle the problem, so that it can't watch us all at once," I said.

"How do we circle it?" Jacob asked.

"Well, first of all I want to refer you to a colleague of mine, who is a superb psychotherapist. You and he will talk."

"Don't you do psychotherapy?" Jacob asked.

"I do but this man is better than I am with someone like you," I replied.

"What do you mean, 'someone like me'?" Jacob asked. "What kind of case am I?"

"I mean someone who is as quick and creative as you are. Honestly, I think you would talk circles around me. But this man is quicker than I am."

"OK," Jacob said. "But you seem plenty quick to me."

"That is because we're not doing psychotherapy," I answered. "When you start getting close to the part of you that doesn't want to change, that's when you'll need someone more adept than I am."

"OK," Jacob replied. "I'll take your word for it. What else do you want me to do?"

"I want you to start an exercise program. Do you exercise now?" Jacob shook his head, no. "OK, you need to start. Pick something you like and try to do it at least every other day. It is much harder to worry if you get regular exercise. I also want to look at how you sleep and what your diet is. Do you drink?" Jacob nodded. "How much?" I asked.

"It depends," Jacob replied. "Probably too much."

"Well, the problem with alcohol is that it is a depressant, and it is toxic to your brain. In the short term it may help with your mood but in the long term it only makes you worry more. How would you feel about giving it up?"

Jacob looked away. "I'm beginning to wonder if it was such a good idea to have come here after all."

"I know it will be hard," I went on. "And you don't have to do it all at once, but this is what I mean by coming at your problem from many different angles circling the problem. If you're drinking, whenever you get close to changing your life the part of you that doesn't want to change can just close its eyes and look forward to the next drink."

"OK," Jacob said. "What else? Do you want me to find God or something like that?"

"Religion is your own business but, to tell you the truth, there is lots of evidence that people who pray and have religious faith worry less and live longer. Are you religious?" I asked.

Jacob chuckled. "I'm your average nonbelieving Jew," he replied. "What do you recommend for us?" he asked with a wry smile.

"Meditation?" I suggested. "Have you ever tried that?"

"No, but I guess I could learn."

"That's the spirit," I said to Jacob.

"Uh, Dr. Hallowell, was that a pun?"

"No."

"You are beginning to overwhelm me a bit," Jacob then said. "You almost sound more like a camp director than a psychiatrist," he complained, not unpleasantly.

"I'm sorry," I replied. "You think maybe I should have a whistle around my neck? I can imagine all this is daunting. I'm just trying to lay out a plan that covers enough ground to work for you. These are all only suggestions. I don't mean to sound dictatorial."

"That's OK," Jacob said. "Actually, it all makes sense."

"Good," I said. "I also think you might benefit if I prescribed some medication for you. Prozac is good against the bees of perfectionism. It can help stop people from ruminating so much. Why? I don't know, exactly, but studies have shown it to be true. Prozac blocks serotonin reuptake. So somehow, serotonin and ruminating must be related. As with most treatments in this field, we do not know *exactly* why they work, but we go on hypotheses and empirical studies. In other words, it's been tried on other people like you and it's helped them, so it might help you."

"Prozac," Jacob muttered. "Doesn't that make some people violent?"

"There are a lot of myths about Prozac," I answered, "and that is one of them. Yes, some people have become violent while taking Prozac, but that does not mean that one can never prescribe Prozac. The number is so small and the benefits so far outweigh the risk that we use it often these days. It is not a cure-all but when it's used properly it can make a big difference, particularly with people who are stuck, like you."

"What do you mean, 'stuck'?" Jacob asked.

"I mean your self-doubts and your perfectionism are like mud you get mired in. Your wheels spin, your engine gets hot, and mud flies everywhere, but you don't move. That's being stuck. Somehow or other Prozac often let's you put aside those self-doubts long enough to get some traction and get moving."

"When would you want to start all this?" Jacob asked.

"After you've had some time to think about it. Let's make another appointment."

Jacob thought about it and did indeed go ahead with the comprehensive plan we had outlined. It included psychotherapy with a man who was able to combine what is called cognitive-behavioral therapy with insight-oriented therapy in a marvelous way.

What is cognitive-behavioral therapy and how does it differ from insight-oriented therapy, and how do both of them differ from what your wise old grandmother might have told you? Basically, therapy differs from advice in that in therapy the patient gets involved in a process of discovery—discovery of new knowledge, techniques, feelings, connections, or insights—while advice, however wise, is just advice.

There are now many kinds of therapy, and mental health professionals try valiantly to describe them precisely, although the boundaries among them are quite blurred. Insight-oriented therapy is the granddad of all of them. It is the legacy of Freud's "talking cure" and has come to designate the guided investigation of one's past, present, and future with a trained therapist, the goal being to increase one's awareness or insight. It is useful in treating a wide range of problems, problems with intimacy, with work, with mood, and with worry. However, sometimes it is too vague and never-ending.

Therefore, more specifically defined therapies have been developed to address particular kinds of mental distress. One of these is called cognitive-behavioral therapy and it is particularly useful in treating different kinds of worry and anxiety. The cognitive part specifically addresses one's thoughts as the patient tries to learn new, more positive patterns of thinking and talking to himself. The behavioral part teaches new actions, new behaviors in response to the problem at hand. For example, a common component of such therapy is learning relaxation techniques, meditation, or prayer as means of subduing excessive worry.

Jacob's psychotherapy combined both insight-oriented and cognitive-behavioral therapy. This makes sense for many individuals who want to discuss their lives in general as well as deal with a specifically defined problem. I met with him for short sessions and consulted with the therapist I referred him to, to offer my suggestions regarding the problem of worry.

But the most important part of Jacob's treatment was to help him change his daily habits. He needed to quit drinking, get enough sleep, exercise regularly, and eat properly. I spent quite a bit of time educating him as to the health benefits, particularly the mental health benefits of altering how he drank, slept, exercised, and ate. For most people, education is more effective than lecturing. Education is most effective one-on-one, live doctor conversing with live patient.

Jacob soon agreed he wanted to make some changes. He got excited about the fact that these changes were not for his moral improvement, but they could actually reduce his worrying and help him get his writing done.

He was able to quit drinking on his own. This is unusual. Most people need the help of twelve-step programs, but Jacob had an aversion to such groups. Instead, he quit without that kind of help, using instead the education and encouragement he received from his therapist and from me.

He also took up tennis and found a fellow librarian with whom he played three times a week after work. He soon grew to love tennis and also found pleasure in the friendship he made with his opponent. The more he played tennis the more he enjoyed exercise in general, and he started to go for walks after dinner, take stairs instead of elevators when he could, and go hiking on weekends. As happens with many people, exercise became a tonic for him. It became a healthy replacement for alcohol. Indeed, both alcohol and exercise produce changes in brain chemistry; those produced by exercise are obviously better for you.

As he exercised more and drank less, he found it easier to readjust his sleep pattern. He stopped staying up so late at night, in part because he felt ready to go to bed and in part because he was starting to ruminate less.

As to food, I gave him grandma's advice: eat a balanced diet, and don't eat too much. The question of diet is an interesting one. There can be no doubt that diet influences our brains. The problem is we don't know yet what kind of diet is best. It's likely that the diet that makes one person think and feel best will not necessarily be the diet another person might need. There is great individual variability when it comes to the brain. A growing number of books recommend one diet or another to enhance mental functioning, and most of these books are written by reliable experts who make excellent arguments. Some of the best of these books include *Spontaneous Healing* and *Eight Weeks to Optimal Health,* both by Andrew Weil, M.D. (Knopf, 1995 and 1997), *The Zone,* by Barry Sears, Ph.D. (HarperCollins, 1995), and *Beyond Prozac,* by Michael J. Norden, M.D. (HarperCollins, 1995).

However, we have not yet definitively cracked the nutritional, dietary brain code. I recommended to Jacob that he avoid toxic substances, such as alcohol, and beyond that, that he watch and observe how he ate. I advised him to use himself as his own experiment, trying to see what diet worked best for his own mental and emotional well-being. This is good advice for everyone.

Finally, medication played a role in Jacob's treatment. He took 20 mg. of Prozac per day and complained of no side effects.

Within three months Jacob was writing again. Within six months he and I decided that he didn't need to see me anymore and I lost touch with him, although he continued to see his therapist. I have been looking on the newsstands and bookstands for his name, but have not yet found it there. I don't doubt that one day I will.

Jacob's is a success story. Not all worriers can find relief so quickly. Sometimes they find no relief at all, but that is rare. Usually a combination of methods works. In Jacob's case it is impossible to say what did what. Maybe it was the Prozac. Maybe it was the psychotherapy. Maybe it was abstinence from alcohol. Most likely, however, it was the combination of medication, psychotherapy, abstinence, exercise, sleep, and diet, which produced a new state in Jacob's mind, a state in which he could allow himself to write.

The key, as is usually the case, was for Jacob to approach his problem not as an inevitable part of the human condition, or as some immensely complicated sequela of his upbringing, or even as a necessary part of the process of writing, but instead to approach his problem as a challenge in "brain management." What could he do in his day-to-day life that would affect his brain so that it would behave the way he wanted it to?

The starting point of this book is to acknowledge that worry can hurt and that there are better solutions to excessive worry than simply to endure it. To manage our minds skillfully and to manage worry well, we must take a dualistic approach, looking at both the biology and the psychology of an individual's life. None of us need be consumed by worry. There are positive steps we can take. We can never dispel worry but we can master it and ride it out well, rather than having it ride over us.

2 "Worry Is Good"

Worrying is the most natural and spontaneous of all human functions. It is time to acknowledge this, perhaps even to learn to do it better.

Lewis Thomas

I was playing squash one Sunday morning with Jeff Sutton, a neuroscientist and a good friend, when I told him I was writing a book to help people who worry too much. He instantly responded, "But worry is good! You have to worry to survive!"

He then went on to talk about worry in the most animated, unworried tones as we warmed up for our game. I soon found out that I had stumbled onto the upside of worry, as championed by Dr. Jeffrey Sutton. "If you don't want to worry, be a plant," he said disdainfully, as he whipped his racquet in the wrist-flick squash stroke, shooting the ball against the wall with a sharp smack. "Everybody has to worry!" Smack! "Life is all about fear. We have to be afraid," he bellowed. "Nature wants us to! If you want to die young, then ignore worry!" Smack! "But even then you can't get away from it. Fear is wired in. Deeper than any other feeling. It's stronger than love or sex or rage." Smack! "Or anything else!"

"Worry is good," he cheered again, as if it were a neuroscientist's battle cry, while he leaped to make another shot. For the time being our conversation stopped, as we both focused on the game.

Jeff Sutton, of course, is right. Worry is not altogether bad. Without worry we die. While some people may suggest that worry is "neurotic," they also realize that some amount of worry helps us survive. It warns us of danger and urges us to take corrective action.

"Worry is really a very advanced form of brain activity," Jeff went on to say after our match. "Most highly successful people worry a lot," he said. "That's part of the price they are willing to pay. Worry gives them an edge. By thinking about all the things that can go wrong, they can take steps to prevent them. But it takes a smart person to think of all those things. You have to be smart to be a good worrier."

"You're telling me excessive worry is a badge of intelligence?" I asked.

"No, I guess not," Jeff allowed. "We all worry—smart and stupid alike. Worry is fear and the only living organisms without fear are vegetables, not animals. Who knows, maybe even plants experience some kind of feeling of fear when danger is near. Maybe when they see Aunt Matilda coming out with her shears they scream in some plant fashion of screaming. Who knows?"

"But no one likes to do it," I went on.

"You haven't met my mother-in-law," Jeff said with a grunt.

Worry *is* good, up to a point. One of the classic graphs in all of psychology is the performance-anxiety curve put forth in 1908 by Yerkes and Dodson. It shows that as anxiety increases, performance improves, *up to a point.* Beyond that point, as anxiety continues to increase, performance declines. The curve, which is important enough to be the only graph you will see in this book, is shown on the next page.

Business people know the positive value of worry. One of the most articulate—and successful—proponents of worry is Andrew Grove, CEO and visionary leader at Intel, a now fabulously successful company—that almost wasn't. Grove steered Intel from a swerve where two wheels went over the cliff to its center-lane position today. He has just written a book that will probably become a classic in the field of management entitled, *Only the Paranoid Survive.* The book is not as

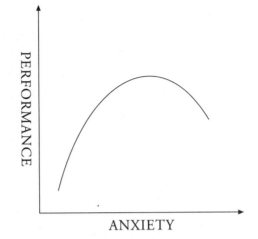

menacing as its title; indeed it is an invitation to success. Be creatively paranoid, Grove urges. Anticipate every alternative. Be active in your pursuit of worry lest it be active in its pursuit of you. Encourage your subordinates to disagree with you, to point out when the king has no clothes rather than to endorse your every viewpoint blindly. Better to hear bad news from your own people than read about it in someone else's victory speech. The work of anticipating bad news—i.e., the work of worry—can be useful. The major point Grove makes in the book is summed up in the subtitle: "How to Exploit the Crisis Points That Challenge Every Company and Career." Don't run from worry, he warns. Embrace it. Dissect it. *Learn* from it. Positive thinking is fine but don't let it blind you from seeing possible danger. Be *positive* about your ability to deal with what is *negative.* Otherwise you will go the way of the millions who choose to ignore danger until it is too late. Grove sees in failure the roots of triumph. "Success," he says, "is only a disaster away."

The annals of business are full of stories of leaders such as Andrew Grove, who know how to worry wisely and well. In their book about how to start your own company, *Fired Up! From Corporate Kiss-Off to Entrepreneurial Kick-Off* (Viking, 1996), business consultants Michael Gill and Sheila Paterson entitle one of their chapters, "Worriers Make Winners." They interviewed many successful entrepreneurs. Hoping to find out what one *should* worry about in running a successful company, they asked these people what they worried about most. They found that no one *topic* of worry predominated, but rather that worry became a constant companion, a welcome prod. They did not spend their time trying to flee or quell worry, but rather to deal constructively with the *substance* of the concerns their worries raised. Instead of seeing worry as an unpleasant state of mind always to be avoided or minimized, they saw it as a useful warning signal, a special kind of competitive edge. If they could sit still and listen to their worries and then act effectively to deal with those worries, in other words, if they could *worry better* than their adversaries, they would prevail. They used worry to break complacency. Gill and Paterson found, "Worrying about *achieving* rather than simply getting along in a corporate world is the *single* most important characteristic of all successful entrepreneurs. Worriers who worry about achieving their goals are sure to be winners."

Gill and Paterson quoted a wide range of successful men and women. One of the most interesting was Tim Moser. His field? Race cars. "Obviously it takes a special kind of worry for such an entrepreneur to survive and to succeed," Moser said. "Most racetrack entrepreneurs I know nurture a special sort of fear: one that inspires action. The ideal fear is one that leads to a positive response. Fear that leads to forward motion. . . . Everyone is afraid. It is how you *use* that powerful emotion that distinguishes the winners from the losers." Gill and Paterson cite a study designed to determine if any one quality of driving could predict winners. The result was unexpected. The study found that while "all drivers were worried about going into a particularly tricky corner, the losers downshifted to cut their speed and ease their fears, while, on the contrary, the successful drivers *stepped on the gas.* The winners were just as concerned as the losers, but it was their reaction to their worry that was different. For winners, worry is a reason to take some *positive* action."

I have stressed a baseball metaphor in this book: the importance of playing a ground ball, instead of letting it play you. To successfully field a ground ball when you are playing an infield position in baseball, you should run at the ball instead of backing up on it, which is most people's first instinct. Similarly, most people's first instinct in taking a curve in a high-speed automobile is to slow down, but the drivers who win the races say they actually speed up. Whether it be fielding a ground ball, driving a race car, running a business, or living a life, the most successful approach is to attack a problem before it attacks you.

Gill and Paterson—and the many successful people they interviewed—stress the importance of creating growth out of worry. Don't look back, they say; don't grieve over lost opportunities; use that energy to find new opportunities. They emphasize that all successful entrepreneurs worry; indeed they say, "Fear is the *fuel* [emphasis mine] that makes the entrepreneurial person a success." They use fear for forward progress, not for backing up. Use worry to make you do well, to prod you to achieve, not to hold you back. When you come to a tricky corner, *step on the gas!*

"But that is absurd," comes the retort. "You'll crash." Maybe you will. But you're likely to lose if you try to play it too safe. Athletes will tell you that if you ski defensively, or play football always trying to avoid getting hurt, or play tennis timidly, you'll fall, get hurt, or lose. A secret we learn from sports—from race car driving to baseball to tennis and golf—can help us in life, especially in regard to worry. It is this: GO FOR IT. Don't let up. Don't back off. Don't, at the moment of crisis, change your whole style and start to backtrack.

You cannot micromanage yourself in those few seconds of make-it-or-break-it—what athletes call "crunch time." The broken-field runner doesn't stop to think, "Shall I swivel my hips right and dart left, or shall I dart left and save the hip movement for the next turn?" If he did, he would be tackled before he took another step. At crunch time, you simply have to go for it. Trust your instincts. Speeding into the curve is not the time for a committee meeting. The meetings should have happened long before. Preparation matters, of course. Preparation is crucial. All those boring, exhausting, punishing practices. All those boring, exhausting, punishing committee meetings, or hours spent studying, or late nights preparing proposals. Whatever its form, preparation is key. But at the moment of performance, you have to be able to *trust* in your preparation and let the forces that you can't consciously control be your guides. You will not crash if you are well prepared, if you let yourself go for it. Not if you've done it before and you know what you're doing. Not if you've failed and tried again.

This link between worry and failure is a critical one. I have found in my work with thousands of children and adults who have learning disabilities of one kind or another that the worst learning disability is not attention deficit disorder or dyslexia or any of the other conditions with fancy names. The worst, most damaging learning disability—also *by far* the most common, affecting *100 percent* of the population at one time or another—is *fear*. Simple fear. Fear of failing. Fear of looking stupid. Fear of being ridiculed or rejected. It starts in school, but it certainly does not end there. It can continue throughout life, holding people back time and again from trying something new, from learning a new skill or trying some advanced technique or starting a fresh career. Failure in any endeavor should be *applauded*, because only if a person is made comfortable with failing will that person be willing to try again. As Andrew Grove said, success is only a disaster away. If the person is not ashamed to fail, he will be willing to use his fear constructively to move forward, to speed up through the curve, instead of using it defensively to slow down. Failure is good if you learn from it. Indeed most successful entrepreneurs say success is 90 percent failure. If you don't fail, you're not trying anything new, you're not pushing the envelope, you're just playing it safe. So failure is good. Worry is good, too. In fact, failure and ongoing worry can make an unbeatable, if paradoxical, recipe for success.

The more you worry, the better you do, *up to a point*. The key is to know how to stop at that point.

Too much worry leads to a host of medical complications, from depressed immune function, to heart disease, to gastrointestinal disorders of all kinds, to an array of different types of headaches and musculoskeletal pains about the body. It has even been found that anxiety disorders in adolescent girls can result in stunted growth! Furthermore, excess worry impairs judgment, induces fatigue, increases irritability, and in general makes a person a less effective leader or worker. You need to learn to worry well so that worry does not become destructive, consuming you instead of arming and alarming you as it should.

3   The Basic Equation of Worry

Increased Vulnerability
+ Decreased Power
_____
= Increased Worry

Harry Dunlop was driving himself mad with worry. On the face of it, there was no good reason for this. He was a fifty-two-year-old family doctor from the Boston area who had given up his medical practice to become a consultant to other doctors and hospitals struggling to adapt to the changing face of medicine. He was in great demand. Married for the second time, he and his wife were happy, and and he even got along with his ex-wife without difficulty. His two daughters were in college and were both doing well. So what was his problem?

"I never let up on myself," he said in his slight Southern drawl. Having grown up in the hills of North Carolina, he had never let go of his Southern accent altogether. "Maybe it was being brought up Baptist, maybe it is just the curse of my birthright, but I never have a moment's peace. Most people when they arrive in their hotel room to begin a vacation throw open the curtains and admire the view. I close the curtains and start to feel guilty for not working. Or I start to look for what's wrong with the room. Or I begin to wonder what problems could be developing back home. It drives my wife crazy. 'Can't we ever just relax and be happy?' she asks. After fifty-two years of life on this planet, I'm afraid for me the answer is no, I can never just be happy. Live in the moment without torment in my mind? I can't do it. I always seem to have to be worrying about something."

"Even when things are good?" I asked.

"Especially when things are good. I look at my life now and realize that things are good most of the time. I'm lucky, very, very lucky. And don't think I don't know it. But I worry even when there is nothing to worry about. You see, I'm the kind of person who *has* to worry. I believe if I don't worry, then bad things will happen for sure. I think of worrying as voodoo magic that staves off bad spirits. I don't dare *not* worry!"

Harry was a big man, at least 6'4", and he had a beard like Ernest Hemingway. With his sweet, deep voice, he had a commanding, even charismatic presence. He came from a rural family with little education and much religion. His upbringing was strict but not brutal. His education was just barely adequate until he got a scholarship and went off to Harvard. There he found a new life. "I could never go back home again," he said. "Harvard opened up a whole new world for me. But it also forced me out of the old one. It's sad in a way. I lost my family. I mean, they're nice folks and I still see them, but they are far from who I am now. All this fancy education changes you, you know."

"Yes," I said a bit ruefully. "So you weren't troubled as a child?" I asked.

"Not as much as now. But I was troubled. I remember my mother telling me to just go to sleep, nothing was out there that was 'gonna git me.' Yes, I worried as a child. But it really got intense in Cambridge, at college. I can remember sitting up to all hours with friends drinking Jack Daniel's, and after they went to bed I had to drink the rest of the bottle to quiet down my mind."

"Did you become an alcoholic?" I asked.

"In college, yes. I stopped drinking in medical school, because I would have flunked out if I hadn't. By the end of college I was drinking all day. But in medical school, I stopped. Then starting up my practice, getting married, having the kids, getting divorced, getting married again, all that kept me busy and I didn't drink. Still don't. I could start tomorrow, though."

"Don't," I said.

"Don't worry, I won't. But what can you do for me to stop my mind from finding problems everywhere? I'm fed up with it. I want to write a book about my life in medicine, tell stories about what I've seen, and I think it could be a good book, but every time I sit down to write it, I freeze up. The computer screen looks back at me and I go off on some damn worry."

"Like what?" I asked.

"Like anything. Will I ever get another consulting job? Which is absurd because I have a waiting list about six months long. Or I worry, will I be able to make the tuition payments? Or will my wife still love me tomorrow?"

"Do you have reason to doubt that she will?" I asked.

"No, none at all. That's just the point. Most of these things come out of nowhere. I make them up. My mind can't stand peace and quiet, so it goes out hunting for problems and sure enough it always bags a few. I can turn a rainy day into an omen of disaster. Sometimes the worrying goes off into self-criticism. Instead of worrying about something real, I just start attacking myself or my work. I didn't do this right, or I did that wrong. I'm weak or stupid or bad. Just beat up on myself. There is this very critical voice inside me. I know it well. I call it the preacher. When the preacher gets started, I know I'm in for it. The preacher gets up into the pulpit and just lays into me."

"Why do you listen to him?" I asked.

"I have no choice," Harry replied.

"But you do have a choice," I countered.

"It feels as if I don't," he replied. "That's the bind. The preacher holds me in my pew and pours on his words, just as if he had my neck in a vise. When he's finished there is very little left of me. I'm reduced to nothing."

"You'd think a preacher would want to lift you up," I mused.

"Not this preacher. He just wants to beat me down."

"Of course, he *is* part of *you*, since he's in your head. You'd think since you invented him you could destroy him as well," I offered.

"I have tried to destroy him," Harry replied softly. "The best I can do is distract him and make him go away for a while. Then, out of nowhere, when I'm sitting at dinner with Sheila or I'm driving down the highway, he pops back into my mind and the sermon begins again."

"Have you ever seen a psychiatrist before?" I asked. "Ever tried any medication?"

"No and no. Unless you count alcohol as medication."

"Just wondering. Considering how much pain you've lived with, why haven't you ever consulted a psychiatrist?"

After a long pause, Harry replied, "That's complicated."

"How so?" I asked.

"I don't know if you'll understand this, because I'm not sure I understand it myself, but it has always felt as if I'd be cheating if I took medicine or talked to a psychiatrist. I had to deal with the preacher on my own. I thought if I took medication or if a psychiatrist tried to help me with it, well, I thought the job would not get done. It would just be another delaying action. I have to kill him on my own or at least answer to him alone. I don't think anyone else *could* really know him as I do. A psychiatrist would probably diagnose me with depression, give me some medicine, and that would be the well-intentioned end of it, but it would not even begin to get to the heart of my reality. It wouldn't come close."

"Why is it that you wanted to come see me today?" I asked.

"I heard you give a lecture at a medical meeting. Something clicked. You seemed like a nice guy. You seemed like you might understand. The truth is that I didn't expect you to help. I just thought you'd make for good company."

"You think your problem is beyond help?" I asked.

"I'm afraid so," Harry said.

"But *you* control it," I continued. "You *listen* to the preacher. He is your creation."

"It doesn't feel that way. It feels as if he is as real and outside of me as death itself."

"Funny you should put it that way," I commented.

"Yes, isn't it?" Harry said. "Death isn't outside either, is it? It comes from within, death does. But we have no control over it. That's the point. I have no control over the preacher, so it feels as if he's coming at me from the outside."

"Why don't you just tell him to go away and stay away?" I asked.

"Because I can't."

"But why can't you?" I persisted, feeling I had to push the question.

"Because he is my truth. I feel as if I must listen, that it is my duty. He, alone, knows me."

"Harry," I protested, "that's not true. He tells you that you are bad and you're not."

"So you may say," Harry replied. "But when he gets talking, there's no arguing him down. I hang on his every word. I believe him more than I believe anyone."

"What would it feel like to tell him you've had enough of his torture and you're just not going to listen anymore."

"It would feel *won*-der-ful," Harry said, drawing out the word as if to savor it.

"So what if I suggested to you that you tell the preacher to go away?" I asked. "What if I told you to put him out of your mind? What if I worked with you on reshaping your thoughts so there was no room for the preacher anymore?"

"It's a nice thought," Harry replied, "but impossible. It would feel as if I had agreed to some pop-psychology positive-thinking gambit out of desperation, even though I knew it was basically bogus."

"But you came to see me," I noted.

"Yes," Harry said.

"Some part of you thinks that maybe I can help?" I asked.

"Honestly, you just seemed like a nice guy. I think my worrying is as much a part of me as my skin."

"And any therapy would be basically bogus?" I repeated.

"Yes, I'm afraid so. Your remedy is in the category of the basically bogus. Nothing against you, personally. We're just dealing with forces that are much more powerful than anything doctors or psychiatrists can touch."

"How do you know?" I asked him.

"Well, Dr. Hallowell," Harry replied, "people like me have been around since the dawn of time, and people like you haven't been able to cure us."

"Sometimes we have," I replied.

"Not very often," Harry insisted.

"I don't know who has the numbers, but it seems to me we should give it a try. What have you got to lose?" I asked.

"Time. Money," Harry said with a little smile.

"Or maybe something more important?" I observed.

"Like what?" Harry asked.

"Your pain," I said.

"Oh, now you are trying to be clever and tell me I do not want to give up my worrying," Harry countered, almost as if he'd already thought of this himself.

"I'm not being clever," I said, "I'm just stating the obvious. You worry much more than you need to, you suffer with your worrying, and yet you haven't been willing to get help, even though you're a doctor and must know that there is help for what you're going through."

"I haven't got help because I don't believe in your kind of help," Harry replied, somewhat defensively.

"So you have told me," I answered, "and I don't want to push you on this if you don't want me to. I'm simply suggesting that you may feel ambivalent. One part of you may want to get help. *That* part of you may be here for a deeper reason than simply thinking I am a nice guy. Another part of you may be saying no, help is forbidden and useless to boot. That's the part of you that wants to hold onto your pain. It's as though you have this private version of Moby Dick running inside of you and you'll be damned if you'll give it up until you have killed the white whale all by yourself."

"I think there is *some* truth to what you're saying," Harry replied. "So what do we do?"

"We keep at it," I replied.

Harry was a brilliant man with a wonderful life but, like so many people, he was tormented inside. He wrestled with demons every day. He never offered them up as excuses, he got his work done and done well, and he didn't burden others, but he was in pain.

This powerful man felt vulnerable within himself. He felt powerless in dealing with his own self-criticisms as well as his fears about the future. Although the outside world saw him as strong, he felt weak in combating his preacher. Although he was powerful in the eyes of observers, he did not *feel* powerful in dealing with himself. Many, many people suffer like this. Their worst enemy is their own mind.

This is due to the interaction between life experience and their biological makeup. The analogy I like is the one of a violin. Imagine the bow of the violin as life experience and the strings of the violin as our biological makeup. The bow of life's experience draws across the violin strings of biology to produce the music of life. We are left to wonder who is *playing* the violin. In part it is our conscious selves, or what psychologists call the observing ego; in part it is our spontaneous selves, our unplanned and unconscious selves; in part it is God, fate, luck, and chance. What kind of music we make depends upon how we deal with what happens to us in life and also upon what we are made of physically. Acknowledging this balance between experience and biology is crucial to a proper understanding of all mental processes.

In the past, experts have tended to emphasize one over the other: experience over biology or biology over experience. Over the course of the twentieth century we have witnessed this ebb and flow. Before Freud we tended to overemphasize the biological self, while neglecting the importance of upbringing and family. After Freud we tended to overemphasize the importance of upbringing, laying almost all of life's ills at the feet of parents, especially mothers. Now, at the end of the century, we are approaching a midpoint, a balanced view, giving equal weight to nature and nurture, biology and experience.

In the case of worry, the balanced view is especially apt. Some people are predisposed, by in-born temperament, to worry and fret more than others. However, the content of what one worries about is shaped by life experience. It is amazing to me that some people who have suffered tremendously hardly worry at all, but instead sail through life with a natural confidence, while others, who have led secure lives, worry constantly even when there is nothing to fret about.

But the process of worry is similar in all cases. Biologically, worry is a species of physical fear. In psychological terms, a fundamental model is this basic equation of worry: *worry results from a heightened sense of vulnerability in the presence of a diminished sense of power.* If you are worried about a meeting with your boss, this probably reflects a feeling of increased vulnerability and/or a diminished feeling of power in relation to your boss. If you are having hard times with money, you may well find yourself worrying about finances a great deal because you are feeling more vulnerable and less powerful when it comes to meeting your financial obligations.

Particularly exasperating if not frightening is how divorced from reality the process of worry can become. If you are broke and worry about money, it at least makes sense. But, oddly enough, the rich man may worry more about money than the poor man who doesn't give his limited income a second thought. Many people were less concerned about money when they were poor than when they started to earn a "real" income.

In other words, worry may arise not from what is real but from what is imagined. It may derive more from *imagined* peril than from any actual danger. Isn't it strange that people torment themselves needlessly, filling their minds with fear of the most unlikely events? But this is what the worried mind does.

What activates worry, therefore, is not necessarily true danger, but a *feeling* that danger *may* lurk nearby. Worry derives from a *feeling* of vulnerability coupled with a *feeling* of powerlessness. It really doesn't matter how strong or weak one actually is.

If you look at most of the situations in which you worry, you will usually find this basic equation underlying the problem: increased vulnerability plus decreased power equals worry.

We all know people who excel at what they do but never feel satisfied. Some of these people take it a step further. They may have done well in the past but always fear they will not do well *this time around.* They live with a constant fear of losing their skills or not making good on their plans. They brood and ruminate over what might go wrong. They live with an inner pain beyond the reach of the reassuring words of others. "What if . . . ?" they ask over and over again, a throbbing refrain.

Ultimately the treatments of worry address both components in the "basic equation": vulnerability and power. To decrease worry we need to increase the individual's feeling of power as well as decrease his sense of vulnerability. The more powerful and the less vulnerable a person feels, the less he will worry.

What happened to Harry? He agreed to continue to see me for a while, although he remained skeptical. But over time, he found that the voice of the preacher began to subside. Why?

To be honest, I'm not sure. In treating patients, I am never sure of why whatever happens actually happens. All of us in this field have to beware of the logical fallacy of *post hoc, ergo propter hoc,* which translated literally means, "after which, therefore because of which." Just because one event *follows* another, it does not mean the first event *caused* the second. Yet we often cheerfully conclude that it does. If I do a rain dance and it rains, that doesn't prove my rain dance caused the rain. That Harry's worrying subsided after he started to see me doesn't prove that seeing me caused his worrying to subside. In this field, we never know exactly what is going on.

What remedies did we try in Harry's case? We used a combination of remedies. First, I listened to him. I made observations and suggestions, which included my giving rational reassurance. I also reiterated my basic interpretation that his worries were coming from inside him, that he was behaving as if he were a powerless child instead of a powerful adult, and that he was feeling afraid of being punished for having done well because he had no model in his growing up of someone who had done this well. He was in uncharted territory and it was scary.

Cognitively, I worked on encouraging him to tell the preacher to get lost. I told him to tell himself that he was in charge, that he had done nothing wrong and that he would not be punished by anyone except himself. This process of listening, interpreting, encouraging, brainstorming, and reality-testing is what I call psychotherapy.

I also prescribed exercise. Harry went on an exercise plan that included jogging three miles three times a week. He didn't have to pay any money or go to any club. He just jogged around his neighborhood.

I suggested certain restructurings of his life, such as better organization. We took an inventory of how he planned and scheduled his days, how he stored data, how he planned his social life, and how he organized his financial affairs. As we reviewed these areas, certain practical improvements suggested themselves.

Finally, I prescribed medication, in Harry's case the antidepressant Wellbutrin. The reason I suggested medication is that it seemed to me that there was a biological component to what was going on with Harry that medication might get to quickly. I chose Wellbutrin because I thought there was an attention deficit component to his condition. I felt part of his problem was that he let his preacher distract him too easily. Wellbutrin is known to be useful in adults who suffer from attention deficit disorder (ADD) and is also a good antidepressant. I decided to try Wellbutrin with him, instead of, say, Prozac, which I had used with Jacob, because Prozac does not act upon the symptom of distractibility.

Which of these interventions made the biggest difference? It is impossible to say. Each probably helped a little.

In the psychotherapy, Harry was able to connect with me. He had never actually talked honestly with another person for an extended period of time about his inner life. People who suffer like Harry tend to keep most of their pain to themselves. Letting these feelings out makes a person feel better. Why? We don't know. But the whole rationale for psychotherapy is simply this: the extended sharing of one's inner feelings with another person helps ease inner pain. There are many studies that have demonstrated this, and most people's own experience bears it out. When you're worried, it almost always makes you feel better to talk to someone—as long as you don't pick the wrong someone!

In this age of new cures and proliferating "therapies," it is worthwhile to emphasize the importance of simply listening. We live in fast times. We speak in sound bites and converse rat-at-tat. It is hard to get someone to slow down long enough to give you the time you need to speak your mind. Most of us have had the experience of feeling pulled apart inside as we try to get off the telephone, or politely break off a curbside conversation, or excuse ourselves from a luncheon meeting because we had to hurry off somewhere else.

To sit with a person and not feel an inner pressure pulling you away is rare these days. But in psychotherapy you have time to talk. Protected time. At its best psychotherapy remains a superb method for helping people who are in emotional pain. "Tell me about it . . . ," the therapist begins and then listens, giving the other person the chance to tell it all. When was the last time someone gave you that chance?

I listened to Harry. I also talked, because silent therapists usually make people nervous and self-conscious. But most of all I wanted to give Harry a chance to talk and to be listened to.

The experience of explaining yourself—telling your story—to a trained, attentive other person heals pain in most people. However, it is not an easy experience to come by these days. Most people are in too much of a hurry to listen. Some psychotherapists are so weighted down with their own agendas—political, theoretical, or emotional— that they can't listen for long before plugging the patient into one harangue or another. But Harry and I kept an open mind.

As Harry talked, he began to find that, contrary to what he had expected, talking didn't feel like a waste of time. He began to try to make our sessions last longer by lingering in his chair or at the door. He began to need me much less to get the session started or to give him feedback along the way. I could even feel some resentment from him at times when I did speak up. He wanted me to be quiet and listen!

A worried person needs—first of all—to be heard. Many friends, lovers, and colleagues make the well-intentioned mistake of jumping in too soon with reassurances and suggestions: "Why don't you try this?," or "I think you should do that," or "Don't feel so bad." The worried person can't make use of the suggestions and reassurances until he has had the chance to come out with what is on his mind. Good advice for the listener is, don't try to fix the problem; just listen to it.

The listener helps by holding the painful feelings the worried person is conveying. "Here, take my misery and hold onto it for a few minutes, would you please?" It is work to listen. In my professional practice, I am most tired after sessions in which I say the least. That is because as I listen the words go into me. They move me. My insides react as I am told of sorrow and pain and hurt. I may stay silent but my feelings churn. The good listener reacts inside to what he is hearing, even if he talks very little.

You speak. I listen. I take in what you say. You sense me holding your feelings. This causes you to feel relief because you feel heard, understood, and supported. If there is one first step I would recommend to diminish worry, this is it: tell your concern to a good listener. Connect. Even if you get no solutions, it's OK. Solutions are overrated and good listening is a godsend.

The way I worked with Harry, using a combination of approaches from exercise to psychotherapy to medication, is typical of the kind of treatment that works for most worriers who come to see me. Of course, not everyone who worries too much has to see a psychiatrist or other kind of professionally trained therapist. This book will give examples both of the kinds of worry that usually require professional treatment and of those that one can usually treat without the help of a professional.

A good way to decide if you should consult a professional is to consider two factors: the intensity and the duration of your worry. If you worry intensely, much more so than a group of your peers, and if you have had this tendency for an extended period of time, then it is probably a good idea to get a professional evaluation.

Not all worry must be endured. Harry Dunlop had spent most of his adult life suffering with the notion that there was no help, that his mental anguish was just a part of the human condition, or at least *his* human condition, and the best he could do was to live with it patiently. For one reason or another, he always balked at getting professional help, until he found himself sitting in my office one day saying he thought I seemed like a nice guy.

In telling me his story, Harry found relief for his stored-up worries. In taking medication, his accompanying depression abated and his ability to sustain mental focus improved. In getting more exercise, he felt refreshed. In restructuring his life—tending to tasks he had put off, such as financial planning and organizing his desk—he felt less vulnerable and more in control. All these added up to a generalized reduction in anxiety and worry.

People's reluctance to get help often breaks down without their knowing it. The most stubborn, resolutely stoical individual can find help without really meaning to. Harry never came to a sudden realization that he should see a psychiatrist, nor did he crash and burn. Instead he did what many people do. He found help without consciously intending to. He drifted into my office on a detour from his usual route in life. Hi, he seemed to say, you seem like a nice guy, do you have time for me? It happened that I did.

4 Brain Burn

The Biological Basis of Worry

If there is one single emotion at the core of human experience, it is fear. Anger, sadness, joy, ecstasy, jealousy, love—none of these is as elaborately built into us as is fear. Virtually every cell in our bodies and every one of our physiological systems can contribute in one way or another to the human response of fear.

Our brains are equipped to register fear—and worry—more sensitively than any other emotion. Definitely more than pleasure. This is why positive thinking, such a fine idea, is often so hard to do. Our brains do not naturally tend toward positive thinking. Rather they tend toward fear or worry and then anger or sorrow. To be happy, content, and full of pleasure are not mental states for which nature wired us well. As far as nature is concerned, happiness doesn't really matter. Survival does. Happiness is not essential for survival. The only elaborate, reliable circuits in our bodies that involve intense pleasure are the sexual and hunger/feeding circuits; nature attached pleasure to procreation and eating because they are essential for the survival of the species. But happiness at work or in marriage or in repose, just sitting on the stoop at the end of the day? Nature really doesn't care. For that we humans have to reach.

On the other hand, fear, and its complex descendant, worry, rise up within us as naturally as hunger or thirst. Hormones, nerve cells, neurotransmitters, great chunks of the brain, sensors in the skin, reflex arcs, involuntary muscles, even hearts—all these stand on alert twenty-four hours a day, seven days a week, poised to make us feel fear and act upon it.

Our brains are perhaps better suited for the humans of thousands of years ago who were hunter-gatherers, exquisitely wired to detect danger in the external world: a snake dangling from a branch, a shadow concealing a trap, or a twig cracking under an enemy's foot. For most people today, physical danger is not as common as psychological danger, yet our brains remain ready to interpret all danger as physical and to set off alarms geared toward a physical response—fight or flight. As Dr. Aaron Beck, the cognitive therapist, pointed out, we misinterpret today's data in terms of what life was like of thousands of years ago. We misinterpret many signals as threats to our physical safety, and we work ourselves up into a state of fear, as our nervous systems pour out chemicals to prepare us to take aggressive physical action, when all we actually do is sit and stew.

For example, one day you open your bank statement. Instead of finding a balance of $1700, which you expected, you find that you are $96 overdrawn. Holy ____!!!, you say to yourself. You grab the bank statement and pull it close, as if by its lapels. "What do you mean, I'm $96 overdrawn?" you scream at it. This can't be!! Your heart starts beating fast. Your field of vision narrows so that all you see is the printed statement, its figures staring back at you implacably. You start breathing rapidly. Then your mind starts to race. You are ready to attack. But attack what?

What is going on in your brain at this moment? A lot. Seeing the overdraft sets off a cascade of events, quickly reaching the state you recognize as worry. Even creatures with the smallest brains, such as fish or birds, can be startled. As fear grows from a simple startle into the much more complicated process of worry, more and more of the brain gets involved. But at the heart of the process, buried deep at the bottom of our brains, just atop the spinal cord, right next to the centers that regulate our breathing and heartbeat, we find the brain stem, the apparatus that regulates our deepest reactions of fear.

Biologically speaking, worry is orchestrated in the brain. While pure fear may be reflexive—someone scares you and you jump—worry involves more than a spinal cord reflex arc. Worry is not instantaneous, like a reflex, but it gradually grows, like long, long thought.

Full-fledged worry requires the participation of the whole brain, not just the spinal cord or the brain stem. For example, when you open your bank statement and see the amount you owe, your startled reaction may then develop into a prolonged worry. Where will I get the money to pay this off? If I pay this, how will I be able to pay the other bills? What is happening to me that I allowed our finances to get so out of hand? Can we sustain our current standard of living or is there going to be a big crash? Will we have to move? Most of us know this all-too-familiar cataclysmic cascade of worries, set off simply by opening a bank statement or a bill.

On the other hand, sometimes worry can rise up out of a bit of information that originally produced no reaction at all. This is the slow burn. For example, someone may pass you in a corridor and that person may squint. After the person has passed you by, you may then casually wonder, *What did that mean? Why did she squint? There is no sun in here. Was it a wince of pain? Does she feel pain when she looks at me? Does she know something bad that is about to happen to me? Was she making fun of me? Was she warning me?* Instead of ignoring such a trivial piece of data as the wince of a passerby, you may fix on it, personalize it, and then "catastrophize" it. The mind can take any seemingly innocuous event and turn it into what *feels like* a crisis.

What is happening in the brain? Our best evidence is that such "fixating" on a problem does indeed have a physical basis. It can begin with a clump of neurons deep in the brain, called the amygdala, the regulator of our fight/flight response, as well as other functions. Fixating on a problem may begin when the amygdala senses danger. It then sends off alarm signals to the prefrontal cortex, the front part of the outer layer of the brain. When the prefrontal cortex receives alarm signals from the amygdala, it starts analyzing the worry, which then creates a reverberating circuit between the two that is extremely difficult to intercept. The prefrontal cortex signals back to the amygdala that the prefrontal cortex is worrying. The amygdala perceives this signal as more danger, so it sends more signals of alarm up to the prefrontal cortex, which causes the latter to keep worrying and sending back down to the amygdala more signals that it is worrying, which the amygdala perceives as more danger, and so it sends back up to the cortex more signals of alarm, which in turn . . .

This may be happening in the brain when you watch someone sink into a state of worry. We have all seen "the worried look." It is a frozen pose, and it takes only a few seconds to set in. You can see it creep across the face of your loved one as he is sitting in his favorite chair. He puts his paper down and stares off into space and in a few moments he looks . . . worried. His eyes narrow ever so slightly at the corners. He appears to be staring at something, but there is nothing there. His brow furrows a bit as the index finger on his right hand begins to tap but the rest of his body is still as a rock. He is not aware of his surroundings because worry has seized his brain. He is in a toxic trance.

The loop between the amygdala and the prefrontal cortex is just one part of a vast electrical-chemical-magnetic network in the brain, which we have only barely begun to understand. However, we do know that the process of worrying is real. We have known that for thousands of years. It can envelop a person like a net. A person can get so tangled up in it that he is unable to move, psychologically speaking. He can hardly take a step without the net pulling him back.

Most of the hundreds of people I polled for this book, when asked, "Would you describe yourself as a mild, moderate, or severe worrier?," responded moderate or severe.

Some, however, responded mild and a few went on to add that they think worry is a waste of time. One woman said, "I simply analyze a problem, do what I can to solve it, then forget about it." Why is this sensible approach so difficult for most people?

Until recently, we have underestimated how large a role physiology plays in worry. Now scientists are gathering compelling evidence of the physical basis of worry such as the recent study that isolated a gene that influences serotonin production in the brain and thereby might determine whether a given individual will be born a worrier or constitutionally bold and confident. Led by Dr. Dennis Murphy at the U.S. National Institute of Mental Health and Klaus-Peter Lesch of the University of Würzburg in Germany, the study focused on a gene that regulates a molecular pump influencing serotonin production.

If you carry this gene you may be one of those people who always must worry, almost as if there is a socket in your brain which requires that a worry be inserted into it at all times for life to feel complete. You almost feel out of touch with reality if you are not alarmed and worried over something. You scan the horizon *looking* for something to worry about to insert into your worry socket. You may have had an ideal childhood and a tranquil life, but still you never know a quiet moment.

As I mentioned in chapter 1, this study made front page news in the November 29, 1996, issue of the *New York Times*. In reporting their study, the researchers cautioned, however, that the problem is not as simple as blue eyes, short stature, or other genetically determined traits. Personality is vastly more complicated than those physical traits and therefore so are the genetic influences that must be taken into account. Experience plays a pivotal role in determining how strongly a gene may be expressed and, furthermore, the expression of a gene can be modified by life experience. Nonetheless, the biological evidence underlying worry is new and important.

One of the most dramatic bits of evidence of the biological basis of worry came from the National Institutes of Health, where a series of children were reported to have developed motor tics and full-blown obsessive-compulsive disorder (OCD) following strep infections. These children were called PANDAS, not because they looked like little bears, but because PANDAS was an acronym for their medical diagnosis, "pediatric autoimmune neuropsychiatric disorders associated with streptococcal infections."

What's this all about? These children got sick with a strep throat.

But then other symptoms appeared totally unrelated to a usual strep throat. The children developed motor tics (involuntary movements of the body such as twitches of the facial muscles or arms and legs) and symptoms of OCD in which they were deluged with intrusive, unwelcome thoughts and felt compelled to carry out strange rituals to stave off imagined consequences. These children had not had any such symptoms prior to their strep infections, so they were altogether new, apparently brought on somehow by the strep infection. But how?

The doctors were naturally intrigued. Being at a research center, they could perform various kinds of brain scans, which allowed them to look at these children's brains in different ways. They found that when the symptoms of OCD emerged, a part of the brain called the caudate nucleus had swelled up. The caudate nucleus is located deep within the brain, near the centers that regulate fear and the startle response. It is connected to the amygdala, which we have already identified as being part of the worry circuits. Part of what are called the basal ganglia, the caudate nucleus is a kind of gateway and relay switch to other parts of the brain and is involved in regulating movement— hence the tics—as well as in relaying signals of alarm and distress— hence the intrusive thoughts and compulsions.

Even more fascinating is what happened after the children underwent plasma electrophoresis, a process that cleaned away the antibodies to strep that had been in their blood. After the blood was cleared of these antibodies, the tics and the symptoms of OCD went away. The children stopped worrying! Furthermore, when the brain scans were repeated, it was found that their brains had returned to normal. The caudate nuclei had shrunk back down to their proper size!

This example shows how a purely physical event, in this case a strep infection, can cause a psychological syndrome, in this case excess worry and OCD. The point here is not that everyone who worries should go out and take penicillin or undergo plasma electrophoresis, of course, but rather that when we worry, certain centers in our brains may become overactive or misshapen.

The implications here might be that the inveterate worrier should seek out medical treatment or at least be aware that his excessive worrying is not all due to how he was raised or to the external influences on his life. For example, some people when opening their bank statement toss it aside if they see an overdraft and think, Oh well, I'll just take care of it. Others go berserk. The difference between the two responses may be as much in biology as in training.

There is more evidence. Brain scans have shown that people who ruminate and perseverate on their worries have excess activity in what is called the cingulate cortex within the brain. The cingulate cortex must quiet down to allow you to "change the subject" as you think, to change the focus of your conscious stream of thought. If you have difficulty doing this because you are ruminating, the cells in your cingulate cortex may be working overtime. They are probably firing constantly. If you could shut them off, your ruminating would likely diminish. In fact, an extreme remedy for extreme worrying is the surgical ablation of the cingulate cortex, called a cingulotomy, which was the most common of the operations popularly referred to as a "lobotomy."

It turns out some of the medications we use to treat ruminations shut down cells in the cingulate. One of the best known is Prozac. As I noted earlier Prozac is a serotonin reuptake inhibitor, that is, it increases the amount of available serotonin in the brain. This correlates with a number of changes in mood and behavior, such as an improved sense of well-being, decreased aggression, and reduced worrying and ruminating. However, the decrease in worrying and ruminating takes longer to occur than the mood changes. This is because the drug is not merely changing the concentration of the neurotransmitters. It is also extinguishing the firing of some nerve cells in the cingulate, and this takes longer to bring about.

The information continues to pour in, as brain research goes on every day around the world. We have discovered that there is some physical basis for worry and it is exciting to speculate as to what else might be going on.

For example, why did Allison Barnes (the doctor described in chapter 1 who was sued by her patient/friend) never fully get over the experience? Why did she still feel fear when she opened her mail even years later? Why did she still flinch when a patient expressed dissatisfaction? Why did her heart beat faster when she drove past any court house?

The explanation could be as follows: When Allison first opened the letter telling her she was being sued by Jim Tracker she felt a burning rush of emotion. Her vision narrowed, her heart rate increased, and her breathing became rapid. She felt intense anger, fear, and sorrow all at once. She felt her world caving in around her. Emotion overwhelmed her. This left a scar as surely as if the letter had been a dagger plunged into her back. The scar was not just psychological. It was physical too.

While Allison read the letter her endocrine system, her nervous system, her cardiovascular system, and her respiratory system all went wild. She pumped out a huge bolus of adrenaline under such high pressure that it burned a hole in her brain, so to speak, a hole she could never repair. The adrenaline surged to subterranean sites such as the amygdala, the hippocampus, and parts of the deep brain called the archecortex. These deep sites then relayed their intense fear to the upper brain, the neocortex. Once that happened, once the relay from the archecortex to the neocortex was complete, the information was permanently placed, like a tattoo or a bad burn. Like the memory of boot camp or any other intense experience, it stays with you forever.

When people are emotionally overwhelmed by an event, as Allison was, they can never fully forget it or put it aside. It becomes impossible for them ever to "get better" completely because their brains have been changed. The experience has branded them.

The difference between the person who gets overwhelmed and the person who doesn't may actually lie not in strength of character but in differences in the brain's sensitivity to adrenaline and to other stress modulators and neurotransmitters. When we speak of someone as being "sensitive," the physical basis for it may be the fact that his brain is more sensitive to the effects of adrenaline and other neuroactive substances.

Furthermore, if a person is given a beta-blocker, a drug that blocks the effect of adrenaline, during the upsetting episode, the episode will not have the same lasting effect. For example, if Allison had taken a beta-blocker just before she read the letter from Jim Tracker's attorney, she might not have suffered as much lasting psychological damage.

Similarly, some people are more sensitive than others to the brain's natural stress modulators, which are activated by the transmitter GABA (gamma-amino butyric acid). People who have a good supply of GABA or have brains that are naturally very responsive to GABA may be the people who are naturally cool and calm, possessed of an innate equanimity. The classic drugs used to treat anxiety and worry, such as Valium, Xanax, and others in the benzodiazepine category, activate GABA and GABA neurons. In other words, just as you can be born a worrier, you can be born a nonworrier. If nature gives you lots of GABA and GABA-sensitive binding sites, you may be cool as a cucumber, regardless of your life circumstances.

The key point here is to note a physical basis for what we have historically considered issues of "character." Bravery, confidence, grace under pressure may be inborn as well as learned. Skittishness, fearfulness, and lack of grace under pressure may have as much to do with not enough GABA as not enough grit.

But whatever is going on can always be altered. Brains are plastic. They can change, and if they have changed in a negative way, there is nothing to say they can't change back in a positive way. Later in this book we will look at various ways of changing the brain positively, but the kind of "brain burn" Allison suffered is very hard to cure completely.

Part of my work with Allison—the "cold towels" and "chicken soup" of my remedy—included helping her understand the physical nature of the injury her mind had suffered, the brain burn she had suffered. Seeing it as a burn that needed to be treated, she didn't have to revise her whole view of life. She could say to herself, "My brain has been burned and that is why I flinch when I read my mail, but I don't have to be angry at the whole world or worry about everything."

Even if one does not suffer a brain burn via a sudden outpouring of neurochemicals in an overpowering moment of emotion, still one may be an inveterate worrier. Some people are simply born to worry. They are genetically wired to be more aroused, neurologically, than others. What does being aroused mean and how does it influence worry?

People who are aroused are on guard. They are alert, looking here, looking there, tense, ready to take action instantly. These people's autonomic nervous systems, the system over which we exercise no voluntary control, are cranked up higher than other people's. Blood pressure, heart rate, respiratory rate, and even the electrical properties of the surface of the skin may be different when one is aroused. If one is aroused most of the time, one is wired to worry.

These people who are highly aroused on a genetic basis are also slow to get used to their surroundings and to relax. Physiologists say they are slow to "habituate." That is, they do not slow down and relax when they get used to their surroundings as most of us do. Instead, they remain highly aroused, on alert all the time.

Professor Jerome Kagan has done pioneering research with these kinds of people in his studies on the nature of shyness, following his subjects from before they were born into early adulthood. He has found that children who are high-strung and highly aroused early on often become shy and inhibited as adults, while remaining internally tense. Kagan can sometimes predict *when a child is still in his mother's womb,* based on fetal heart rate alone, whether or not that child will grow up to be tense, shy, and a worrier, or whether that child will develop a more relaxed nervous system and an outgoing personality.

Dr. Hans Eysenck, another pioneer in the field of the biological basis of emotion, differentiated in the 1960s between extroverted and introverted individuals on the basis their baseline of cortical arousal (cortical, referring to the outer layer, or cortex, of the brain, which receives its stimulation, at baseline, from lower centers in the brain). He found that all people were happiest when they were neither too aroused nor too calm. However, some people had a low baseline level of arousal, so they needed to seek more than the average amount of stimulation in the outside world to come alive, so to speak. These were the extroverts. Other people had a high level of baseline cortical arousal to begin with. They wanted only a little more stimulation from

the outside world in order to feel at their best. These were the intro-
verts.

Furthermore, Eysenck defined the difference between neurotic and
stable individuals physically on the basis of the reactivity of their autonomic nervous systems. The more intense the autonomic reactivity,
the more neurotic on a physical basis the individual was thought to be.
In addition, such an individual would be much slower to habituate to
whatever stimulus was causing the autonomic system to react. High
autonomic excitability coupled with a slowness to habituate characterized the individuals with the physical trait of "neuroticism." He was
not referring to our popular definition of neurotic; rather high-strung
is perhaps the closest popular expression. Eysenck became one of the
main developers of behavior therapy to help such people learn to mod-
ify their highly reactive nervous systems. While in some ways his work
is out of date, it remains a model of creative thought on the physiology
of emotion.

The physical perspective on worry, which we shall return to
throughout this book, helps explain why some people react so strongly
to certain kinds of crises, while others do not. We cannot lay all the
causation at the feet of parents or life experience.

Worriers seem to inherit a neurological vulnerability that life events
can then trigger. While some people are born confident, others are
born insecure. While some people are born calm, others are born
wired. While some people are born plunging forward, others are born
holding back. You may be born with a specific characteristic or you
may be born with a vulnerability to develop it later on, in the face of
the stresses life usually presents.

If you are "by nature" a worrier, can you change? Is worry wired too
deep for anything to be done, so that you must stoically accept your
lot in life? The answer is that you *can* change. You cannot give yourself
a new brain but the brain you have can be redirected in certain ways:
retrained, reassured, bolstered, and reset.

Dr. David Barlow, an authority in the field of anxiety research, puts
the physical data into perspective this way: "The one robust finding is
that anxious patients are chronically hyperaroused and slow to habitu-

ate. They are continually vigilant and ready for action. This may reflect a genetically determined neurobiological hyperactivity; a chronic cognitive state of relative helplessness, associated with chronic apprehension over future events; or a combination of the two" (*Anxiety and Its Disorders,* by David H. Barlow, Guilford Press, 1988).

Barlow's statement brings us nicely back to what I have called the basic equation of worry. Whether physical or psychological in origin, worry seems to derive from the combination of heightened vulnerability and a diminished sense of power. Both the body and the mind, genetics and life experience, are factors in this basic equation.

We are wired to feel fear and to worry. These responses are built in at the deepest levels of our neurological foundations. What we should do is learn to modulate these feelings, not try to eradicate them.

5 The Infinite Web of "What-If?"

The possibilities. This is where worry begins. In possibility. In imagination. In "what-if?" The same place dreams begin. The happy capacity of mind that allows a person to conceive of great success and wonderful outcomes also causes that person to worry. This is because the possibilities are endless.

I have a patient who calls these negative possibilities SBPOWs, pronounced like spouse, because she says her husband is responsible for most of them. The acronym stands for "spontaneously branching polymers of worry." My patient, Becky, runs a business as well as a household. "Today I called in," she said, "and my office manager told me she had talked it over with her assistant, David, and they had decided that the fax number needed to be changed and that we had to get a second line. That was a good idea, I thought, and I told her so. Do it, I said, and I hung up. Then after I hung up the SBPOWs began. What did she mean, *she and David* had decided? That was my original worry. Simple enough. I wondered to myself if my office manager was teaming up with her assistant to take on more authority than I want them to. I felt threatened. Fine. I should have been able to calm myself down. A part of me did, in fact, calm down. I told myself I was actually glad that I had empowered David and Karen to take on authority and make decisions, and I reminded myself that Karen did run it by me first, and it was only the phrasing that irked me.

"But another part of me then went wild. The SBPOWs began. The original little worry started to branch spontaneously with a vengeance. It was like a pattern of frost that shoots instantly across a cold pane of glass. These worries go wild on contact with your brain. In the blink of an eye, they multiply exponentially, so that in seconds I am fighting with an enormous net of dangerous, intricate detail, all stemming from that one, original little worry. You can't believe how fast it happens, how I can go from dealing with one worry to having to fight a jumbled mess of them."

I asked Becky if she could possibly reproduce in words what happened in her brain in those few seconds it took for the first worry to multiply.

She took a deep breath. "Whew!" she said, "I guess I could but it would be frightening. Maybe it would be helpful though. Do you want me to try? OK, I'll try. OK, so in this instance it starts with the phone call and my taking exception after I hung up to how Karen and David had decided together about the new line for the fax without asking me first. Then instantly my mind goes off in all kinds of directions. I envision EXACTLY where I imagine them standing, next to the elevator, as they make this decision. I see Karen's face and I see David stroking his chin. Then I feel in the pit of my stomach a sense of being excluded and I feel jealous and angry. Then I think how small and petty of me and I flash momentarily onto my uncle who always used to say, 'The world wants to be fair if you let it.' He would have told me not to worry about Karen and David. Then I feel guilty for worrying, but then I flash onto Warren Barnes, who has been trying to steal my clients for months now, but I haven't been able to deal with him directly. I feel a surge of anger at him and at myself for not telling him to back off, and I imagine picking up the telephone and calling him.

Then I see myself in conversation with him and I feel intimidated, which annoys because I know I'm smarter and harder-working than he is, and so I tell myself not to let him scare me just because he's a man. Then I have a few intrusive thoughts on the lowly place of women throughout history, and then I imagine a hopeful look on my daughter's face and how I'm determined that things will be better for her, which then makes me wonder, for reasons I don't understand, if she had a good day in school, and I hope no one was mean to her, even though I have no reason to believe anyone would have been mean to her, since the other children are usually very nice to her, and she is a popular girl. But I wonder, what if they weren't nice to her today? I tell myself I shouldn't worry about how popular Dinah is just because I always struggled to be popular, and I realize it is Dennis, my husband, who tells me not to worry about this, and I wonder why he can't just let me have my own relationship with Dinah, then I see his face and I remember I love him, then I worry why I had such an unkind thought about him, and I look back at the telephone and think about calling Warren Barnes, which reminds me of how insecure I am, and how maybe it's a family trait, as my mother was never very confident herself, but I then tell myself that that wasn't her fault, now was it? And I wonder what if I don't call Warren Barnes. Is he going to take away my business, even though I am better than he is? Then my uncle's words come back to me, that life wants to be fair if you let it, but I remind myself that my uncle never ran a business. All those thoughts, Dr. Hallowell, in the space of a second or two. The thoughts come in much faster than it took me to tell you about them. That's why I call them spontaneously branching polymers of worry. They race through my mind as if they were run by electricity. It's exhausting."

"Whew!" I said to Becky. "You must wear yourself out!"

"I do," she answered. "I wish I knew how to stop them. I made up the word SBPOWs one day when I was driving in the car with Dennis, and he made some trivial remark, which set off one of these reactions. I described the reaction to him but he just laughed, so I named the whole process after him as my way of blaming him for it. Actually, naming it helped a bit. It helped me put it somewhat at a distance.

Dennis thinks everyone has SBPOWs now and then. Do you think he's right?"

"Now and then, yes," I replied. "But it sounds as though you make these branching polymers all the time. By the way, where did you come up with the word polymer? Do you have a chemistry background?"

"Lord, no," Becky replied. "It's just the word that popped into my head. Must have picked it up from a magazine article or something, I guess."

"Well," I went on, "it is just more evidence of how imaginative you are, a trait common among worriers."

"Why's that?" Becky asked.

"The imagination is a two-edged sword," I replied. "You can use it to dream up good stuff or you can use it to dream up bad stuff. Unfortunately, you usually don't have much choice as to what happens in your mind, so you dream up good and bad."

"You mean I can't control this?" Becky asked.

"No, I didn't mean that at all. I'm just saying that as of now, before we talk about any remedies, it might feel to you as if you don't have any control. You feel you just have to take on whatever thoughts your mind brings in, including the SBPOWs."

"Right," Becky replied, with a certain gloom.

What Becky called her SBPOWs, I call the "what-ifs?" They are the relentless stream of thoughts that can rush in and amplify a simple worry, as Becky so vividly demonstrated. A single worry can kindle a whole bonfire of anxiety. When the what-ifs take off, there can be no end to them. This is partially because real life offers no end to the what-ifs. Take any situation and you can imagine it branching in a hundred different ways, then each branch itself branching, and so on as the design grows unmanageably complex. It is also because the what-ifs are fed by our very powerful fear system. Nature wants us to think of the what-ifs so that we keep ourselves out of danger. As I pointed out before, the fear system nature equips us with is potent. It is built deep within us and never shuts down.

The price we all pay for having a cerebral cortex on top of our animal-like brainstem is, in part, this ability to use our imaginations to worry—to torture ourselves, to ask, over and over again, What if? If we had only a brainstem, we could still react with fear, but we wouldn't be able to brood over danger, and we certainly wouldn't be able to torment ourselves with preposterous scenarios that don't stand the faintest chance of ever actually happening. This is part of the price we pay for having imaginations: we worry.

But just as we do not want to be like Candide, believing that everything will work out for the best in this best of all possible worlds, neither do we want to live like Cassandra, anxiously anticipating (if not demanding) the worst outcome everywhere we look, starting every day convinced that nothing will work out, entering each new encounter with a feeling of preordained doom.

The human imagination, at times the great tool of creation, is at other times our bane, as it snoops into the crevices of life to find, or even to create, phantoms and devils of every species and style, ready to tease and torment us as we attempt to pass the day in peace. *Pathological* worry resides not *out there* but *in here.*

So captivating is the tease of negative possibilities that the mind returns to them again and again, drawn by a strange curiosity. The worrier always wants to examine what can go wrong. He is like the driver who must slow down and look at an accident on the other side of the road. He is horrified by the accident, but he cannot look away. He cannot pass it by. He must look. Why?

Because of fear and curiosity. The same reasons worriers worry. Worriers must put their hands into the darkest corners of life and feel around to see if anything will bite. They cannot leave those corners alone. The driver who stops to look at the accident does not relish what he sees; quite the opposite. But still he has to look, drawn by the same magnet that draws the worrier to the worry. The magnet that draws the worrier to the worry is the magnet that draws us all to examine whatever we fear. If we can see it well, we might learn to avoid it.

It is also true that there is something ghoulishly interesting about what can go wrong in life. We contemplate our own demise. As much as we hate to see life's mishaps, they fascinate us. "O-o-o-o, look at that," we say, "isn't it awful?" and we move closer for a better look. The minute we hear of a disaster, we want to hear more. We hear of a death and we want details. We hear of a bankruptcy and we want details. We hear of a divorce and we want details. Even if we know that the details will upset us, we seem to want to know more.

The worrier turns this macabre curiosity onto his own existence and begins to dissect what can go wrong for him. The possibilities are endless. How many mistakes can he make? How many different ways can he go broke? How many different ways can someone betray him, in business or in love? How many different ways can he get sick? How many different accidents can befall him? How many ways can the vacation go wrong or the lease be misworded or the sale be a cheat or the car be a lemon? How many different kinds of trouble can his children get into? How many different ways can he die? The possibilities are endless.

They are almost thrilling, in a negative way. It is *exciting* that life is so cursedly uncertain. What can possibly go wrong now?, the worrier anxiously asks and of course his mind races making many replies.

The worrier is like a jealous lover. Both seize upon a detail and then fall victim to a devious process of mind. Out of one small fact they create an entire web of imagined details and possibilities, a theory of what is happening—or might happen—based upon one bit of truth and a slew of wild imaginings. I call this "the infinite web of what-if." The more advanced the process, the less apt it is to yield to reason or reassurance. Both the worrier and the jealous lover fear they will lose what they prize, and the irony is that their fear may actually cause that loss. This is the waste of worry: to suffer unnecessarily and to create problems that otherwise might never have been.

The what-if reflex can defeat a person. A patient of mine named Gerry, for example, began to wonder if he suffered from some deep desire to sabotage himself because every time he came up with an idea for a new business, his mind went crazy drumming up all the reasons he couldn't/shouldn't/wouldn't ever do it. "What is it with me?" he asked in exasperation. "Do I want to fail?"

Gerry did not want to fail, but I could see why he wondered. Here was a man with great talent and ambition, who was stuck in a job well below his capabilities. At age forty, he was working as a production assistant at a TV station. In the opinion of his peers, his wife, and supervisors, his ability should have taken him much farther.

The predicament of underachievement is a common one and can have its roots in many different places. Some people underachieve because they are depressed (and some people are depressed because they underachieve). Some people underachieve because they have a substance abuse problem (and some people have a substance abuse problem because they underachieve). Some people underachieve because they lack confidence (and some people lack confidence because they underachieve).

Deeper psychological roots usually entwine the mind of the underachiever as well. Was one parent or another particularly intimidating? Does he fear getting what he wants because it will mean having to give up a dependent position he secretly cherishes? Does he feel some unnamed guilt that holds him back whenever he is on the brink of success? Does he fear punishment if he wins, or might he fear that he will hurt someone else with his victory? These fears can hold a person back.

But the final common pathway for underachievement can often be excessive worry. A person can hold himself back by poring over the dangers of a new idea.

In Gerry's case, every time he had a new idea, his inner critic tied his hands. For example, once he had an idea for starting a restaurant, but he quickly negated that by telling himself that restaurants usually fail. He had an idea for starting a temp agency, but he heard the competition was too stiff. He had an idea for teaming up with his brother-in-law in the flower business, but he worried about working with a partner, especially his brother-in-law. He thought of writing a book about all he had seen in the TV business—and he had seen a lot—but he worried that the book might make enemies. He then thought of writing a mystery novel, but nixed that by deciding he couldn't write well enough and that all the worthwhile plots were already taken anyway. He thought of setting up a tutoring business for the many kids who were not getting what they needed in school, but he decided he didn't have the know-how to do that. Ironically, a friend, with much less know-how, stole this particular idea and did very well with it.

Gerry needed to learn how to take a risk. How do you help someone learn to do this?

Reassure him? Yell at him? Do something to make him mad so he'll forget how afraid and worried he feels? Give him a few drinks? All these methods have been tried, often by spouses or business associates, and some have even worked.

In Gerry's case, what I did was believe in him. It was not something I had to fake. I really did think he was a very talented man. I told him so explicitly more than a few times, but I do not think it was my telling him that helped. I think it was that he felt it. He could feel that I believed in him. This feeling built up over time. After we'd been meeting for about six months I could sense how Gerry looked forward to our appointments. He would come in with newfound enthusiasm and talk easily and openly.

If there was a magic to the treatment it was not so much the insights we developed about his life but the relationship we forged. Gerry knew I admired him, believed in him, and liked him. Somehow, that changed him.

A year into treatment Gerry started his own production company, specializing in making video products for businesses. He drew upon the many contacts he'd made in TV and soon was drawing business from out of state, out of New England, and even out of the country. He was an overnight success in a field more known for overnight failures.

How had therapy changed Gerry and given him the ability to take the risk he needed to take? How had he changed from a worrier to a doer? First of all, he did not change all that much. He still worried a lot. It was just that he found the courage to take one big risk, to go out on his own. How did he find it? In sitting with me, a person he didn't know, he found someone who saw him differently from the way he saw himself. My view of him became like a brace, which gradually straightened his spine, even as he strained against it. After a while, he didn't need the brace of our relationship any more. He went out on his own.

It takes a certain close-your-eyes-and-jump attitude to get past all the what-ifs, to take action in the face of negative odds, to make a sales pitch to a skeptical audience, and to put your best foot forward when you're not sure you have a best foot.

After you have calculated the risks and taken precautions, and after you have sought out wise consultation and sound advice, and after you have considered the options and carefully weighed your decision . . . you must jump! You have to do it to get where you want to go. You have to act. Finally, this is the way out of the infinite web of what-if. You leave the frightening world of your imagination and enter the world of actual deeds. Something ventured, something gained.

6 How Much of a Worrier Are You?

A Self-Assessment Quiz

> *We are, perhaps, uniquely among the earth's creatures, the worrying animal. We worry away our lives, fearing the future, discontent with the present, unable to take in the idea of dying, unable to sit still.*
>
> *Lewis Thomas*

Everyone is a worrier some of the time. But are you an excessive worrier? How can you get a handle on how much worry is normal and how much is too much? How do you know when to get help?

You need to look at how you worry. Are you a mild, moderate, or severe worrier? We don't have instruments to make these measurements, so we offer some guidelines here.

While we do not have a meter to measure worry, nonetheless people can rate themselves in terms of the intensity of their worrying as compared to that of their peers. In order to quantify how much you worry and find out how severe a worrier you are, I suggest that you take the following quiz. In response to each of the questions, give yourself 0 points if your answer is "rarely or not at all," 1 point if your answer is "sometimes," 2 points if your answer is "often," and 3 points if your answer is "almost every day." The questions that are starred (*) at the end (numbers 46–50) represent major risk factors for becoming an excessive worrier. Each of these questions should be answered simply "yes" or "no." Give yourself 3 points for each "yes" and 0 points for each "no." Answer all the other questions on the 0, 1, 2, or 3 scale just described.

SCORE	QUESTIONS
_____	1. Do you wish you worried less?
_____	2. Do worries pop into your mind and take over your thinking, like annoying little gnats?
_____	3. Do you find something to worry about even when you know everything is OK?
_____	4. How much did you worry as a child?
_____	5. Do others comment on how much you worry?
_____	6. Does your spouse (or person closest to you) tell you that you worry too much?
_____	7. Do you find that worry clouds your judgment?
_____	8. Do you tarnish good times with worry?
_____	9. Do you dwell upon a time or times you were unfairly sued, slandered, unexpectedly fired, downsized, or otherwise victimized by injustice?
_____	10. Do you worry that good friends will turn on you?
_____	11. Do you think about death and get frightened?
_____	12. Do you worry about your health in a way that you know, or others have told you, is excessive or irrational?

_____ 13. How often do you worry about money?

_____ 14. Do you know or do other people tell you that most of your worries are irrational?

_____ 15. Do you become immobilized by worry?

_____ 16. Are you more concerned than you wish you were with what others think of you?

_____ 17. Do you develop physical symptoms in response to stress?

_____ 18. Do you tend to brood over possible danger rather than doing something about it?

_____ 19. Do you drink or use other drugs when you get worried?

_____ 20. Do you find yourself unable to make use of reassurance when you worry?

_____ 21. Do you ruminate, i.e., go over the same worry again and again?

_____ 22. In the midst of success do you find yourself feeling apprehensive, wondering what will go wrong?

_____ 23. When you are alone, is some degree of fear your resting state?

_____ 24. Do you feel that it is dangerous, almost like tempting fate, to feel confident and secure?

_____ 25. Are you inhibited and/or shy?

_____ 26. How much do you procrastinate?

_____ 27. Are you plagued by a feeling that nothing can work out well?

_____ 28. How often do you feel that something bad is "about to happen"?

_____ 29. Do your daydreams tend to be gloomy?

_____ 30. When you sort through your mail, do you feel a sense of foreboding, wondering what bad news may have arrived today?

_____ 31. Do you avoid confrontations?

_____ 32. Are you insecure?

_____ 33. Are you alone more than you'd like to be?

_____ 34. Do you look for what is wrong with your hotel room or your rental house/condo the minute you enter it?

_____ 35. Do you find compliments and/or reassurance hard to take?

_____ 36. Do you feel that nobody knows "the real you"?

_____ 37. Do you find yourself drawn to negative thoughts even when you're otherwise in a good mood?

_____ 38. Do you wonder if someone is out to get you or is trying to take advantage of you?

_____ 39. Do you tend to dismiss as superficial people who are cheerful or optimistic?

_____ 40. Would people describe you as imaginative or creative?

_____ 41. Is it hard for you to shake off criticism, even if you know the criticism is inaccurate?

_____ 42. Do you fail to live up to the standards you set for yourself?

_____ 43. Do you feel an unmet need for reassurance?

_____ 44. Do you lose perspective easily, worrying over some relatively minor matter as if it were a major concern?

_____ 45. Do you feel compelled to worry that a certain bad thing might happen, such as a business deal falling through, or your child not getting picked for the team, or your financial situation collapsing, out of an almost superstitious feeling that if you don't worry about it the bad thing will happen, while if you *do* worry about it, your worrying might actually *prevent* the negative outcome?

_____ *46. Did you ever suffer physical, sexual, or psychological abuse?

_____ *47. Did you have few secure attachments to other people as a child and/or would you describe your childhood as unstable?

_____ *48. Do you have symptoms of obsessive-compulsive disorder, e.g., habits or ritualistic behavior that you cannot resist and/or intrusive obsessive thoughts that won't go away; or symptoms of panic attacks, e.g., sudden episodes of intense feelings of panic accompanied by physical symptoms of sweating, elevated heart rate, and rapid breathing; or symptoms of recurring, intense anxiety?

_____ *49. Do you have a family history (in your parents and/or grandparents) of depression or obsessive-compulsive disorder, or panic attacks, or anxiety disorders, or substance abuse?

_____ *50. Do you have any medical conditions that have been ascribed by your doctor at least in part to excessive worry?

The minimum score on this test is 0. If you scored 0, I'd like to meet you. You must be a supremely secure and confident individual—or maybe you fudged your answers so as not to worry!

The maximum score is 150. If you scored 150, it is good that you are reading this book.

A rough breakdown as to the meaning of your score would be as follows:

0–25:   Low. You are not an excessive worrier.

26–75:   Potential Danger Zone. You may have some tendencies toward worry that this book can help you with.

76–150: Danger Zone. If you worry this much, consider consulting a professional. This much worry is not good for you physically, emotionally, or spiritually, and it can impair your life at home, at work, and especially when you're by yourself.

Part II

Toxic Types of Worry

7 When Pain Can't Be Forgotten

Worry, Old Bones, and Broken Trust

Perhaps the most common cause of toxic worry is pain a person can't let go of. This doesn't necessarily constitute a medical or psychiatric diagnosis but it surely creates problems in everyday life. Why does anyone hold onto pain? No one knows for sure. A painful event occurs and often memory can't let it go, so it gathers up into a major worry. The memory of the event lodges in the mind and festers. There it stays, keeping the person awake, not letting go.

One of the original meanings of the word worry is "to gnaw." Used this way, the word describes what a dog does to a bone: he *worries* it, chewing on it all day long. This is also what people sometimes do as they worry: they chew and gnaw on a problem, devoting full focus to it, like a dog with a bone ignoring the sun as it makes its way across the backyard and ignoring the rest of life as well. Just as the dog won't let go of his bone as he worries it, so the worrier won't let go of his worry, biting and chewing into the quick of his life, nipping and picking, looking for meat, but only finding old bone and remnants of blood.

Sometimes it is a very old bone indeed the worrier chews on. The bone gets buried and dug up and buried and dug up and buried and dug up, as the same old pain gets reworried over and over again. As Yeats wrote, "Men relive their sins, and that not once but many times." The process is reminiscent of the joke, "Q: What is Irish Alzheimer's? A: You only remember your grudges." But it isn't only the Irish who hold onto old pain; it is everyone.

Why? Why can't people just let their pain go? The dog worries his bone for pleasure, but people do not. People hurt when they worry. So why don't they give it up? There are many reasons, but one in particular is very common. Many people can't let go of pain because the only way to let go of it once and for all is first to feel it through and through. Many a person fears this would be overwhelming. They keep the pain alive, oddly enough, by not letting it in.

The sadness she never felt is the worry she keeps feeling now, I thought to myself, as I talked to Liz Brightman in my office. During that visit she told me her father had committed suicide in a mental hospital when she was ten years old. She said she and her sisters and her mother went to the funeral. After the funeral they all stopped for lunch at Mc-Donald's. Then Liz's mother took them all to a carnival "to have some fun and forget." Her mother never talked about her father again. The children didn't either, sensing from their mother's lead that such talk was out of bounds.

Liz told me this stark story as if she were telling me tomorrow's weather report. I didn't push her or inquire for more details out of respect for her need to keep her distance from a terrible event. But I did shudder inside at what a price she had paid for this distance. People tend to pour the present into a mold they have made out of the past. It is difficult for anyone to break the mold and begin to experience life in a brand-new way.

Liz Brightman came to see me originally "to find a better way to live." She had no intention of talking about her father; she just wanted to be happier. She was preoccupied with worry about a multitude of insignificant problems in her life, as well as a few significant ones. She was thirty-eight years old, single, working as an administrator in an environmental engineering firm, and she lived by herself. She was, as she put it, "a nervous Nellie," worrying about everything under the sun.

When we first began psychotherapy, what Liz wanted most from me was reassurance. She wanted me to tell her that everything would be OK. She said she sensed danger much of the time, even though there was no real danger around her. I gave her reassurance as best I could. Indeed, there was not a great deal in her life to worry about from an objective standpoint. She had a boyfriend whom she thought she loved, she had a job she said she liked, she was in good health, she had sisters she loved, and a mother still living whom she got along with well. I told her that it seemed to me life would be fine for her, but I wondered what her worrying was all about.

When she told me about her father, I began to understand the roots of her present worrying. The funny thing was, she understood it too and, really, she always had. A few minutes after she told me about him, she said, "You think it's weird how we dealt with my father's death, don't you?"

"I guess it must have been the only way you all could think of," I said.

"Yes, but it screwed us up. Why didn't we deal with it more at the time?"

"Can you tell me?" I replied.

"Well, my mother said what else was there to do but to go on. So we went on. My sisters and I and my mother. Then she met my stepfather, and we went on some more, further and further on. And on and on. My father kept receding into the past, like a rowboat that had fallen off the big ship. I never even cried."

"Twenty-eight years ago," I mused. "Can you still see the rowboat?"

"No," Liz said. "I lost sight of the rowboat a long time ago. In fact, I don't remember much at all about my father or even about my life before my father died."

"Do you think maybe we should go looking for that rowboat?" I asked.

Liz was holding back tears. "Yes, I'd like to do that," she said. "I can see the red hat with that long black visor that he always wore outside."

"Is he in the rowboat?" I asked. "What's he doing?"

"Next time we'll get to it," she said, dabbing her eyes. "Let's talk next time. I'm not used to this." Even as she brought it up she needed to push it away.

"You've never talked about it with your family or anybody?" I asked.

"Sometimes I talk about it with friends. Someone will ask me about my father. If I feel comfortable with the person, and that's not often, I'll tell the truth. I'll say it, like I said it to you, my father committed suicide in a mental hospital. It's a real conversation stopper. Once in a while they'll ask another question, like, why did he do that? And then I'll say I don't know, his diagnosis was depression, and they'll feel foolish or embarrassed for having asked, and one of us will politely find a way to change the subject. I'll usually want to reach out and apologize to whoever it is for having told them about it, because it really is one of those revelations that a person just doesn't know how to respond to. Even I don't even know how to respond to it, except I know it must be important."

"And do you suppose you've always known that?" I asked.

"Yes," she said, quietly.

"Yes, of course," I said. And that was when I thought to myself that the sadness she had not felt was the worry she continued to feel, like a dog worrying a very old bone.

Many people's worries really are old bones still buried at home. Sometimes people use worry in the present moment not as a means of getting to the meat on these bones but as a *defense* against feeling the pain that was buried long ago. Such worry defends these people against a deeper emotion, often sadness or shame. Worrying becomes a painful way of avoiding even deeper pain.

It wasn't hard for either Liz or me to understand all this. There was not some brilliant "Aha!" interpretation. Liz came in to see me knowing she had not finished something all those years ago. She knew that she had been pushing something away but knew that at the same time she had been wanting to let it in. She had been wanting to cry.

It is remarkable how easily this can happen. You can know what your problem is but behave as if you do not know. You almost convince yourself but never completely. You can know in your heart that the solution to your problem lies in traveling north but still spend your whole life deliberately going in every direction except north.

As you go on, a little voice inside tells you every day that the answer lies in going north, and you do hear the little voice but you do not heed it. You do not tell anyone else about it. You do not tell your spouse or closest loved one. You can even be in psychotherapy, paying money ostensibly to discover what you should do to solve your problems in life, and never tell your therapist that you actually know what you need to do to solve your problems: go north. But you do not share this. Instead, you spend your time in therapy worrying about one thing or another. Such worry becomes a grand diversionary tactic, a "symptom," a means of distracting you and your therapist or loved one from what you—and you alone—*know* is the direction for solving your problem.

Why do this? Why not just go north? Because you imagine going north will hurt too much. So you pretend not to know that this is what you know you need to do.

In Liz's case, going north meant talking about her father. She needed to let herself feel all that she felt back then but pushed away. She needed to remember, to see the red hat and the black visor and all the rest, and find the rowboat that was drifting behind her big boat somewhere far away. She needed to cry. For many people this is the act they fear the most. They do not want to cry; most of all they do not want to cry in front of someone else. Crying feels humiliating, too out of control, too vulnerable, possibly overpowering.

Liz had spent her life since her father died not feeling what she needed to feel. She knew she needed to feel what she was avoiding, but she didn't want to. The longer that she didn't feel it, the more her not wanting to feel it became a habit she couldn't break. It became part of who she was.

But because there was a hurt inside her that hadn't come out, she gnawed at it every day. She worried. She prevented herself from having feelings about the most painful thing that had ever happened in her life by worrying about all the other things that had happened or could happen. She became anxious over little things to avoid dealing with the big thing. She worried so as not to cry. She worried so as to remain "strong." She worried so as not to lose control.

How Liz and I worked on this together would make another book. It is not a simple matter, like saying, "OK, Liz, cry." The longer she hadn't cried, the harder it became to cry. Of course, crying was not the whole story. But crying mattered. She needed to let it out in front of another person and in front of herself, to discover that her world would not fall apart when she did it and that there was no shame in it. Indeed, there was great strength and courage. She needed to find out, firsthand, that her tears could heal her.

Once she had heaved up the big thing, it amazed her how the little things shrunk back down to size. Once she had talked about her father, and cried about her father, and revisited him and those years, she felt better. She had gone north and she came back a whole person.

The details of Liz's voyage have no place here. However, the fact that she took the trip does. Many people who worry too much are avoiding what is really bothering them. They, like Liz, have some business they need to take care of but are afraid or ashamed, and so they keep pushing it away. Tomorrow, next year, someday. A moment or a deed or an event from the past has shaped their lives, and because they have not talked about it or reacted to it fully, they are crippled by it. They have not cried or confessed or done what they need to do to put an end to it. So it lives on, too long, in the form of worry about everything else.

If you are such a person, you know it.

At its most severe, past pain can reach the point of a psychiatric diagnosis: post-traumatic stress disorder (PTSD). How long do bad things last? Sometimes forever. How bad can they be? Sometimes so bad that after the traumatic event, the sufferer never lives a happy day again. This is the painful lesson we have learned from studying victims of trauma.

.   .   .

When is trauma so severe as to warrant a diagnosis of PTSD? The text-book definition, from the diagnostic manual most mental health professionals use, called DSM-IV, goes as follows:

The person must have been exposed to a traumatic event in which both of the following were present:

1. The person experienced, witnessed, or was confronted with an event or events that involved actual or threatened death or serious injury or a threat to the physical integrity of self or others.
2. The person's response involved intense fear, helplessness, or horror. In children this may be expressed instead by disorganized or agitated behavior.

For example, a soldier returning from the Vietnam War starts to suffer from flashbacks of watching his buddies getting shot. He witnessed death, could do nothing about it, and his mind stored the memories in a dynamic cell, releasing them in the symptoms of PTSD. A little girl is repeatedly fondled and touched inappropriately by an older relative. She feels utterly helpless. Her mind's only way of dealing with the trauma becomes for her to go numb inside and appear constantly distracted and difficult to engage.

Most mental health professionals extend this textbook definition of trauma to include any event that ends up being experienced as traumatic, as in the case of Allison Barnes (from chapter 1, the physician who never got over getting sued). A person can be traumatized in everyday life without being exposed to a life-and-death situation. In a technical sense such an individual does not qualify for the diagnosis of PTSD. However, he experiences all the symptoms and distress of one who does.

Does this mean that every little toe-stub can be called a trauma? Are we opening the floodgates of diagnosis to include as traumatic injuries skinned knees and every sort of hurt feeling? No, the point is that there are no objective criteria to measure or predict the subjective response a given individual will feel to a given event. Some children can survive repeated life-threatening beatings and be psychologically OK years later. On the other hand, some individuals never get over a betrayal by a friend. Even though this betrayal may neither have been life-threatening nor have "posed a threat to the physical integrity of self or others," nonetheless it may have changed forever the life of the person betrayed. That person may reexperience the betrayal every day, think back on it involuntarily, dream about it, go to great lengths to avoid reminders of it, feel numb inside because of it, and be excessively aroused and hypervigilant, like a kicked dog, for years after the event—in other words experience all the symptoms of PTSD without "qualifying" for the textbook diagnosis. The unfortunate fact is that bad events of any dimension can have lasting, severely toxic effects.

After the traumatic event, what happens? Most people, thank goodness, heal naturally. But some people, in the wake of trauma, find that they are simply not able to put the event to rest. It continues to come up, either in dreams or in waking life, in highly disturbing ways.

Following the trauma the individual may find that even years later she still reexperiences the event in a variety of ways, such as flashbacks, nightmares, or random associations with the event, avoids reminders of the event and feels numb at its mention or even distant suggestions, and habitually feels increased arousal and vigilance even though the traumatic event smolders decades in the past. These three symptoms—reexperiencing the trauma, avoiding all cues and reminders of the trauma, and feeling physically vigilant and on guard most of the time—constitute the defining triad of symptoms associated with PTSD. The event burns a brand into the brain, a brand that keeps sending out signals of pain and alarm long after the original trauma is past. Even in animals, a trauma can persist long after it is over in real time.

How do we treat a person—or even a dog—who still flinches years after the original event? Is there any way of undoing the damage? A good answer comes from Maya Angelou, who wrote, "History, despite its wrenching pain, cannot be unlived, but, if faced with courage, need not be lived again." For both the person and the dog, love provides the surest anodyne. However, it must be skillfully applied, especially at first, and it helps to supplement the love with some expert advice and safety.

I know a woman who lost a ten-year-old son to a fatal illness. Losing a child seems to me to be about the worst thing that can happen to anyone. Four years later she tells me the loss still hurts and she thinks about her son every day. But the anger and bitterness have passed. Why? How? She doesn't know. She is a loving woman who reaches out to people easily. She is also the kind of person who thinks, as she told me, that everyone has something good inside. She makes it possible for others to love her, even when she is feeling angry and bitter inside. I think these are the qualities of spirit that make it possible for her to get by. She also believes in God, although she's had her moments of doubt. However, she tells me that for many other parents who lose their children, the anger and bitterness never pass. The death takes all the hope out of their lives.

Why these different responses? Why do tragic experiences turn some people against life forever? Ultimately, we do not know. But there are some steps that a person can take that can reduce the chances of the worst outcomes.

First of all, making contact with another person almost always helps, as long as that person is kind.

Second, the process of grieving usually helps. Whether it is a lost lover or a lost job or a lost friend, let the grief come out. An old teacher of psychotherapy in Boston, Dr. Elvin Semrad, said that a person must try to "acknowledge, bear, and put into perspective" the pain he carries. This way you are more likely to be able to put the pain behind you once and for all. All loss should be mourned.

Third, if you feel guilty, find forgiveness. On the other hand, if you feel vindictive, find your way instead to forgive. Both guilt and a thirst for revenge keep old hurts alive and can put the mind into a frenzy of worry, but forgiveness is the antidote for both. Where you find forgiveness depends upon your own ways and customs. But almost everyone can find forgiveness—how to give as well as receive it—if they look hard enough. It can take a lifetime and require what seems like divine intervention, but it is worth the search. Even if you never find it, keeping yourself open to the possibility of giving or receiving genuine forgiveness is better than sealing your soul over in hopelessness.

How much worry is spent in the service of old pain, kept alive by guilt or a desire for revenge? Too much. If you can, try to see that you hurt yourself more than anyone else by devoting too much of your energy to guilt or to fantasies of revenge.

Beyond these balms, professional assistance is often indicated in PTSD. The point of the treatment is to detoxify the old pain, no matter how long ago it started. There are various techniques as well as medications that can actually do the job quite well.

Most of them have been mentioned or will be mentioned in chapters to come. For PTSD the combination of cognitive-behavioral therapy (CBT), eye movement desensitization and reprocessing (EMDR), and medication can make for an effective detoxification of old hurt.

In CBT, which will be described in more detail in the chapter on panic attacks, the individual is asked to reexperience the original event—in his mind—with the therapist present. As the patient brings the old pain back to mind, he is asked to stay with it, instead of reflexively pushing it away, which is his natural tendency and desire. However, by staying with it, by intentionally allowing the full scenario of the original trauma to take center stage in his mind and stay there, he finds that his anxiety escalates to a peak and then starts to decline. This is because the human physiological response to stress cannot stay in a state of red alert much longer than forty-five minutes. The system simply runs out of neurotransmitters and hormones, like an engine running out of fuel. At this moment the sufferer can discover his ability to visualize the trauma *without fear*. He can envision the traumatic scene and feel calm inside because his physiology has run out of the chemicals that send the messages of extreme alarm. In this panic-depleted state, the sufferer can *experience* the trauma without fear. Experience being the greatest teacher, this detoxified experience teaches the individual that the original trauma need no longer hold him in its power. He has detoxified his own experience by using his own fantasy life and his willingness to bear with intense anxiety over forty-five minutes in the presence of a therapist. He has "washed out" his own brain of its negativity.

As this proceeds he can then learn new thoughts to set in place in his memory structures. He can fortify his brain with these new thoughts, as if they were sturdy beams. Thoughts like, "It was not your fault," or "He has no power over you now," or "You are in charge from here on."

For example, I worked with a woman who had been sexually abused by a stranger many years ago. The incident continued to haunt her. At first she did not want to talk about it at all. But over time, she found that it helped to describe to me what had happened, to recall all the details and hold them in her mind as I held them in my mine. She found that as upset as she became at first, as the minutes passed her fears subsided. By bringing the traumatic moment back from the past into the present and feeling it once again completely without pushing it away, by reexperiencing it completely in a safe place, she was able to stare it down, so to speak. She was able to pluck its fangs. She made it spend its poison until it had none left. She found out that by feeling it through and through, in the present, it lost its hold on her imagination.

These techniques can be painful and must be attempted only with a trained professional. But done right, they are safe. They are like mind exercises, which require professional guidance at first but can be practiced on your own over time.

EMDR also seems to be able to cleanse the mind of toxic memories. Although no one understands why it works, there are many published reports of its efficacy. In EMDR the patient is asked to follow the therapist's moving finger as the patient recalls a traumatic event. There seems to be something about the eye movements occurring simultaneously with the remembering of the trauma that serves to drain the poisons out of the memory. Somehow, the visual tracking activates some process in the brain that otherwise does not come into play. It sounds strange but often seems to work! The best hypotheses are that EMDR equilibrates the two hemispheres of the brain. The eye movements allow the painful material to "spread out," so to speak, and move between the two hemispheres. This leads to a reduction in pain, just as lancing an abscess does. [For more discussion, see the book *EMDR,* by Francine Shapiro (the developer of the technique) published by Basic Books, 1997.]

Finally, medication can help PTSD. In the acute phase, right after the trauma, it is probably a good idea *not* to talk about the event too much, if at all, and instead to make the individual feel safe, powerful, and at ease. Medications such as the benzodiazepines, for example clonazepam (Klonopin) can help in this regard.

Over the long term, after the individual has been stabilized and reassured that the danger is over, the tricyclic antidepressants, such as amitriptyline (Elavil), or the selective serotonin reuptake inhibitors, such as fluoxetine (Prozac) can help reduce the frequency and intensity of upsetting symptoms.

For example, I worked with a man who came to see me two years after losing his business in bankruptcy. Although he was now gainfully employed once again, he had been traumatized by the loss of his business and he brooded over it every day. Talking about it brought marginal relief. However, when I started him on Prozac, the results were dramatic. He stopped ruminating within a month and reported, "I am a new man." While we all should be skeptical about dramatic cures, it proves to be the case that Prozac, and the other medications in the same category such as Zoloft and Paxil, can, sometimes, radically reverse ruminative depressions and the pain of PTSD.

The best approach combines nonmedication methods with medication. In true PTSD it is best to seek the guidance of a professional. This is a condition, as most of the states of worry discussed in this book, for which we have developed practical and effective treatments. While the memory of severe trauma almost never disappears, with proper treatment it need not be a life's preoccupation.

8   The Worried Child

Children worry. Sometimes adults forget how many worries fill even the happiest childhood. This is because childhood is a time of "firsts," of doing so many things for the first time. The first of anything is a little scary. The first day of school. The first sleepover. The first piano lesson. The first class in a foreign language. The first kiss. Exciting moments, but all potentially fraught with worry.

In some ways, worry is what makes childhood so memorable. We remember how much we worried about such little things. Being popular. A pimple. Grades. Hitting a baseball. Being picked for . . . anything.

No one should try to take all the worry out of childhood. As much as we want to protect our children, some degree of worry is part of their adventure. Part of the fun of riding the roller coaster is getting scared in advance. Getting into mischief, worrying about what happens in the dark in the woods, worrying about who lives in the haunted house—these worries enliven childhood. They're part of the fun. With any luck, children learn to get information to inform their worries and to help calculate their risks. They learn how to get comfortable with a certain amount of danger and when to pull back or go for help. In other words, they learn how to worry well. This is an invaluable skill in adulthood. Children learn how to do it by practicing, not by being protected from all danger and all worry.

Many of the common worries children carry are wild exaggerations of the dangers of everyday life. Even young children from affluent, sheltered areas worry about robbers and thieves, personal safety, and imminent danger. It is not abnormal for a child to worry about disaster and catastrophe, as long as these worries do not become preoccupations.

A child's growth includes the development of perspective. With perspective, worries can be set aside or given their proper weight. Sometimes, however, children lose perspective. Sometimes they worry too much. Sometimes their worrying crosses the line between the normal adventure of childhood and a state of excessive fear.

What are the kinds of worry children develop that parents should be concerned with? There are three main categories. The most common, category 1, includes worries related to problems with connectedness. Category 2 encompasses the worries parents and others impose upon children. Category 3, less common but not at all rare, takes in diagnosable emotional problems involving worry.

Children who feel disconnected tend to worry. Children need a sense of connectedness in order to feel safe and secure—a sense of being connected to some entity larger than themselves. They need to feel a part of it, held by it, and protected by it, and they need to know that it will always be there for them. What kind of an entity should this be? Traditionally, it was the nuclear family: mom and dad. However, as families have changed, children are finding their sustaining connections in newer family arrangements. It doesn't really matter who is there, as long as the people involved provide the child with a strong feeling of love and constancy. A child needs to be able to take a sense of "I love you and I'll be here no matter what" for granted. If he can't, then he'll start to worry, and this kind worrying is bad for him.

Why is it bad? It is bad because it retards his emotional and intellectual growth. If at age six he is wondering who will make him dinner, or who will pick him up at school, or more basically who loves him or what trouble has he caused, then he will start to restrict his spontaneity. He will start to manufacture his responses in accordance with what he thinks will "work." He will create an inner world full of exaggerated fears and disastrous consequences, which will further restrict his ability to feel confident, take chances, learn, and have fun. Instead of developing an attitude of "can do," which is what all children should develop, he'll start to develop an attitude of "might not" or even "can't do."

I once treated a boy I'll call Charlie, who you would have thought had it all. His parents were wealthy and famous. His siblings were strong and accomplished. But Charlie, being the youngest by ten years, hadn't fit in with the plans of the family as a whole, and so he was sent away to boarding school in the fifth grade. While he had many of the advantages of having a strong family, he was one of the loneliest, most worried boys I ever met. I consulted at his school, where I would see Charlie once or twice a week for therapy sessions.

During these sessions we often went for walks together or threw a ball around outside. Charlie was preoccupied by worries about his performance at school and was also often homesick. He worried if his parents were OK, if his family would still be there when he got home, and whether his being sent away to school meant he was not loved. We didn't talk too much, as Charlie would get nervous and just want to play catch. After a while he became quite attached to me and to other adults at the school. I could feel his enthusiasm as he ran up so see me. Not many fifth-graders run up to see their therapists. Charlie and I basically became buddies. I became sort of a father-substitute, along with probably half the faculty at the school.

He would tell me he understood why he had to be at the school, although he thought it was "a gyp" that his brothers and sisters had been able to stay at home when they were his age. "If we didn't have so much money," he said one day, "I'd have had to stay at home."

But the money was there and so he was sent away. All in all, given the unavailability of his parents at home, it was probably a good idea.

The school supplied the connectedness he couldn't get at home, although it was ironic that his disconnection from home was his main worry.

He found connections at the school, but school-bred connectedness is not quite the same. I could see, over the four years I knew Charlie, that by the eighth grade he had developed a certain shell, a slight cynicism that I believe was born of being sent away. Instead of worrying so much, and instead of feeling homesick, Charlie affected an air of slight disdain. But no matter how much he rationalized his situation to himself, and he was a good sport, not wanting to blame anyone for anything, it became increasingly hard for him to understand why he had not occupied a place of higher priority with his parents.

"I would have rather been allowed to stay home," he said to me more than once. As he grew older he began to develop an interest in books and saw himself in various characters. "Do you think I'll ever feel secure?" he asked me one day.

"Yes," I replied, hopefully.

"Well, I don't."

Charlie went off to prep school in New Hampshire, and I lost touch with him. I have known many Charlies. Often they do well in that they achieve a lot, but there is usually a sadness that follows them all their lives. These children are not hard to find: children with all the material advantages, children with good but too-busy parents, children who ache simply for the relationship they see other children having with a mom and a dad.

Without sustaining connectedness, children become afraid. Various studies, most recently those by Dr. Judith Wallerstein, have correlated broken homes with depression and anxiety in adult life. Without basic security, children lose their bearings. They develop awkward defenses and lose the sense of innocence and playfulness so characteristic of healthy children and so vital to their development. They become precocious, taking on the habits and manners of adults. They become depressed. They lose heart.

Connectedness costs nothing but time. It is the royal jelly of emotional health. Far more important than grades in school or athletic prowess or innate intelligence (whatever that actually means), a feeling of fundamental connectedness naturally leads to a calm kind of confidence, which in turn correlates with happiness and success in adult life.

What can a parent do to develop this feeling of connectedness in a child? It is really quite simple. Spend time with the child. Love the child. Do not burden the child with adult worries and concerns. Provide consistent rules, regulations, supervision, and schedules. Eat dinner together. Read aloud. Take trips together. Make frequent contact with extended family, neighbors, and friends. Make sure your child gets to know his neighborhood. Take him into local shops and stores. Take him to the local library and fire station and police station. All these concrete steps build a sense of connectedness. The child sees, talks to, and experiences his connections. This is much more important than lecturing your child or even telling him how connected he is. Show him. Do connectedness, don't just talk it. Make his life a connected one and he will feel the power of the connections and be sustained by them. It makes a world of difference.

Ironically, in an effort to take especially good care of their children, some parents create the very worries they wish to prevent. This is the second large category of children's worries: those that parents and others instill without meaning to.

Billy was brought to see me because his fifth-grade teacher told his mom he seemed sad. His mother said she was seeking my help but we had to make it brief because her husband was opposed to any form of psychological assistance.

"Why is he opposed?" I asked.

"He believes in discipline. Mental toughness is what he calls it. He is a police officer himself, and he wants Billy to learn how to gut it out. That's his phrase." Billy's mother, whose name was Iris, looked tired.

"How do you feel about it?" I asked.

"Well, I'm here," Iris replied. "But I don't want to start a family feud. I love Tommy—that's my husband's name. We just don't see Billy the same way. He thinks I spoil him. But I know I don't. Billy is just dying to please his father, but no matter what he does his father still wants more from him. Nothing he ever does is good enough. Tommy says that was the way he was brought up and it worked for him. 'You gotta be tough in today's world,' he says to me. 'It's for Billy's own good.' "

I met with Billy myself and he was a trooper. Trying to be a good sport, trying to tell me everything was just fine, he couldn't help but let me see he was as fragile as an eggshell. He bit his nails, he tapped his fingers, he looked here and there, he answered me in monosyllables, and he did everything but crawl out of his skin, he was so anxious. After we'd spent an hour together I'd learned what I needed to learn.

"I've got to talk to his father," I said to Iris after I'd met with Billy. "Your son worships his dad. If we're going to help Billy, it has to be through his father."

Iris immediately started to cry. "I knew I shouldn't have come here. Tommy will flip out. You don't understand. He's a good man. But he'll never come in here. Why did I do this?"

"Iris, it'll be OK," I said gently. "Please let me help you and Billy. I have dealt with lots of dads like Tommy. I know he's a good man. Would he let me visit you at home?"

Iris wiped her eyes. "You could come to our home?"

"Sure," I replied. "Doctors still make house calls now and then. You could tell me the school wanted me to meet with you together to discuss his progress."

"I think I could talk him into that," Iris said, and I could see the wheels of her mind start to turn.

When I went to the house, a triple-decker, Tommy opened the door of the second-floor apartment they occupied. He was a tough-looking guy with a pockmarked face, a short, wiry build, and sandy blond hair. He was wearing a sweatshirt and slacks. He waved me into the living room where Iris was already seated on the couch. Tommy sat down next to her, and I took the easy chair beside the TV.

"Doc, I gotta tell you I do object to you seeing my son without me knowing about it. Just to get the cards on the table."

Iris started to speak, but Tommy put his hand on her knee as if to say don't speak.

"I can understand that," I said. "Actually, that's why I'm here now, because I think you have to know what is going on."

"I don't need some shrink to tell me what's going on with my own son," Tommy fired back.

"Maybe not, Mr. Finnegan, but you need someone to tell you," I replied in a quiet voice.

"You know, the only reason I haven't thrown you out yet is that I promised Iris I'd hear you out, but I can tell you you've blown your chance already with me, if you ever had one."

"It's not my chance with you that concerns me, Mr. Finnegan, it's your chances with Billy. He loves you more than he loves anything or anybody, but you are breaking him down in ways you just don't see. I've heard from your wife how much you love him and how hard you are trying to instill good values and proper discipline in him. All I'm trying to tell you is that your good intentions are starting to backfire."

"Is that it? You done?" Tommy asked me, looking at his watch.

"No, I'm not," I replied. "If you're such a tough guy, why are you scared to talk to me about this?"

"I'm not scared," Tommy shot back, "certainly not of you."

"Then what is it you're scared of?" I asked. Iris was looking pretty nervous at this point. The tension in the room was high.

"Nothing that's any concern of yours. Who do you think you are, anyway, coming in here, talking like this?"

"I think I'm someone you want to talk to," I said to Tommy, taking a big risk. "I think you wouldn't have let me come here otherwise."

"Oh yeah? What do you think I want to talk to you about?" Tommy asked, in a sort of snarl.

"Your life," I replied, risking it again. "How hard it is, how you don't want life to be as hard for Billy as it's been for you."

Tommy stared at me. The room was dead quiet for ten, maybe fifteen seconds. I was saying a silent prayer. Then I hit the jackpot. Tommy smiled, just a little bit, but a smile nonetheless. "You're OK," he said. "I'll talk to you. But not tonight. Not now."

Sometimes you have to go to the mountain. Once Tommy had decided I was OK he came to see me. We talked about all the pressure he was under and had been under, and we talked about how his father had treated him, and we talked about how much he loved Iris and Billy. It didn't take him long to see that for all his good intentions Billy was not the sort of kid who needed a kick in the pants, as Tommy said he had needed. Billy was the kind of kid who needed a pat on the back. Especially from his dad.

When Tommy started to understand this and give Billy what he needed, Billy's sadness lifted. Tommy felt better, too. He also admitted to Iris that he'd been wrong.

Iris and Tommy deserved a lot of credit for what each of them did. Many parents couldn't have pulled it off. I'd have been out on my ear.

Parents can make their kids worry too much. Sure, children need discipline, now more than ever. But they also need encouragement and reassurance. A tense and nervous child will not learn well, nor will he grow properly.

Well-meaning parents who constantly push a child to succeed can create malignant instability within the child. What you want a child to come out of childhood with is not a straight-A average, but a straight-A attitude. That is what correlates with success in adult life.

The third large category of worried children includes all those who have a diagnosable, brain-based condition. The spectacular advances medical science has made over the past twenty-five years have given us a much better understanding of certain kinds of worry in children that are genetically based and amenable to specific treatments.

The most common of these in children are separation-anxiety disorder (SAD), generalized anxiety disorder (GAD), obsessive-compulsive disorder (OCD), and social phobias or shyness.

As a group it is important to note that these conditions used to be lumped under such headings as "disturbed child" or "bad parent." Until quite recently, children who had any of these conditions did not receive diagnosis and treatment; rather they and their parents were subject to ridicule and blame.

The great good news of the recent advances in brain science is that these children and their parents can get rid of what I call the "moral diagnosis," i.e., bad, weird, or strange, and benefit from the much more helpful and accurate medical diagnosis. The moral diagnosis leads only to increased shame and pain, but with a medical diagnosis comes a rational plan of treatment, and the chance to get better.

What do these conditions look like?

SAD is an exaggeration of the anxiety all children feel upon leaving their parents. Most children can say good-bye to their parents by age four and go off and join a peer group, without too much fuss, which is why preschool often starts around age four. However, some children have tremendous difficulty in doing this and cannot part with their parents without an inordinate to-do. This problem can appear at age four or it may show up later, as the child experiences more challenging demands, say at age six, when he starts first grade, or at age eight, when he takes his first piano lesson, or at age ten, when he joins some club.

Sometimes peers will ridicule such a child, as he clings to mommy, not letting her go. Sometimes parents will feel ashamed of such a child and wonder what they have done wrong. Teachers or grandparents will mutter about "still being tied to mama's apron strings," and everyone will feel inept.

However, SAD is brain-based and can be treated effectively and rationally. It is a kind of panic response, mediated by excess activity in the locus ceruleus, a part of the brain we encounter again when we take up panic in adults. Basically, the locus ceruleus is a group of nerve cells in the brain that pump up the fear response. Some children have this set too high, so that when they are asked to leave their safety net, they panic. They cannot separate.

Treatment includes both psychotherapy, in the form of behavioral interventions, and medication. Such treatment needs to be provided by a professional, usually a child psychiatrist. It is effective, and quick. Results can be expected in a matter of weeks.

It is worth pointing out that in the days before we had the diagnosis of SAD, we relied on shame and ridicule as our mainstays of "treatment." Of course all this did was compound the problem and create truly disturbed children, parents, and families.

The child with GAD looks quite like the adult with the same condition. Ben Miller in chapter 1 had GAD. The child with GAD is consumed with worry. He may live in a normal family, have completely calm and undemanding parents, and yet feverishly require perfection of himself at every turn. This is the child who worries about the history test weeks in advance, who spends hours at night doing and reviewing homework, who stays up late checking his work and gets up early to make sure nothing has been overlooked, who worries more than even the average adult about everything that might or could go wrong in life, and in general denies himself a childhood by worrying all the time.

Sometimes, of course, such a child is the creation of what I have called "disconnectedness." However, we may see GAD in children who are richly connected because it can arise through one's genes. A child can be born a worrier.

Treatment for GAD also works well. It involves the same steps in children as in adults—cognitive-behavioral therapy and medication. While parents often fear medicating a child, the medications we use to treat GAD are very safe, especially medications like Prozac or Zoloft, and they can be dramatically effective.

It is important for a parent to recognize how much damage excessive worry can do to a child. Excessive worry is bad. It retards growth emotionally and cognitively. There is even evidence that excessive worry can actually retard a child's physical growth. A study done by Dr. Daniel Pine, published in the June 1996 issue of the journal *Pediatrics,* followed 716 children aged nine to eighteen over nine years. The girls who suffered from anxiety disorders grew up to as much as two inches shorter than the others. Oddly enough, the study found no such correlation for boys, supporting the idea that boys and girls differ in their physiological responses to worry.

A third brain-based syndrome of worry in children is social phobia.

This is an intensification of ordinary shyness, in which the child may be afraid of all social situations, or just selected ones, such as gym class or public speaking or other specific situations.

In all cases, the child can be helped. While the best approach with shyness is simply to help the child accept who she is without pathologizing the state, if the child avoids all social contact with others, shyness becomes disabling. A combination of behavioral therapy and medication can help dramatically.

But is this right? What if the child is so extremely shy because she is so sensitive? What if her avoidance of others is based upon an acute appreciation of how painfully cruel people can be to others? What if her fears of being embarrassed in public are based upon experience? What if she is right? Is it correct to "medicate away" or otherwise "treat" a child's sensitivity?

In extreme cases I think it is, for several reasons. First, the extremely shy or socially phobic child is in great pain. Second, her condition limits her ability to grow emotionally. Third, her sensitivity will not be reduced by treatment but will simply be balanced out. As cruel as people can be, they can also be kind. It is worth it for a child to get a shot at making friends.

The medications we use, both the antianxiety medications and the serotonin reuptake inhibitors, work pretty well and have few side effects.

Other treatable conditions of worry in children are discussed in chapters about adults. OCD, PTSD, ADD, and panic can all be present in children and adolescents. The same treatments we use for adults work for children as well.

Most worry in children is normal, benign, and a formative part of childhood. However, extreme worry may signal a condition for which a parent should seek help. Again, the most common causes of such worry are disconnectedness or the parents' inadvertently instilling worry in the child. The biologically based conditions are not rare, however, and respond well to the treatments we now have available.

9   **Worry in Pairs**

Wife and Husband, Parent and Child

Worry can reverberate between two people like a live circuit, resulting in heightened anxiety for both parties, which was why Kelly MacMahon came to see me.

"I just can't stand what my husband is doing to himself," she said to me desperately. "He is eating himself up with worry. Ever since he left Pool-It he's been crazy, crying about everything he might lose." Kelly was an attractive thirty-eight-year-old woman, the mother of two young children and the wife of Jerry, who had just left a swimming pool company where he had worked for fifteen years to go into business on his own.

"Why did he leave Pool-It?" I asked.

"Because B.J. Pinckney, the man who owned it, hired his stupid son-in-law to run the company instead of Jerry. Jerry had worked for him for fifteen years on the assumption that he would take over one day. Then B.J. brings in this inexperienced, retarded son-in-law of his, and Jerry just couldn't stand it. He had all the expertise he needed to go out on his own, so he did. He has all the contacts. We've only been on our own three months and he already has more business than he can handle."

"So why is he worried?" I asked.

"That's a g-o-o-o-o-d question," Kelly replied in her smooth Southern accent. She and Jerry had moved up to Boston from Florida fifteen years before, at B.J.'s urging, but Kelly had never lost her accent. "He just keeps going over and over all the things that can go wrong. I don't know why. Maybe it's just the shock of being self-employed. But I can tell you, it gets tiresome! At least it does for me and I can't help but think it does for him, too. It must, because every now and then he just loses it and starts to cry. My husband is a tough man, Dr. Hallowell. He played football at FSU and he is a typical jock, I guess you'd say. You know, he's not into feelings very much. But now, he is just consumed inside with all this worry."

"It started when he left the company and went out on his own?" I repeated.

"That's when it got worse. But he has always been on the uneasy side. You see, his daddy died when he was ten years old, and he has never really been able to believe that things will ever be OK ever since then. That's what drives him and motivates him, I guess. But now, it seems to be just tying him up in knots. Maybe I see it more because he works at home now. I don't know. We are doing well financially, as I told you, but at what a price! The other day, he was complaining that he didn't have enough free time to get to learn the new software for his computer. The next day when I saw him working on his computer, I said, 'Good, you've found some free time to work on your new software.' He looked up at me with these terrified eyes and said, 'No, this is bad, I shouldn't have free time. It might mean no more orders are going to come in.' That's when I decided to come see you. I thought he was going crazy. I heard about you from one of my friends. Do you understand people like Jerry? I sure don't."

"I think I do. But tell me, do you think Jerry would come in to see me?"

"He would if I asked him to. But I thought maybe you'd just have some suggestions how I could take care of him myself. Plus, I thought maybe you could help me. I'm afraid I'm losing patience. I just want to tell him to cut it out!"

"That might not be a bad idea," I replied with a smile.

"Really? But he's such a little puppy dog when he gets like that. I'd be afraid I'd devastate him."

"But he's a tough football player, too," I reminded Kelly.

"They're all big babies at heart," she answered, absently looking out the window.

"Who are?" I asked.

"Men," she replied, still gazing out the window. Then she looked back at me. "Oh, I'm sorry Dr. Hallowell, I hope I haven't offended you."

"Not at all," I said. "You're probably right."

"He's just so sensitive," Kelly went on. "He's the kind of man who stops to move a turtle off the road so it won't get run over. I've seen him do that more than a few times."

"But maybe he needs to see you not take all this worry as seriously as he does. Maybe if you told him to cut it out, he'd feel reassured. You'd basically be telling him that since you're not upset, there's nothing to be so upset about, wouldn't you?"

"I've tried saying that," Kelly replied. "Because he always can think of something that *might* go wrong. He has this built-in radar for anything that could *possibly* go wrong. He could probably worry that the sun might rise in the north if we're not careful. It's amazing."

"But the company is doing well," I commiserated.

"I know! That is what is so strange. Do you think he is going crazy?" she asked.

"Absolutely not," I said firmly. "People do not go crazy this way. They just suffer."

"He is doing that," Kelly said with a sigh. "So am I."

"You're caught up in it."

"I surely am," Kelly replied. "His worrying dominates my life. His mind takes over my mind. That isn't fair! I resent it. I get mad at him inside but then I feel guilty, like he's in such pain I should somehow make it all better for him, or at least I shouldn't get mad at him because I do love him and I am his wife; but damn it all, he is just making me miserable. Oh, I *hate* it when I do this," Kelly said, wiping back tears.

"It's good to cry," I said.

"Well, then I must be really good because I cry every day now. I am just so frustrated. It would be one thing if he was worried because he had cancer, something that really deserves worrying about. But this worrying over nothing just makes me crazy. I'm losing respect for him and that's the worst thing of all. I have to respect him if I'm going to live with him. What can we do?" she pleaded.

"Well, it is a big jolt," I replied, "going from the security of a company to being out on your own, particularly if you've never done it before. It is happening to lots of people these days, what with downsizing so rampant. In Jerry's case, as you pointed out, he has the long-standing insecurity that started with his father's dying when he was only ten. So what is going on is understandable. But what to do about it. What have you found so far that helps . . . if anything?"

Kelly paused. Then she said, "Holding him. Sometimes he just asks me to stay in bed five more minutes and hold him. Sometimes he sobs a little and sometimes he actually falls asleep like a little baby. That's when he's most relaxed. But I can't hold him all day!"

"No, I suppose you can't," I replied. "I wonder how else he can feel held."

"Golf," Kelly said. "He loves golf. But he doesn't play anymore because he says he can't afford the time."

"Tell him to make time," I replied. "The exercise will help, but even more important is just having the diversion, getting outside, doing something he loves."

"But what do I do with all his anger?" Kelly asked. "He wants to blame me all the time. He'll say, 'If you just would blank, then everything would be OK.' Blank could be something as stupid as take out the trash and do the dishes or something major like get a job. But he'll really carry on about it, until he gives up and says he knows he's wrong and he apologizes. I'm telling you, I am tired of this! Does that make me a bad wife?"

"Of course not," I replied. "But that's the insidious thing about irrational worry. Your rational response makes you feel guilty! But you don't need to feel guilty. He needs you as a reality check."

"Is there any cure for what he's got or do we just have to tough it out?" Kelly asked.

"There isn't a cure but there are treatments."

"Like what?"

"Well, you've mentioned two. Holding him and golf. We've got to get him back out on the golf course. Also I think it would be good if he came and talked to me. I imagine some medication would help him as well, but he and I can decide that together after we meet."

"What medicine?" Kelly asked, a little skeptically. "Not Prozac, I hope."

"Well, actually Prozac and the others like it such as Zoloft and Paxil are very good for ruminative worriers," I replied.

"But I read they are dangerous. They can make you suicidal or violent."

"Only once in a blue moon," I replied. "And I'll be following him closely, so if there are any problems we can stop the medication right away."

"But how does it work?" Kelly asked. "Is it just going to drug him up? A martini could do that!"

"No, it's not like alcohol at all. In fact, alcohol makes ruminations worse in the long run because alcohol is a depressant. Prozac and other similar antidepressants are much more specific. They don't impair your mental abilities or your level of alertness. What they do, technically, is increase the amount of a certain neurotransmitter called serotonin in your brain. How does doing this work on ruminations like the ones Jerry is suffering from? We're not sure how but it does. There is some evidence that two of the switching stations in the brain called the cingulate cortex and the caudate nucleus can't quiet down in people who brood a lot, and this results in the relentless, repetitive thoughts that make up ruminations. Prozac helps these switching stations go back to normal without altering other mental processes. That's why it works so well. It is not an 'upper' or a 'downer' but instead a normalizer. It can help," I concluded, cautiously. "It is not a cure but it can help."

"You mean all his fretting and backing and filling might be biochemical?" Kelly asked.

"Partially, yes. And the good news is that we have medications that can address the biochemical problem. But there are other measures to consider, too. For example, talking to me—or someone else like me—can help."

I ended up meeting with Jerry and Kelly alternately. They both needed help in adjusting to Jerry's new situation. Finally I referred Jerry to another therapist for more in-depth work on residual feelings from his childhood, but by then the crisis of worry had passed. The medication—we chose Prozac—had helped, as had golf!

Most of the time when one member of a couple is intensely worried, the other member gets drawn into the process as well. It can be upsetting and destructive for both parties. Certainly one good reason most adults pair off in life is to find someone to worry with, but when the worrying becomes extreme and/or one-sided, outside intervention can help reestablish a balance.

The process of destructive worry in couples *begins* benignly, in empathy and concern. But when one member obsesses over a danger he feels and worries constantly, the other member of the couple begins to wear out. This is when help is needed. Kelly was in as much distress as her husband. Although she came to me looking for help for him, she needed help for herself, too. She was trying hard to hang in there with her husband, but she knew something had to change.

Something also had to change between my patient, Beth, and her daughter, Abby. This situation represents another common example of worry that ties two people up: worry between a parent and a child (although the process may just as easily start up in other pairs, such as close friends, teacher and student, boss and employee, even owner and pet!). Beth's nine-year-old daughter Abby was chronically anxious. To hear Beth describe the problem at first, it sounded as if Abby was suffering from a kind of generalized anxiety disorder.

But as Beth told the story in more detail, it became clear that Abby got anxious mainly in reaction to what she perceived to be her mother's state of mind. She was exquisitely tuned in to what she thought her mother *might* be feeling.

"For example," Beth explained, "I was driving home from grocery shopping yesterday and I saw Abby watching for me out the kitchen window as I drove up. The minute I got out of the car, she rushed up to me and asked, 'What's wrong? Why are you frowning? Did something bad happen?' The fact is I *had* been thinking about some harsh words I'd had with Bob, my husband, that morning. But I wasn't *terribly* upset, I hadn't been crying in the car or anything like that, I had only been having some mildly disturbing thoughts. But somehow Abby picked up on this and got very upset. It was as if she had a secret detector for any negative feeling I might have, and once she detected something, she got upset. How did she know what I'd been thinking about? She could see me from the kitchen window and must have inferred from the slight frown on my face that I was in total despair. It's getting so that I don't dare be even a little sad for fear of totally upsetting her. Bob says it's just a phase. He says she is too attached to me."

"How do you feel?" I asked.

"Honestly? Honestly, I secretly agree with Abby. I think we are sort of joined at the hip, emotionally. I think we do have a sixth sense for each other, but I don't know that it's such a good thing. I think we need to put more distance between us or we'll worry each other sick."

"You can sense her moods?" I asked, "more than the average mother can?"

"I think the average mother is pretty attuned, particularly to daughters," Beth replied. "But I am even more so. When she worries, I fret. When she has had a bad day at school I can see it in her face instantly, I can hear it in her tone of voice, even in the way she clears her throat. I am much more attuned to her than I am to my husband." She paused, then added, "Thank God. I don't think I could take it if I had this kind of a connection to anyone else. It is just too much to worry about, without enough control."

Sometimes a child can be so attuned to a parent's emotional state that even the slightest change in the parent throws the child way off. It can happen in the other direction as well. A parent can be so concerned about—and exquisitely aware of—a child's feelings that even the *slightest* sign of emotional distress throws the parent into turmoil.

These situations call for rebalancing. Restoration of perspective. Reassurance that sticks. How does anyone provide this?

One member of the pair—or preferably both—needs to disentangle from the worried nexus. Exaggerated fears, like Abby's, often develop from excessive closeness and what one member of the pair feels as total dependency on the other. It is important for each member to reestablish some reasonable independence. While closeness between mother and daughter is one of life's great blessings, too much of that closeness can overwhelm both individuals. Clear statements need to be made by the mother that it is OK for the child to be independent and that mom needs time to herself as well. These statements sometimes need to be made over and over again. For example, Beth might say to Abby, "I'm OK. It's all right for me to feel sad sometimes, just as it is OK for you to feel sad sometimes. Even though we love each other, I am not you and you are not me. If I am sad, that does not mean you are in danger and it does not mean I am going to go away, or that Daddy is going to go away, or that anything bad at all is going to happen to you or to me or to any of us." At first Abby would probably listen apprehensively to these words. But as they are repeated, and as mom does indeed not overinvolve herself in Abby's life, trying to prevent or assuage every moment of pain, Abby will likely begin to give up her fearful fantasies and learn how to reassure herself when she's worried about something in her own life as well as about mom's feelings.

But if mom gets in too close, if in her efforts to help Abby she joins Abby in her anxiety, she can effectively prevent Abby from learning how to separate and comfort herself. Then Abby will probably continue to manufacture her fearful fantasies. Why? Because she then does not have the chance to realize that it is safe not to. She cannot discover that she can take her eye off her mom. She has not yet tested her own independence sufficiently to understand that it is OK for her to be happy when her mom is sad. She has not yet fully discovered that she is a separate being unto herself. Her fear that in some way she is responsible for her mother's moods sets off a panic inside her. She has to work overtime to keep watch over her mom. She becomes excessively vigilant in trying to detect what her mother might be feeling. She develops prodigious powers of empathy in her mighty attempt to constantly monitor her mother's moods. She becomes almost a child version of an overprotective parent, watching, sensing, and fretting as she anticipates her mother's every feeling. And her mother's response—Can't she ever just leave me alone?—is similar to the response of the overly protected child.

What should Beth do? Back away from her child. Let Abby feel a little anxious for a while but in the process discover that it is safe for her to back away too.

Beth tried this. She reassured Abby that she was OK. She took an almost business-like approach. "I'm fine, honey," she'd simply say in response to Abby's troubled questions, "now tell me about your day." At first Abby became even more worried, but gradually she could see that her mom was not in trouble and that, indeed, her mother really didn't *want* to talk about her every little mood. Gradually, Abby developed a more livable distance from her mother, so that she could let her have her own feelings without being overly anxious or worried about them. This gradual disentanglement worked wonders. When, over time, Beth saw that Abby was feeling relieved, it became much easier for her to continue to back off. She gave Abby reasonable reassurance, then let Abby discover for herself that both mother and daughter could love each other without having to live in each other's skin.

Bob, Beth's husband, needed to help Beth back off a little from Abby by getting more involved with Abby himself and by encouraging and reassuring Beth that she was doing the right thing. As Beth backed off, Bob moved closer to Abby, while also offering support to Beth. This helped balance out the family dynamics.

Such worry between a parent and a child can preoccupy, and unbalance, an entire family. Usually, someone outside the parent–child pair needs to intervene, to help both back off.

. . .

While the examples in this chapter are of husband and wife, and parent and child, worry can infect pairs of many kinds. A boss and an employee, a coach and a player, a teacher and a student, a friend and a friend, a therapist and a patient, a lawyer and a client—these are just some of the many pairings that worry can throw off course. While concern between the people involved is natural in all of these pairs, when that concern becomes excessive or one-sided, it can get in the way of whatever the pair is trying to do.

When excessive worry arises in any pair, it is an alarm signal. If both members of the pair hear it, they should discuss it. If only one hears it, the situation is even more serious. The one who hears it must make it known, somehow, in some safe forum, so that the worry can be balanced out, and the poisons removed. Ignored too long, unspoken worry can destroy a relationship of any kind.

As William Blake wrote some two hundred years ago:

I was angry with my friend:
I told my wrath, my wrath did end.
I was angry with my foe:
I told it not, my wrath did grow.

And I watered it in fears,
Night & morning with my tears;
And I sunned it with smiles,
And with soft deceitful wiles.

And it grew both day and night,
Till it bore an apple bright.
And my foe beheld it shine,
And he knew that it was mine.

And into my garden stole,
When the night had veiled the pole;
In the morning glad I see
My foe outstretched beneath the tree.

—"A Poison Tree," 1794

10 Worry at Work

It Can Make You or Break You

One of the most common causes of harmful worry in the workplace is a difficult boss. Most of us have had a boss somewhere along the line who ruled by terror and intentionally planted worry in the minds of everyone in the company. The person at the top can create a culture that is radioactive with worry. Some bosses mean to do this. They believe that fear increases productivity. Some bosses do it instinctively (it is the only way they know) and some do it because they have learned it from previous bosses or even their own parents.

Look at a company I'll call Bull Run. Bull Run was a young investment firm specializing in managing the finances of physicians. The key to the success of the company was the soliciting of doctors to sign up for their services. Started by a former physician and Civil War buff, whom I'll name Duane Spate, Bull Run shot up in profits during the eighties, but started to plateau in the nineties.

Duane was a thoracic surgeon, who had found the growing liabilities and insurance woes of medicine becoming too much to take in the early eighties. Entrepreneurial in spirit, he looked around for a business to start. His father had been in investments, so Duane had spent many hours when he was growing up learning about money from his dad. Knowing that most of his colleagues in medicine needed financial advice but lacked guidance in getting it, Duane traded on his credibility as a doctor to get the business of other doctors.

He did well. Starting out on his own, he built the business rapidly—so rapidly that in six months he hired an assistant and in five years he had sixteen people recruiting clients for Bull Run. But this is when Duane started to become cruel. His basic personality shifted into a new gear. He was already a control monger and could be abrasive, but as his company grew and he no longer had to deal directly with clients, he lost the civility clients required and his controlling, abrasive qualities took over. One-on-one with a potential client he had been able suppress the obnoxious parts of himself, but now with his own people under him, his employees at Bull Run, he became a tyrant.

I heard stories of his management style from a patient who worked for Duane. He described Duane's impromptu public "evaluations," which he conducted at Bull Run's required Friday afternoon staff meetings. All the company reps would be present, along with support staff and Duane, a total of about twenty-five employees, gathered in the bunker-like meeting room, where they sat, ostensibly to go over the week's activities and plan the next week's agenda. Duane's right-hand man, C.J., would run the meetings, as Duane sat in a corner, observing, eyes flashing around the room. When he got in the mood to do an "evaluation," he would suddenly leap from his place, interrupting whatever was being said, and bark out the name of one of the reps.

The reps lived in fear of this moment. One day the unlucky man was a rep named Howard Jarvis. "Jarvis," Duane bellowed, "time for your evaluation." Then Duane began to pace around the room, like an attorney on a TV show making his summation to the jury, lacing into Jarvis with relentless sarcasm and ridicule. Everything about Jarvis became fair game. His ears, his nose, as well as his weight, the appearance of his wife, the patterns of his speech, and the make of his car. Duane said such things as, "Jarvis, have you ever stood close enough to someone to smell their breath as you're making your pitch? Well, let me tell you that most dogs' breath smells better than yours. How can you expect to make a sale if you stink? And have you ever evaluated your wife's appearance when you bring her to the physicians' open houses? Jarvis, spend some money on her, will you?" Then he smoothed it over with lines like these: "I'm only telling you this for your own good. I know how to win the Super Bowl because I have been to the top of the mountain. I have won all the prizes you all are shooting for. I have made my first million and my second million and my third. Jarvis, you know you are panting right now to be where I am and, young man, I want to take you there, but you must FOLLOW ME. Do you hear me, Jarvis? You must follow me, and do what I tell you to do. I cannot go out there and do it for you. If you want to get to the top of the mountain you must do what I say. I can give you the tools but you must use them. Right now you are a sorry sack of garbage, aren't you, Jarvis?" At this point Jarvis was expected to nod. "But if you listen to me you will get to the top of the mountain. And if you don't, you will carry your sorry self straight out of my sight because I cannot stand the sight of losers. I can guarantee you that."

Howard came to see me not long after that particular episode. When I heard about Duane's style, I asked Howard why he didn't quit.

"Duane is right," Howard said to me. "I do want the bucks, and he seems to know how to get them. But it's killing me to work there. He pits us against each other, humiliates us all the time, and fires people without warning."

Bosses like Duane, who create such overtly hostile working conditions, often hold onto employees through a strange kind of bonding process.

What is this process? Why do so many people work for people they can't stand? Why did Howard put up with such abuse? For the money, he said. But the money didn't roll in, in the bundles it was promised. Indeed, Howard made paltry commissions on the business he brought in, having to give a lot over to Duane in the form of "training commissions." He lost most of the revenue he generated. Why stay?

"Because someday the big bucks will come," Howard said.

"Have you known other reps who got big bucks through Duane?" I asked.

"C.J. did. Well, sort of. He makes seventy-five thousand a year."

"That's big enough to go through all this?"

"I don't know," Howard said, as he began to reconsider and come to his senses.

But he had taken leave of his senses for a year and a half. He had worked for Duane for that long, making little money and suffering in the process. He was an intelligent man with a college degree. What in the world kept him there, I would ask.

The promise of the big bucks, he insisted. But it seemed to go deeper than that. He seemed afraid to leave. It was as if Duane had instilled a fear in Howard, a fear of leaving Duane, as if he needed Duane to succeed. By so thoroughly dominating and humiliating Howard, Duane had systematically stolen away his gumption, reducing him to an insecure mass of worry.

I gradually proposed this theory to Howard. "You think I *want* to stay with him?" Howard asked, incredulously. "That's ridiculous."

"But you do stay," I replied.

"I don't have another job. I have rent to pay, my wife and I would like to have kids someday, and we'd like to have some money put away."

"Howard, you are free as a bird. You could get another job. But you choose not to."

Howard frowned. "I don't want just another job. I don't want to sit in the cheap seats my whole life. I want the big bucks. If I have to put up with Duane to get there, so be it."

"But what if he's sold you a bill of goods? C.J. is the only one earning good money, and even what he earns isn't the big bucks you're looking for, right?"

"Right," Howard said.

"Honestly, Howard," I went on, "with your ambition and drive and intelligence, you really could make big bucks someday if you wanted to."

"Do you think so?" Howard asked, as if I had just told him something he'd never believed before.

"Yes, I do," I replied. "But not with Duane."

"I stay with Duane because I'm afraid to leave," Howard said. "That's the truth of it. I'm afraid what he says about me is true, that I am just garbage and that without him I'll never learn how to make it to the big show. My God, I can't believe how he has changed me in a year and a half."

"He's a predator," I said.

"It's weird," Howard went on. "As much as I hate him, sometimes when I'm out having a beer after work I find myself almost admiring him, like he's my father or something and I want to please him, to live up to his expectations. He's really gotten into my head. You're right, I don't dare leave him, I want to stay with him, like maybe someday I'll do the job right and he'll pat me on the back."

"Don't wait too long," I said gently.

Strange as it may seem, bosses like Duane and employees like Howard are common. Particularly these days, when job security is rare, and turnover is frequent. A boss like Duane holds onto Howard by exploiting Howard's worries. Not only his legitimate worries about the economy and job security but, at a much more fundamental level, his worries about himself.

This is what is so insidious about such bosses. Everybody worries about the economy and that kind of worry makes sense. But what the Duanes of the world exploit is the employee's inner worries and insecurities. Duane senses Howard's self-doubts (such intuition is a skill these bosses have), seizes on them, magnifies them, and after totally demeaning him, holds out the possibility of success someday, but only if he follows Duane.

Duane is extreme, but bosses like him abound in more subtle guises. This kind of exploitation can occur in business at the very highest levels. Top executives might not be willing to put up with the explicit abuse Howard was willing to endure, but even top executives put up with more civilized forms all the time. I have treated a half-dozen such executive-level men and women who felt tied to a Duane-like boss by explicit promises of future rewards; but the stronger, implicit bond was psychological, built upon their own worry and self-doubt. "I don't dare break away," they all said to me in one way or another. "I can't do it. I'm not good enough."

How did they know they weren't good enough? Their Duane told them so. But the most powerful Duane was really located within themselves. Their own worry and self-doubt is what gave the external Duane his remarkable power.

The bond you can feel to such an employer is of triple strength. The first strength, the easiest to see and understand, derives from the promised reward, the "big bucks" envisioned someday or the fame just around the corner. The second strength, less apparent but still overtly felt, derives from worry about finding other jobs, that is, general job insecurity. The devil you know, the reasoning goes, is better than the one you don't know. But it is the third strength, the manacle forged by the employee's own worry, that binds most tightly. This third strength, the strongest bond of all, derives from the employee's self-doubt, his or her own internal fears. This is a powerful and dangerous force. As potent as positive thinking may be, negative thinking can be even more powerful, especially when you turn it against yourself. The power of negative thinking is what keeps millions of people in jobs they hate. They are held back by their own internal worry that they can't make it anywhere else, and that they're lucky to have any job at all, that they basically couldn't hack it on their own.

An abusive boss, like Duane, exploits this by accentuating the employee's insecurities. This leads to a kind of voluntary slavery. You volunteer by saying to yourself, "I'm not that good." The boss pounces, saying, "Exactly so! You aren't that good. But if you work for me, and do what I tell you to do, someday you might be!" Sadly, this is a bargain from which only the boss usually gains.

You can sell yourself short in this very same way even if you don't have an abusive boss like Duane. How? You make one up! You can create such a boss, just by believing that you have one. Through a common process of mind you can attribute to your boss intimidating qualities you have had to deal with before, in other people in places of authority. You bestow upon your current boss abusive qualities he does not in fact possess. This can happen subtly, imperceptibly, over a long time. Intelligent, otherwise shrewd people can fall prey to such distorted thinking, which renders them fearful and worried about their boss, a boss *they have created out of their own past experience.*

The net effect is the same as if the boss were like Duane: you imagine he is persecuting you, so you live in a constant state of worry and fear but don't dare quit because you worry you can't make it somewhere else. You become trapped in a prison you yourself have made. As Howard was bound to Duane, you become bound to your job and your boss by your own fears. Your worry allows you no exit.

But since you erected the prison out of bars of worry, so too you hold the key to get out. All you have to do is use it. Most people have much greater inner strength than they ever call upon and much greater resourcefulness than they realize. I have found this again and again in working with people during periods of great stress, grief, fear, or loss. I have been filled with awe in watching how people deal with the worst things that can happen in life, the death of a child, a fatal disease, public disgrace, or financial ruin, to name a few grim examples. People rise up like great spirits, calling upon strengths they never knew they had. They have to learn of their strength through tragedy.

If you are tied to a job you don't like by your own worries that you are not good enough to do anything else (or bold enough, smart enough, young enough, talented enough, *anything* enough), ask yourself this key question: *How do I know?*

How do you know you're not good enough? Do you actually *know* it or do you just fear it? How accurate is your assessment of yourself? Probably quite distorted. Self-appraisal is hard to do. You should ask a few other people who know you well for their assessments of you. People often assess themselves as less capable than they actually are, and their self-doubt keeps them down much more than lack of talent.

Common reasons people stay in jobs they don't like are money, inertia, fear of change, or special benefits. But perhaps most common of all is the bind that self-doubt creates, the feeling of worry that immediately overcomes you when you imagine trying to do something else. "Oh, I couldn't do that. Not me." *But how do you know?*

Breaking free requires more than just a change of heart, but that is where it starts. Then you can move into the structured approach of EPR outlined in chapter 23: Evaluate, Plan, Remediate. Evaluate yourself. Reappraise. With the help of a friend, spouse, or counselor make a list of your strengths and vulnerabilities, this time being fiercely vigilant not to sell yourself short. It helps to have another person at your side to stop you from staggering down the same old alley of self-doubt.

Don't feel that you must solve the entire problem, as you appraise yourself and make a plan. As Peter Drucker says, "Don't solve problems. Pursue opportunities." Appraise yourself and make your plan not by setting it out and connecting every dot but by opening the door to an opportunity, then giving yourself a chance to walk through.

Howard and I followed this method together. "So what do you think you can do?" I asked.

Long pause. "I'm not sure any more," he said quietly.

We had to go back to his days pre-Duane and reconstruct his view of himself. We had to go back further than that, recalling talents he had given up on, dreams he had laid to rest, and ask the question, "Why did I give up on that?"

Time and again we found no good reason. Just the refrain of, "I didn't think I could; I worried I'd end up in the poor house."

But Howard had ambition and talent. He just needed to reawaken it. Gradually we named his talents, and the list grew, from grilling steaks to making other people feel comfortable to being willing to work until he dropped to having a good head for numbers. As he got into a more positive frame of mind, over some months, we began to plan, to brainstorm, entertaining various ideas as to what he wanted to do next. The key here is to let yourself go, to let yourself be "unrealistic." The final plan can come later. The first stage is just digging down and unearthing all those ideas you put away long ago, as well as coming up with new ideas that may have just occurred to you, now that you are in the right frame of mind to think constructively.

During Howard's brainstorming he kept coming back to the idea of opening a restaurant, "something like 'The Charcoal Pit,'" he said, sheepishly at first. We both agreed that restaurants were a common fantasy and that they usually failed—but not always.

Since Howard kept returning to this idea, he decided to give it a try. The next step was serious planning. The "P" in the system of EPR, evaluate, plan, remediate. Howard now had to set up a plan to make his restaurant possible. Again, not solving the problem totally, just setting it up so he could pursue the opportunity. Deciding on a site. Opening up the question of financing. Thinking about the "look." Clientele. Contractors. Once he had a plan, he began to set it in motion, while still keeping his job with Duane.

Soon, however, doing that became impossible. Howard couldn't do what was needed and still keep up with his day job. So he quit. Not without some last words, which Howard relished. Indeed, quitting was his first reward in this process of change, and the meeting itself was a meeting Howard said changed his life.

"You should have seen Duane," Howard began, gleefully. "His jaw dropped as if I'd just told him to kiss my butt. We were standing in his office, just him and me, and he told me I needed to make plans to work late for a few weeks to offset lagging accounts. I said to him, really nonchalantly, 'I'm afraid I can't do that, Duane.' Then I just waited. I knew saying I couldn't work late was totally forbidden. Having said it, I was now supposed to be falling all over myself trying to offer some explanation, but instead, I just kept my mouth shut. Let him speak next, I thought. That was fun. I knew I was quitting, so it didn't matter anymore. I haven't enjoyed anything that much in a long, long time.

"Duane looked at me like I was out of my mind. 'What do you mean, *you can't?*' Duane almost whispered in the hushed voice he often used just before he yelled at someone. 'Well, you see,' I explained still nonchalant, 'my evenings have suddenly become tied up. I've joined a bowling league.' This was pure b.s. on my part. But boy, did it have an impact.

"Duane took the bait. He yelled at me so loud he jumped off the floor, and his voice squeaked. That was funny. 'WHAT? YOU CAN'T WORK BECAUSE YOU HAVE JOINED A BOWLING LEAGUE? YOU SORRY SACK—' I cut him off dead before he could finish the insult. 'QUIET!' I yelled back. And I'll be damned if he didn't shut right up, like I'd socked him in the jaw. Must have been the first time a rep actually stepped in his way. 'Duane,' I said, now in a normal tone of voice, 'I'm just busting you. And you took my bait.'

"Duane stared back at me. He had changed. I could see it. I went on, 'I have not joined a bowling league. However, I am tied up in the evenings, and in the daytime, too. I am quitting this job to go out on my own. I want to thank you for making me hate you enough to come to my senses and see what an asshole you truly are, and what a jerk I was becoming by staying here. Goodbye.' With that, I left, a free man.

"On my way out the door Duane sputtered that he was about to fire me anyway, and that I would fail out there without him. But we both knew he wasn't about to fire me. I was one of his best reps. When he lost me, he lost a good slave, and he knew that. As to whether or not I'll fail on my own, who knows? But no matter what happens, it was worth it.

"What felt so good wasn't just breaking free, it was watching the look on Duane's face, seeing him break the way he used to make all of us break. He didn't cry, the way he made some of us cry, but what he did do was just as satisfying for me. When I told him to be quiet, and he shut right up, I knew the game was over. I had won. In that second, my life changed. Suddenly, I was in charge again. All the energy I had was focused in that room right then. It was all there, my whole wad. And I used it to rise up and strike down this man I had thought was invincible.

"You know, the amazing thing about it was that it was so *easy.* I didn't need any more strength than it takes to sneeze. Well, I guess I did to get up the nerve to do it, but once I had the nerve, it was a piece of cake. *A piece of cake.* Once I laid down the law, Duane turned into a child. Once I made him know that I was not afraid of him, he became afraid of me! I could see the change in his eyes, right then and there. Man, what a rush. The whole meeting couldn't have taken more than five minutes, but what a five minutes! That's all it took, but man, that felt good. I can't believe how good that felt. I don't care if this restaurant falls flat on its face, I'm better off now no matter what."

In fact, Howard's restaurant did not fail. Following the plan he had set up, Howard moved into step three, the "R" of EPR, or remediation. Using both friends and consultants wisely, Howard learned his new business quickly. Now a free man, he had the extra energy of a man who doesn't want to go back to jail. He worked eighteen to twenty hours a day, often sleeping on a cot he had in his office at the restaurant. He schmoozed with the customers, he got to know the delivery people personally, he drove his pick-up to the flower market every morning when it opened, then to the fish market, then back to the restaurant, all in an effort to learn as much as he could himself, directly.

Soon he said goodbye to me. Howard's restaurant did so well that the last I heard he was petitioning the zoning board in another part of the city to open a second Charcoal Pit.

Certainly you should not blithely throw away a good job, or even a bad job that is paying your rent, in the name of some vague, romantic notion or "positive thinking." But neither should you suffer in a bad job because you have determined, by a private, uncertain calculation, that you are not able to do anything better. The Duanes of this world only have their power because you give it to them.

Of course not everyone who leaves his or her job will find success right away. But what Howard said makes sense for millions of people: he was better off having left no matter what happened next.

Duane, like many bosses, thought he could use worry to his advantage by creating an atmosphere of fear. He believed that he could scare his people into producing better results. But this is rarely a wise use of worry.

While work should provide a major source of satisfaction in life, worry eats at the heart of many people in business today, and in workplaces in general. Cynicism is rampant. Many employees—at all levels—are sick in their souls with the feeling that something fundamental isn't right.

What's wrong? What are people worried about? They feel increasingly disconnected at work. Alone. On their own. Not an integral part of some larger mission, but instead a cog in someone else's big wheel. It's more than a fear of getting fired, I think, although that is certainly a part of it. The people I talk to complain of a concern deeper than losing their jobs, a concern they expect to encounter in their next job even if they lose their current one. It is a feeling of being left out. They worry that they don't belong, or they won't belong for long, as if they are caught in an unstoppable game of musical chairs. When will there be no chair left for them?

Getting fired is bad enough, but the feeling of being unwanted can be worse. Beyond a fear of being "downsized," there is a widespread disconnection in workplaces these days. Employees yearn to join in, to belong, to connect; they want to give their all to a team, if only they could find one!

Trust is breaking down at work, as cynicism mounts. People feel jaded as they listen to streams of positive management philosophies, then encounter another wave of downsizing the next day. Their cynicism speaks words like these: "Let's face it. Management is bunk, nothing but fads and slogans, trying to get us to work harder for less pay. When you come right down to it life is pretty simple—win or lose; kill or get killed. No matter what they say, everyone is out for the same thing: the biggest score they can get, so then they can get out and do what they want. Quality, dedication, loyalty—those are words for suckers."

The boss gets up and gives a plausible talk, turning nice phrases, wearing a lovely business suit, her hair just so, or wearing his strongest power tie, his hair just so, and the boss says all the right things in all the right ways, but the junior executive or the middle manager or the on-line employee sits back in the audience and thinks, "Yeah, *right*. Tell the little joke you memorized, smile the little smile, then when we get the zinger, now or in a memo, we'll be softened up for it, right?"

They look at a ruthless manager like Sunbeam Corporation's Albert "Chainsaw Al" Dunlap, so-named for his sawlike cost-cutting, as the only kind of manager you can trust—because he comes right out and tells you he'll get rid of you if he can.

The net effect of all this worrying is that huge amounts of potentially positive energy get wasted. As Dee Hock, founder and former CEO of VISA said, "Without question, the most abundant, least expensive, most underutilized, and frequently abused resource in the world is human ingenuity."

Why does this happen? Why do so many people worry at work instead of using their talents most creatively? Often the reason has to do with shortsighted management. Managers who treat employees like robots turn people sour. Policies that cleverly disguise the truth, so that a worker thinks he is being promised one thing but then is given another, make people lose faith.

But isn't fear a great motivator? And if fear and worry are *not* the best motivators, what are?

To answer these questions, let's go back to the brain. One of the many interesting facts we are discovering through the use of the new techniques, such as MRI and fMRI, which give still photographs and moving pictures of the brain as it thinks, is how the brain communicates *within itself.*

Nature has set up the brain so that cell to cell, the connections are very sparse, just as the direct connections between individual telephones are sparse. This reduces static, noise, heat, interference, and energy expenditure, which is important considering that 100 billion cells are involved! But while each individual brain cell is not plugged into many other individual brain cells, regions of cells are very widely plugged into other regions of cells. If any one cell needs to be in touch with another part of the brain, it can be, through the network it's a part of, just as individual telephones can. Regions of the brain are in constant contact with other regions of the brain, so that at any given time, the whole brain can coordinate what it is doing. This is important, since the brain is *always* multi-tasking: regulating breathing, body temperature, heart rate, balance, physical movements, speech, and fantasies, not to mention creating whatever it is we call "thought."

Once a brain message is initiated (and what exactly initiates a nerve cell message that ultimately becomes an abstract thought remains pretty much a mystery), brain messages pass through sorting points, or switching stations.

Interestingly enough, one of the most popular switching stations is the limbic system, the brain's deep regulator of emotional expression. Bundles of nerves from all over the brain pass through here. It is like the boiler room of the brain, located deep in the basement, but all the pipes have branches that pass through.

We haven't always known that the emotional regulator of the brain is so connected with much of the rest of the brain. In mapping out the brain's "exchanges," we are starting to realize how wide the influence of the limbic system truly is. To use a communications analogy, from the Federal Express system of routing all packages through one central city, the limbic system is the Memphis of the brain.

So what? What does all this have to do with worry in the workplace and whether or not fear is a good motivator? Actually, a lot. It implies that the emotional state of a worker influences his performance more than we have known. If all the thinking circuits have to pass through the emotional center, then what goes on in the emotional center will influence the kind of thinking that gets done.

Still, someone might argue, "Fine. Emotion matters. But fear and worry are emotions. I want all my employees to feel the emotion of fear, because then they'll work best." Many managers believe, or at least act as if they believed, that the way to get the most out of their people is to pit them all against each other, and make them compete in an atmosphere of fear and imminent doom.

Until recently, the neurosciences have not helped settle this debate. We have known of the performance-anxiety curve mentioned earlier in this book, which shows that performance improves as anxiety increases, up to a certain point, after which, as anxiety continues to increase, performance starts to decline. But we have not known how much anxiety to shoot for, or how other emotions come into play.

As we learn more about the complex relationship between emotion and thought, we see that while fear may motivate well in the short term, in the long term it gets in the way of performance. Survival-level fear does not promote smooth and effective thinking in the workplace; it impedes it.

Intense fear takes over the brain, and the rest of the body as well.

For reasons of survival nature has put fear at the top of the list of messages our brains will listen to. When the survival-level fear alarm goes off, everything else steps aside. When deep fear strikes, you think of nothing else but. Creative thinking that is unrelated to the fear ceases. What takes center stage is managing your survival.

In extreme fear-and-worry states the amygdala, the brain's center of fear, which is located in the limbic system, sends out signals that demand the attention of the frontal lobes, distracting them from whatever else they may be doing. Beyond a brief startle, fear becomes toxic. It becomes an overwhelming preoccupation.

But don't smart business people worry a lot? Yes, but they worry wisely. The focus of wise worry is not on daily personal survival; it is on ways to make the company do better, or make oneself perform more effectively. When people feel reasonably safe, they worry productively, not in a state of amygdala-driven terror, but in a state of frontal-lobe mediated creative thinking. This is not survival worry—although in the long run it makes the best plans for our survival.

But still, can't some fear be useful? Don't some people thrive in an atmosphere of intense competition? Don't some people perform best when the stakes are really high? True. However, these people are feeling not fear but stimulation. They are feeling not afraid but "pumped up." They are charging toward a goal.

Some people can only function well in an atmosphere of high intensity. Traders in the commodities exchange, emergency room physicians, race car drivers, and trial lawyers thrive in high-stimulus situations. There is a physiological basis for this. At baseline these people are underaroused physiologically, and so they require more than an average amount of stimulation to become fully aroused. They are naturally drawn to highly stimulating jobs and highly competitive situations. But it is not fear that is motivating them, but *intensity*, the high stimulus of the moment.

What is the difference between fear and intensity? Physiologically, fear and intensity are quite similar, both involving an outpouring of adrenalin. But cognitively, at the thinking cortical level, they are different. The person who feels overwhelming fear is thinking, "I hate this. I can't wait for this to be over." But in the exact same situation, another person may think, "I love this. I would live in this state forever if I could."

I once treated two medical residents, both in training to become emergency room physicians. Ernie was worried he had chosen the wrong field. "Every time an ambulance pulls in I tense up. I get worried it will be a case I can't handle. I get concerned that I'll make a mistake or miss something or the nurses will think I'm incompetent." The fact is, Ernie was regarded as highly competent, and was ranked number one on his residency training exam. But the highly stimulating scene of the ER made him feel frightened and anxious. So much so that he eventually left the field and went into dermatology.

Hank, on the other hand, didn't score as high as Ernie on the tests, but loved the ER scene. "When I hear the sirens I get turned on. Even if I'm out having dinner, and an ambulance speeds by, I have like a Pavlovian response, and I want to get up and run to the hospital. I love the action. In the rest of my life I'm bored or half-asleep, but give me an emergency, and I come to life." Hank's problem was the opposite of Ernie's. He needed to learn how to be engaged when he wasn't in an atmosphere of danger and high stimulation.

There are more Ernies than Hanks. For most people, intense pressure and threat do not create helpful high stimulation. They create a harmful distraction. The Hanks of this world, who thrive in dangerous situations, have a different physiology, which derives from their genetic makeup. Their brains use the outpouring of adrenalin brought on by a highly stimulating, dangerous event to "turn on," to focus. While most people become distracted, nervous, or worried in such situations, these people actually become more calm and better focused. They *need* more pressure to function best.

Such people can use high-tension worry in work to make them work better. But for most people, alarming worry gets in the way.

But how can one avoid being subjected to fear tactics at work? Aren't all businesses necessarily cutthroat, not people-oriented but profit-oriented? Isn't business basically mean?

Not the *best* businesses, as it turns out. Not the ones that last. Arie de Geus, a retired Shell executive, has written a new book called *The Living Company* (Harvard Business School Press, 1997), which examines the question of what makes businesses endure. He and his team studied twenty-seven corporations that have lived a long time, one hundred years or more, and compared them to the majority of corporations, which are dead within twenty years of incorporation. Indeed, *one-third* of the 1970 Fortune 500 companies had merged, broken apart, or been acquired by 1983, so they no longer existed as independent entities!

What makes a company escape such a fate and endure on its own? De Geus found that the corporations surviving more than one hundred years were run as "living companies" where profit, like oxygen, was regarded as "necessary for life but not the purpose of life." The living companies "know that assets are just means to earning a living." The purpose of the company is to live, sustain life, and endure—and this sometimes means putting people before profits.

De Geus found that the "living companies" shared the characteristic of valuing people more than assets, and worked hard to develop trust among employees. "In the living company," states de Geus, "the essence of the underlying contract is mutual trust."

De Geus documents that long-term success depends upon employees who feel they belong in the company and identify with its values and purpose. The managers see their roles as stewards, whose responsibility is to leave the company in better shape than they found it. In today's world even using such words as "stewards" or "community" may seem out of date, but the history of business shows us that long life for a corporation depends upon such words being put into action. The people who do not grasp this will be out of date themselves. The companies that last know that the human connection is what makes any group great over time, be it a family, a neighborhood, a school, a city, or, yes, a business. Arie de Geus continues, "The feeling of belonging to an organization and identifying with its achievements is often dismissed as soft. But case histories repeatedly show that a sense of community is essential for long-term survival."

What happens when that connection is missing? What happens

when the people in charge neglect the living part of the company and only nurture profits? The company starts to lose its cohesion, its culture, its sustaining sense of who it is. Profits may mount and roll in for a while, but the history of business has shown they do not last. If you invest in your people, assets will grow; but if you invest only in your assets, your people will leave.

Most of us have had a boss somewhere along the line who ruled by terror and intentionally planted fear in the minds of everyone in the company. The man or woman at the top can create a culture that is radioactive with worry. Some bosses tend to do this. It is their strategy. They believe that fear increases productivity. Some bosses do it instinctively; it is the only way they know. And some bosses do it because they have learned it from previous bosses, or even their own parents.

These days, creativity is a key component of production, as our new technologies still await their most creative applications. Innovativeness and creativity usually thrive in an unworried workplace. Elspeth McFadzean, a researcher at Henley Management College in Henley-on-Thames, England, has carefully examined what conditions enhance creativity in the workplace.

McFadzean's research led to her making a number of recommendations for enhancing creativity, including simply making sure that the work environment is enjoyable. Her research found what most people would intuitively confirm: that you are more creative and open to new ideas when you are not feeling worried or defensive.

Furthermore, experts in learning tell us that learning begins, and depends upon, a positive mental attitude, an attitude not of fear but of safety and a willingness to be wrong. Positive emotion enhances learning. As Priscilla Vail, a world-renowned learning specialist, says, emotion is the on/off switch, "either closing or opening pathways to thinking and learning." Now, more than ever, businesses are learning corporations. A positive emotional attitude turns learning on; a negative state turns it off.

But isn't some worry useful at work? Indeed it is. Good worry is a key to success. Good worry is informed anticipation. The good worrier in business is described in these terms: "shrewd," "savvy," "one step ahead," "thorough," "a stickler for details," "an excellent planner," "sleeps with one eye open," "vigilant," or "never unprepared." No one in business should aspire not to worry, only to worry well.

The best way to do this is to set up a workplace environment that is as free of psychologically toxic elements as possible. We all know what environmental toxins are. Psychological toxins are just as dangerous. They poison the mental atmosphere. They create destructive worry.

Bad character is probably the most common psychological toxin in the workplace. A boss like Duane, for example. Or anyone whose personality is destructive to other people. Everyone has character flaws, but some people unfortunately are so deeply flawed as to make work miserable for everyone around them. These people should be screened out. As Herb Kelleher, CEO of Southwest Airlines, says, "Hire for attitude, train for skills." It is amazing how much damage one poisonous person can do to a business.

What can you do if the character of one of your co-workers is the major source of your worry in the workplace?

If the other person is the boss, as in the case of Duane, your best move may be to quit—or to keep as much distance as you can. But if it is a coworker or a middle manager, you have more options. The following steps might help:

TEN TIPS ON DEALING WITH DIFFICULT CO-WORKERS

1. Keep your distance. Try not to associate too much with someone you find difficult.
2. Observe carefully how others deal with colleagues you find difficult. Notice who gets good results, and how they do it. Whatever those people do, do yourself.
3. Don't get sucked into a feud. Feuds at work develop like flashfires; the only difference is that feuds last much longer. Once a feud develops between two people at work, it can be almost impossible to stop it without removing one of the people from the job. You don't want that person to be you.
4. Beware of how irresistibly *magnetic* an annoying person can be.

We all know people, at work or elsewhere, who captivate us with their positive qualities. But the opposite can happen, too. A person can captivate you with their *negative* qualities. Evil is often more interesting and compelling than good-naturedness. You may find a co-worker *so* obnoxious you can't leave him alone or get him out of your mind. You start rehearsing angry speeches you want to make to him. You drive to work thinking of how you are going to tell him off, and you drive home from work planning the following day's attack. You feel you just have to respond; you can't resist taking his bait. The problem is that it's you who suffers. Next thing you know you're putting huge amounts of energy into fighting with someone you'd be better off ignoring. Try to recognize this is what is happening, so you can redirect your attention and energy, no matter how irresistibly annoying the other person might be.

5. It could be worth trying to work the problem out. If you can go out for a cup of coffee and establish the ground rules for some sort of working relationship, everybody wins. Possible? Sometimes. Hard to do? Always. But just remember your days out on the playground as a child when you were told to "work it out on your own." Sometimes you actually did.

6. If you can't work it out, try setting some limits. Tell the other person to leave you alone, if he is bothering you. Better to be a little assertive than to steam in silence, then erupt one day and make yourself look bad. Some difficult people respond to feedback, because they are not aware they are bothering you in the first place. Furthermore, it is only fair to ask a person to stop what he is doing before you take him to court, literally or figuratively. Stick up for your rights, but ask nicely first.

7. Speak to your supervisor. Do this in confidence, and only when you have established the rules of confidentiality for the conversation in advance. If you are having trouble with a co-worker, your supervisor might be able to help you work it out, either by moving someone or by mediating. Furthermore, if you can be specific about what is bothering you, it can be doc-

umented and compared against other complaints that might have come in. If the co-worker is ultimately to be removed, input from other workers may be essential. You don't want to be a "snitch," but on the other hand if the behavior is grievous enough, neither do you want to be a victim.

8. As a caution on No. 7, try not to participate in ongoing gossip sessions about the co-worker, or become part of a scapegoating process. Go through established channels if you have a complaint. Never join a lynch mob. A lynch mob is destructive to everyone involved, the process is unjust, and the results of lynching are tragic.

9. Find something good to say about the difficult co-worker, if you possibly can. As long as that person is still on the job, you will do better getting along with him than not getting along, and one good way to get along with someone, at least superficially, is to find something positive to say about him. Just be sure you mean it, at least a little bit. Otherwise it will make both of you feel worse.

10. Remember something that is hard for all of us to remember: we, too, might be difficult at times. We should all ask ourselves now and then, how might I be contributing to this problem?

I think there are realistic ways to encourage people to work together—and worry together—effectively. The key is what I have called elsewhere in this book "connectedness." Connectedness curtails toxic worry, while at the same time, it drives productivity and creativity.

Connectedness is the most powerful antidote we have to toxic worry at work. Conversely, disconnectedness is the most common cause of toxic worry at work. Connectedness means simply a feeling of being a part of something larger than yourself. A family. A neighborhood. A cause. Or, in the business world, a company or corporation. Connectedness seems to have broken down in America over the past fifty years.

It is ironic to see disconnectedness in the workplace because electronically we are more connected now than ever before. But our electronic connections bring with them the challenge to learn how to hold onto human connections as well. To find a human connection, you must be able to feel in your bones that you belong. This requires more than the rapid transmission of data. It requires honest concern.

Consider this from business expert Thomas Stewart. In his book, *Intellectual Capital* (Currency/Doubleday, 1997), he writes,

> A fundamental paradox lies at the heart of the Information Age organization. At the same time that employers have weakened the ties of job security and loyalty, they more than ever depend upon human capital. . . . Community . . . belonging . . . If it sounds like Dr. Spock, don't worry. Organizations can help create bonds of ownership in both implicit and explicit ways that are thoroughly adult. An adversarial relationship with employees . . . may save or make a few dollars in the short run but at the expense of destroying wealth.

Businesses are catching on to the powerful benefits of community, or what I call connectedness.

Fred Smith is an example. He built Federal Express on the idea of connectedness. The Fed Ex managers' training guide states at its beginning, "FedEx, from its inception, has put its people first both because it is right to do so, and because it is good business as well." Predictably, the employees respond in kind. At one time early in the company's history, money was tight. One week, employees received a personal letter from Fred Smith with their paychecks. The letter said that although it was OK to cash the checks right away if you had to, it would surely help the company if those who could afford to would wait a few days. Even to this day, some of those checks have not yet been cashed, and they hang framed in various FedEx offices.

New business books have appeared with surprising titles for hardcore business books, like *The Loyalty Effect* (Harvard Business School Press, 1996), written by Frederick Reichheld, a top executive at Bain & Company, a fiercely competitive consulting firm, and *The Connective*

Edge (Josey-Bass Publishers, 1996), written by Jean Lipman-Blumen, a widely acclaimed consultant to governments and businesses around the world.

Customers and employees both need to connect in a genuine way, not to be treated like robots or machines. The companies that realize this stand a better chance of attracting and holding onto both the customers and the employees they want.

Two kinds of connectedness are vital at work: connectedness to colleagues and connectedness to a mission. If you have a solid sense that you are part of a team, and if you understand and believe in the mission your team is on, and what your goals are, then you will feel connected in the most important ways.

What if you do not have these forms of connectedness where you work? Try to develop them. Few people are opposed to connectedness. The work lies in developing the structures that allow for it to grow.

It is best if leadership shows the way. People naturally want to connect. So you begin by doing it yourself. Saying hello. Setting up lunch dates. Sending friendly or whimsical e-mail. Generally putting out the message you are interested in your colleagues as thinking, feeling people, as people you'd like to get to know better, not just nod at now and then. Humor, spontaneity, laughter—these are irresistible lures toward connectedness, and away from mechanical relationships.

Next, you begin to take an interest in other people's work. "What are you working on?" "Why did you use that color?" "How did that solution occur to you?" And you ask for advice. "What would *you* do if you were in my shoes?" We all want our work to be noticed. When that doesn't happen at work, or when it is only noticed in the context of performance appraisals or criticism, people tend to get defensive, secretive, and worried. The more you can take the lead by asking about others' work, by getting interested, and by valuing the opinions of others, the more connected your workplace will become. Not only will you develop better relationships, but naturally you will all grow more involved in helping each other. Work will improve.

"I don't want to talk to my colleagues; I'm already too busy." "I don't want to help anybody else; I'm too wrapped up in staying afloat myself." "Don't ask me to offer suggestions that would help other people in my office; they're the people I'm trying to beat out!" These are the typical obstacles to developing connectedness: time, pressure, competition.

But if you take the time, you'll find that that connectedness helps reduce the pressure and makes everyone a winner in the competition. Hoarding, working alone, being secretive, playing everything close to the chest is not only really un-fun, it is also counterproductive. Just think of the friends' groups and the Tinkertoys, or the fabulous success at Southwest.

You can develop connectedness in any job—or languish without it in any job, as well. I have treated a number of people making over a million dollars a year who complained that they felt "empty" and even "disgusted" at work because their job was fundamentally "meaningless." When a person talks about feeling "empty" at work, or uses the word "meaningless" to describe his job, I have come to realize this almost always means the person lacks connectedness at work. Most people derive a feeling of meaning from connecting to something we believe in—other people, a team, and/or a mission. Without such a connection, no matter how much money you may make or how famous you become, you will probably feel empty or dissatisfied.

Worry in the workplace is common today for many reasons, some of which we have looked at here. From a difficult boss, to personal insecurities, to difficult co-workers, to the threats of downsizing and global competition, to the constant explosion of technology and other forms of knowledge which can seem to leave so many of us behind, we all can find reasons to worry about our work.

If there is a great antidote to such worry, I believe it lies in the power of connectedness. Without connectedness at work, you worry. With it, you thrive.

11 Worry and Depression

One of the first signs of depression can be ruminative, unproductive worry. It is important to know this because you might simply think you are having a stressful time or that you are having a run of bad luck, when in fact you are clinically depressed. You might not realize that your worrying is a treatable condition called depression. Indeed, many people think of worry as simply one of life's hardships that a person must learn to "tough out." They do not realize that severe, extended worry should not be a part of life any more than severe chest pain should.

People fail to recognize their depression because sometimes they artfully organize their negative feelings into a coherent worldview, a bleak, pessimistic philosophy. It never occurs to them that they are "depressed." Indeed, they would dismiss the term, maintaining they are simply acute observers of the human condition. They regard anyone with a more cheerful view of life as sweetly deluded.

Such people, often extremely bright and conscientious, suffer without knowing that their suffering is preventable. "You think you can strike me down like Job?" they ask of fate. "Do you take me for just another trusting human you can lull into a false sense of security? Not me!! I'll beat you to the punch by worrying about whatever you have in store for me *before it happens!* I'll never feel betrayed because I'll never place any trust in anyone or anything in the first place. I never relax. That way I'm never surprised when you send your disasters out of the blue. I may not be able to stop them, but they won't catch me unaware. I know that every promise can be broken, I know that every friend can betray me, I know that every job can be lost and every prize be taken away, and I know that justice is nowhere to be found."

This is depression, enlivened with wit, vigilance, and cynicism. It wasn't very long ago that all depression was considered just a part of life. To complain of depression was to admit weakness or moral failure. Depression was taboo.

Depression has gradually moved from the moral court to the medical clinic. Women have sought help for depression more freely than men over the past few decades, but now men are feeling brave enough to seek help for this condition as well. Courageous men such as Mike Wallace and William Styron have acknowledged that they struggle with depression and that they have benefited from treatment for it. In so doing they have opened the doors for millions of other men to do the same. A recent book by Terrence Real, *I Don't Want to Talk About It* (Scribner, 1997), poignantly chronicles the many different ways depression afflicts men.

As people grow less ashamed of depression, they become curious to learn more about it. One of the first things to learn is how to recognize it. Depression isn't always obvious. There is no proof-positive medical test for depression, no litmus test, no way to ascertain with absolute certainty that a person is or is not depressed.

In the absence of an absolute test, we professionals must rely on the oldest test in the history of medicine, the individual's history. The doctor asks the patient questions, such as, "How do you feel?" and "When did you start feeling this way?" and "What makes it better and what makes it worse?" These are the questions of diagnosis, whether one is diagnosing appendicitis, a heart attack, or depression.

In the case of depression, the individual may not come right out and say, "I'm sad" or "I'm depressed." If he does, of course the diagnosis becomes much easier. But if he does not, the diagnostician—or the spouse, friend, or relative—must keep his or her ears open, and must know what to listen for. One of the symptoms to listen for is excess worry—worry out of proportion to the actual life circumstances. This is what I call toxic worry—worry that seems unwarranted, unproductive, and yet strangely unstoppable.

For example, I saw a man not long ago who came to see me because he wanted help for his college-age son's learning disability. However, it became clear right away that the man himself was more upset than he knew. He arrived for his appointment twenty minutes late, irritated at the traffic that had slowed him down, and he was angry at the fact that life was presenting him with yet another problem. He was sweating and out of breath just in telling me of his annoyances. I didn't interrupt him because I thought he would be frustrated if he didn't get to talk about his son. However, after about ten minutes I did ask him how *he* was.

"Me?" he replied in surprise. "How am I? Now that you ask, I'm a mess."

"What's going on?" I asked.

He took a deep breath and let it out through pursed lips. Then he took another breath and let that one out more easily. "I have so much going on," he said, "I don't know where to start. Just coming here to see you required major changes and compromises. I'm overextended. I don't know if I can make it. I can't think about it or I'll get overwhelmed. Let's talk about my son."

"How are you sleeping?" I asked, ignoring his request.

"Hardly at all," he replied. "I stay up into the night worrying. It is driving me crazy. But why complain? What can I do but keep trying? I have no choice."

This man—Buck—had a choice but he didn't know it. He was depressed. He was running on empty and was about to run out. It is a fact that some highly responsible men and women such as Buck tend not to recognize depression in themselves because they are too busy to stop and consider their state. They work harder and harder and cut themselves less and less slack until some catastrophic event stops them dead—sometimes literally—in their tracks. They may have a heart attack or a stroke, they may get fired, their spouse may walk out, they may collapse in exhaustion, they may have an automobile accident, they may exercise disastrously poor judgment, or they may accidentally on purpose commit suicide. These are just some of the potential, dire consequences of unrecognized depression.

In a high-achieving man, like Buck, it is not uncommon for the depression to manifest as frenzied worry. This is because he cannot say, "I'm sad." It is not in his repertoire. When he gets the sinking feeling others would recognize as sadness, he recognizes only a danger signal and so he works harder. Since the depression is making him less efficient and less mentally alert, his life begins to unravel and he develops more real problems to worry about. Soon he is enveloped in a continuing crisis, running from problem to problem, desperately trying to hold everything together, sensing that he is failing, knowing that he is not himself yet not knowing what to do about it except to work harder. More hard work further wears him down, which leads to less successful performance, which leads to more worry, which leads to more hard work, which wears him down still further. Alcohol often finds its way into the cycle as the overwhelmed individual makes a misguided attempt at self-medication, which only makes the whole problem worse. If someone else does not intervene, this man will push himself until he drops.

Buck was running, trying to juggle the dozens of balls he had up in the air. Business, children, spouse, social obligations. Buck was trying to keep up with them all. Now forty-six, he had been able to do it all so far; why shouldn't he continue? He was not weak or sick. He was strong. He was just in a tough patch. Or so he thought.

He worried and worried and worried. He shared his worries less and less with his wife because he didn't want to alarm her. She complained he was drifting away and that he was working too hard. He replied that he had to work hard to keep up with all the bills, and with two children in college, it wasn't easy. He rebuffed his wife without meaning to, but in so doing he put distance between himself and his best source of emotional support. He worked harder. He felt desperate. So he worked harder still.

Then, sure enough, a tavern sign caught his eye on the way home from work one day and it started to catch his eye every day thereafter. Two scotches, three, then four, plus a beer seemed to help. He could find some peace of mind. But it led him to fall asleep early, then wake up in the middle of the night, unable to get back to sleep, as he consumed his nights with worry.

It was at this point that he happened to come to see me. He came because he wanted help for his son. If I hadn't asked, he never would have mentioned anything about himself. This is the true meaning of denial: Buck was literally unaware that he was depressed. It was so deeply ingrained in him that depression was not a possibility he couldn't even name it.

Gradually, I drew it out of him. The magic of empathy is that it can awaken feelings in an individual that he is not actually aware of in himself. "It's so hard to keep up with everything," I said.

"You have no idea," he replied. "I have six dry-cleaning outlets and I have to oversee them all. I'm getting sued by a competitor who has a lot more money than I do, so he can just keep the suit rolling. He's trying to kill me with it. I'm on the Board at St. Joseph's and they're having their troubles now too."

"Quite a list," I said.

"That's not even the half of it. My kids, they're great kids, but Tommy has this learning problem and Sharon is just unhappy all the time for reasons I can't understand. She never was like this before."

"Maybe she senses that something is happening to you?" I asked.

"Like what?" Buck demanded.

"Just the obvious. You're overwhelmed. Sometimes kids pick up on this and get sad."

"But she's in college," Buck protested. "I don't see her that often."

"But you talk on the phone, don't you?" I asked.

"Sure, all the time," he answered. "You think she's unhappy because she thinks I'm unhappy?"

"Could be," I said. "Have you two been close?"

"Oh yes," he said. "She reads me like a book. Always has."

"So tell me," I went on, "what's in that book right now?"

"I'm afraid I'm losing everything," Buck said, getting a little choked up.

"Let yourself cry if you can," I said quietly.

"I'm just afraid I won't be able to keep it all going for the kids and for Debbie. Poor Sharon, you really think she's hurting for me? That makes me feel so bad. I love her so much." And now he really let himself cry. I handed him a box of Kleenex and gave his shoulder a little pat.

"Good," I said. "Just let it come out. You've been holding it back a long time."

Fortunately for Buck, he found help before a devastating crisis developed. Many people who are depressed, especially men, do not get help because they push it away. They angrily rebuff people who ask if they are OK because talking about it feels threatening. They are having all they can do just to deal with life without also having to talk about how bad they feel. They do not understand that feeling better can begin by talking about feeling bad.

If you know someone who is especially worried and/or irritable, more so than usual, keep in mind that this may be a mask for depression. The person can be of any age. Indeed, adolescent depression, which is on the rise, often manifests itself as excessive worry.

The stakes in depression are high. Obviously the worst outcome is suicide. Short of that, however, depression carries with it serious side effects. When you're depressed, your performance declines, either at work or at school, and you lose ground. Since the average episode of untreated depression lasts a long time—about nine months—you can lose a lot. A whole school year can be lost to one episode of depression, or several jobs, or a relationship, or a marriage.

Particularly if the depressed person is worried and irritable, other people may begin to stay away. It only takes a few rebuffs for most people to give up on someone who is cranky, worried, and sending out stay-away messages. Hence the depressed person ends up where he or she does worst: alone.

The good news is that depression (and the worry that so often goes with it) is treatable. Medication, psychotherapy, exercise, prayer and meditation, social restructuring (e.g., making dates to see friends, joining clubs where you feel welcome, and leaving places where you do not), techniques of positive thinking and cognitive therapy, group therapy, and humor all can help alleviate depression. The crucial step is to see it for what it is before it does too much harm along the way.

In Buck's case, he got help in time. It turns out that he had been depressed, without having a name for it, for about three months. His drinking had only recently intensified, so it was not that difficult for him to cut back. Alcohol exacerbates depression, as it is in itself a depressant. It is seductive because in the short run it is a good antianxiety agent and makes the drinker feel happy for a little while. But in the long run it makes worry worse and it deepens depression.

In addition to quitting drinking, I advised Buck to begin a regimen of regular exercise. He loved tennis, so that was a natural. Not only did he start to get the antidepressant benefits of exercise, he also got the antidepressant benefits of the social contact he developed with his opponents. Soon he had three regular games a week, with three regular partners.

We also began a short course of family therapy. Father, mother, son, and daughter all came together and talked. I served as referee and timekeeper. The sessions were wonderful for everybody as all kinds of stored up worries got put out on the table, where they could be dealt with.

In the first session Buck, trying to get to the point quickly like many men, pointedly asked Sharon, "So, are you unhappy because of me? If you are, don't worry, I'm fine, I just want you to be happy. If you want me to be happy, you be happy, OK?"

"Oh, Daddy, you think it's that simple? I should go be happy because if I'm happy you'll be happy and that should make me happy even if when I talk to you on the phone you sound like you're half-dead?"

"I do not," Buck protested.

"Daddy, you do. I am so worried about you. You have no idea. Do you realize that I have started to say prayers for you? I haven't prayed in a long time, but I am praying now. What's going on? Why have you changed?"

"Your father is very worried," Debbie added. "But he doesn't even talk to me about it. I can see it written all over him, but when I ask he just forces a laugh and says, 'everything will work out, it always does.' "

"Well, it has, hasn't it?" Buck asked.

"See, Mom, you're another one he just wants to have be happy."

"Is that bad," Buck asked, "that I want my family to be happy?"

"I like this," Tommy piped up. "I thought we were going to spend this whole time talking about my grades in school."

"We'll get to that," Buck said.

"Why don't you want to tell your family how you really feel?" I asked Buck.

"I don't know," he said. "It's not my job. My job is to provide."

"And you feel bad because you're having a hard time doing that," I added.

"Screw you," Buck said, looking at me.

"Buck, that wasn't an insult," Debbie said, jumping in. "He wasn't trying to offend you."

"I know," Buck said. "I'm sorry. I just feel ashamed."

"Daddy, how can you feel ashamed? Look at everything you've done for us," Sharon put in. "We love you and we want to pull together now that times are tough. Can you let us do that?"

"She's right, Dad," Tommy said.

"What do you think, Buck?" Debbie asked.

"I think I'm lucky to have you guys," Buck said softly.

The family sessions went on for eight weeks. Basically what they did is captured in the scene just quoted. They opened up communication and developed the expression of feeling that helped everyone, not just Buck. Worry and depression usually develop when people feel cut off or out of touch. Family therapy is an excellent forum for helping people get the chance to say what they need to say.

Buck also started to take the 20 mg a day of Prozac, which seemed to help and produced no negative side effects.

Within a month Buck was a different man. He had got a ton of worry off his chest, as had his family. He had cried cathartically. He was physically healthier, owing to increased exercise and decreased alcohol intake. He was more effective at work, owing to the fact that he was less depressed. His increased effectiveness at work in itself served as a kind of additional antidepressant because success tends to diminish depression.

Exercise became a permanent feature of his life, as did reduced alcohol intake. The family therapy was discontinued after eight sessions, having served its purpose well. I referred his son to a colleague for the workup of the problem Buck had originally come to see me about. Buck continued to take the Prozac, as most studies show that the longer you take it, the less the risk of relapse.

Buck's diagnosis and treatment serve as a good model of how effective a comprehensive approach to depressive worry can be. In Buck's case, worry was a symptom emerging out of depression, and successful treatment needed to recognize and take into account the link between worry and depression.

12 Intruder in the Dust

Obsessive-Compulsive Disorder

Jerry Mulholland came to see me because a friend of his told him he worried too much and that maybe a professional could help him.

What was striking in Jerry's story was that he didn't realize there was anything that unusual about it. This is the way it usually is with worriers; they think their worrying is "just life."

But Jerry's worries exaggerated the concerns of "just life." He brooded. He ruminated. A chance event could strike his mind like flint on stone and set off a fire of worry in an instant. "For example," he said to me, "yesterday I saw an invoice that was ninety days past due on my office manager's desk. We have the money to pay the bill. Why hadn't he paid it? I couldn't get the thought out of my mind. The manager was out of the office for a few hours so I couldn't ask him. I went back to my desk and tried to do some work, but I kept thinking about the invoice. It was from a supplier. No big deal. But in my mind I kept seeing the invoice, the logo of the company, staring at me as I tried to do some paperwork. I couldn't stop thinking about it. It grew in my mind as time passed. By the time my manager returned I was almost in a rage. I grabbed him and practically dragged him into my office and demanded to know why he hadn't paid the invoice. Poor guy, he looked at me like I was crazy. 'Jerry,' he said, 'let's go look at it. Can you calm down a little?' We went and looked at it, and immediately Hank recognized that this was a bill he had some questions about. He thought there was an error and he wanted to check it out before he paid the bill. Perfectly logical. But I spent three hours brooding on it instead of just putting it out of my mind. This is how I deal with problems all the time."

I told Jerry that there was a better way.

"What is it?" he asked. "I'm not ready to start talking about my mother or anything like that."

Many people think psychiatrists want to blame mothers for everything, probably because for years we did. But Jerry really didn't need to talk about his mother. He just needed to focus with me for a while on how he dealt with perceived danger. His method was to obsess about it. To brood and to ruminate. When he saw something that he thought might signal bad news or possible danger his mind went into a spasm, clamping down on the evidence of the danger and squeezing it, depriving him of the flexibility needed to make wise decisions.

The longer we talked the more examples he gave me. "Just when I think everything is OK, I'll open a piece of mail or see something in the newspaper that sets me off. A letter from a customer complaining is a typical one. I'll read it, send it through the proper channels, and take care of it properly, but it will ruin my day. I'll be unable to think about anything else. I'll start to think, 'What if that customer starts bad-mouthing us all over town? Who does he know? How much damage can he do?' Then I'll start to feel sick to my stomach. Even though I know I've taken care of the problem. Sometimes I'll call the person who complained and basically give them everything they want and more, practically begging them to relent and think we're OK. I've always thought this was just the price of doing business. If you don't worry about pleasing the customer, you'll have no customers."

"Well, Jerry," I interjected, "there's worry and there's worry. Do you think this relentless brooding helps you in any way?"

"No. In fact, I know it doesn't. Sometimes I make a bad decision just to try to make the worry go away. You know, give away the store, just to make someone else happy, even if I was in the right." He told me more stories, stories of spasms of worry brought on by minor complaints, bits of bad news, and small setbacks. Really, any negative news of any sort would send Jerry into a day's worth of brooding, at least. Sometimes the brooding would carry into the night and be his first thought when he woke up in the morning. "You mean everyone doesn't do this?" he asked.

"No, they don't," I said.

"I'll bet everyone in business does," Jerry replied.

"People who own their own businesses worry a lot," I acknowledged, "but there are better ways to worry than your way. The way you worry not only makes you sick, it is not efficient. You are wasting a lot of time and energy brooding. It is like a bad habit you have got yourself into, and now we have to work together to break it."

"That's possible?" he asked skeptically.

"Yes," I replied. "It's possible."

"But not probable," he said.

"What's probable is that we'll reduce this habit—make it less painful and prolonged."

"Even that sounds great to me!" Jerry replied enthusiastically.

Jerry had a version of obsessive-compulsive disorder (OCD). His mind would *obsess* over negative outcomes at the mere hint of one. It became his way of dealing with danger. What he had to do was learn another way.

Later in this book I will detail such a method, which I call EPR, standing for evaluate, plan, remediate. Jerry needed to start to train himself, with my help at first, to see a possible problem, rationally evaluate it, set up a plan to take care of it as best he could, then enact the plan, remediating the situation as effectively as possible.

Learning this new method took practice. Jerry and I had to go through pretend situations, literally speaking the thoughts as they came up, then putting them into the new framework.

For example, I said to Jerry, "Let's imagine you just got a complaint letter in the mail. What do you do?"

"Freak out," he replied with a grin.

"Then what?" I asked.

"Evaluate," he said dutifully. "OK, I look at the letter and size it up. What is the problem? How much of a deal is it? Then I plan what to do. I send the letter through channels, maybe call the customer, even get involved myself depending on the magnitude of what has happened. Then I remediate. Do the plan. Is that right, Doc?"

"That's right on the money. I know it sounds forced right now, but if you practice this every time you sense bad news or start to freak out, you'll find it works like a braking system on your mind as it's going out of control so that you don't obsess all day long. Just bite your tongue and say to yourself, 'OK, now do EPR, step by step.' It gives you a plan, a program, to combat the wildness of your obsessing."

Jerry and I met for a few months working on his developing this new method. Over time it did help. I also added the advice that when he felt a worry attack coming on, he get up and exercise. Some simple exercise, such as walking up and down a flight of stairs a few times or going for a short walk. Exercise can clear the mind and change its state in a short amount of time.

This is perhaps obvious. This is common sense. But why wasn't Jerry following such a plan on his own? Because he had developed a bad habit—the habit of embracing danger, of obsessing on negative outcomes. People can fall into this habit unwittingly because danger is so compelling. Nothing is so fascinating as disaster. More than that, the mind may try to trick itself into believing that it can control the negative outcomes somehow by conjuring them up repeatedly.

In these instances the ways of worry invoke magic. In OCD worry rules the mind like a sorcerer. The individual resorts to superstitious rituals in the hope that the rituals will magically rid him of the dangers he senses and fears. The sufferer of OCD is *obsessed* with a variety of intrusive, unwanted thoughts. He also feels *compelled* to act out certain rituals in an attempt to stave off (imagined) dire consequences associated with his unwanted thoughts. Hence the term *obsessive-compulsive* disorder.

OCD is not rare. It affects from 1 to 3 percent of the population, or between 2.8 and 8.4 million people. We do not have a cure, so the condition tends to be chronically bothersome, but we do have excellent treatments, which can drastically reduce the severity of the symptoms. It is important to note that other conditions often accompany OCD, especially other anxiety disorders, as well as learning disorders, so that when one diagnosis is made others should be sought.

The diagnostic term makes the condition sound more strange than it actually is. In fact, most people have experienced the symptoms associated with OCD at one time or another. OCD is an *intensification* of the fears and superstitions most people live with in mild forms all the time. Everyone must deal with unwanted, surprising, sometimes horrifying thoughts now and then. For example, most people have imagined jumping off a tall building, for no apparent reason, while they were standing atop it, or they may have imagined defiling a beautiful painting while they were looking at it, even though they liked the painting and meant it no harm, or they have been horrified by a gruesome image of the death of some loved one that pops into their minds out of nowhere. Once in a great while this kind of intrusive thought or image bothers just about everyone. But if the thoughts happen all the time, if they seem uncontrollable and deeply upsetting, then we may be in the domain of OCD.

Similarly, most people can cite superstitions or rituals they go out of their way to obey. Not stepping on sidewalk cracks or never walking under ladders are common ones. Not letting a black cat cross your path is another. Many people even have rituals for undoing the damage they fear may have been caused by breaking one of the superstitious rules. For example, I have a friend who tries to obey the superstition of saying, "Rabbit, rabbit," as the first words out of his mouth on the first day of every month. He feels that if he does not do this, something bad will happen or he will simply have a less good month than he would have had if he had remembered to say, "Rabbit, rabbit." It is easy to forget to do this, as my friend must remember to say the words immediately upon awakening almost as he's rubbing his eyes, before he has spoken to anyone else. If he forgets (and *remembers that he forgot* before the day is over!) his rules say he can undo the damage by walking around his block backward. This man lives in Cambridge, Massachusetts, a place tolerant of many eccentricities, but even in Cambridge it is a little strange to see someone walking around a city block *backward*. Even though he tries to make it seem as though he is a casual window-shopper, not too many people window-shop backward around an entire block. Nonetheless, such is the power of superstition that my friend has been willing to endure the embarrassment of doing this more than a few times. He is not crazy nor does he even have OCD. He is simply one of the many millions of people who feel compelled to obey certain rituals, even at the expense of some embarrassment or inconvenience. This may be considered odd, but it is still within the broad bounds of what we call normal.

True OCD is much more disabling than my friend's need to say, "Rabbit, rabbit" the first of every month. True OCD ties the sufferer up in knots, severely limiting what he can and cannot do. For example, I once treated a man who had to hop around on one foot whenever he was waiting in line. This is obviously humiliating, but such was the strength of the compulsion that he felt that he would be in extreme danger if he did not obey it. His solution was never to get into a line, thereby restricting his life considerably. I had another patient who felt compelled to kiss a doorknob whenever he passed one. This was so embarrassing as to be unbearable. Therefore he never went anywhere with other people. Some people with OCD can never do anything but obey their rituals; they become total prisoners to the irrational demands of their superstitions.

OCD provides an excellent example of a kind of worry whose treatment has been revolutionized by our recent discoveries about the brain. Only two decades ago the standard treatment for OCD was to try to ferret out and resolve the psychological conflict it was assumed must be causing such bizarre behavior. People would stay in psychotherapy for years, while still suffering from their OCD. We now know that there is a physical basis to OCD and that it is best understood and treated in genetic and biological terms.

A case of OCD can be quite mild, not really in need of treatment, or it can be disabling. The obsessions can be utterly horrifying, involving graphic scenes of sexual violence or religious defilement. The sufferer feels appalled at what his mind is doing but cannot stop it. The compulsions can be so elaborate as to prevent an individual from functioning in the world. I once treated a man who had to count to a thousand before he left the bathroom. It takes a long while to count to a thousand. He also had to wipe out and then lick any ashtray he saw, including large ones in airports and public buildings. Not only was this horribly embarrassing, it was a hazard to his health. But if he didn't do it he felt he would go berserk, even *commit suicide.* He couldn't *not* do it, as much as he hated the symptom. The upshot was that he never went into places where he might pass by an ashtray. That meant he never went out much.

Usually, however, the symptoms are not that extreme or bizarre. A very common symptom in OCD, for example, is checking. The sufferer must return over and over again to his house or his office or his car to *make sure* he did not forget something, or leave some switch on that he should have turned off. He will have to check a half dozen times before he can finally leave. He checks his briefcase repeatedly before closing it, checks to make sure his wallet is in his pocket hundreds of times a day, calls in for his bank balance three times in an hour, checks outside several times to make sure his car hasn't been stolen while he's waiting in the dentist's office, asks his boss to repeat the assignment he's just been given four times to make sure he's got it right, checks in his rearview mirror so often that he's dangerously unaware of what's in front of him, and a host of other kinds of checking, any one of which is not a great concern, but taken as a total package, becomes a huge impediment.

Similarly, the person suffering from OCD needs to check in with other people over and over again to make sure everything is OK interpersonally. "Do you still like me?" "Are you sure I haven't upset you?"

"Do you think we'll be OK?" "Will you be there when I get back?" "Will you always be there?" The relentless need for reassurance, even in the face of demonstrated loyalty and security, can result from OCD.

We have delved into the genetic and biological basis for OCD elsewhere in this book. OCD provides a physical model for extreme worry. It begins with the mind not being able to let go of a certain fear and then goes on to the mind making up some magical ritual—such as counting or drumming fingers in a certain pattern, or making everything symmetrical on the desk, or singing a certain song—in a desperate attempt to control the irrational fear. As this pattern sets in, actual physical changes can occur in the brain, such as the swelling of the caudate nucleus, as was described in the children who developed OCD after strep infections. We are finding other differences in brain scans in individuals with OCD, and we have seen these changes resolve after treatment, which is pervasive evidence that this condition is not under voluntary or even unconscious control but is rather a medical problem.

Specifically, the caudate nucleus can increase its size transiently during flare-ups of the symptoms of OCD. This has been demonstrated on brain scans. A patient will be scanned and as the scan is proceeding the technician will offer the patient some benign object, such as a clean rubber glove. The scan will show no change. But when the patient is given a dirty rubber glove, the scan shows a sudden burst of activity in the caudate nucleus.

Furthermore, there have been studies showing changes before and after treatment for OCD. Before treatment, subjects showed excess activity or hypermetabolism in the caudate region. After treatment with medication or even behavioral treatment *without* medication, the activity in the caudate region dropped to normal.

Not only does this finding show the physical basis for OCD, it demonstrates by brain scan the effectiveness of interventions that do not include medication. In other words, you can effect physical changes in the brain by talking to someone or by changing behavior.

This and similar evidence in connection with other conditions remind us that treatment should not be "either/or"—either medication *or* psychotherapy or cognitive-behavioral therapy but usually "both/and"—both physical and psychological interventions.

The studies on OCD have taught us a great deal. The physical understanding of OCD is new. Even a decade ago we did not have the strong evidence for the biological underpinnings of the condition we have today. As many of the conditions discussed in this book, OCD was regarded as a purely psychological problem, if not actually a moral failing or a mark of shame.

Now we know that this is not the case. The millions of people who have OCD no longer need to search for the "hidden psychological cause" of their problem because there isn't one; and they no longer need to feel ashamed because they have done nothing wrong, any more than someone with a seizure disorder has done something wrong to bring on the seizures.

While we do not have a cure for OCD, we do have treatments that are effective both for children and for adults.

What seems to work best, for young and old alike, is a combination of medication and psychotherapy. Different medications are used, but they all act upon the neurotransmitter serotonin. When Anafranil (clomipramine) was introduced a decade or so ago, it quickly became the medication of choice for treating OCD. While it does not provide a cure, it is effective in reducing the intensity and frequency of both the obsessions and compulsions. Judith Rapoport has described the story of OCD beautifully in her book, *The Boy Who Couldn't Stop Washing* (Dutton, 1989). Since Anafranil was first introduced, the selective serotonin reuptake inhibitors such as Prozac (fluoxetine) and Luvox (fluvoxamine) have also been used effectively to treat OCD.

Psychotherapy has also been helpful in treatment, particularly cognitive-behavioral therapy. As the term implies, cognitive-behavioral therapy addresses both the cognitions and the behaviors involved in OCD—which makes sense since OCD includes both kinds of symptoms.

Cognitive-behavioral therapy aims to help the patient consciously and deliberately alter his or her thinking—or cognition—and behavior. The method of EPR that I encouraged Jerry to use is an example of this kind of therapy. Other examples would include giving the patient a set of breathing exercises to do when the obsessions came on or a set of relaxation or meditation techniques. Similarly, I might encourage the patient to consciously rephrase negative thoughts, become his own "spin doctor," so to speak, as many worriers habitually and reflexively put a negative "spin" on any situation.

For example, Jerry assumed that any hint of negative news meant disaster. He might rethink a complaint letter as an opportunity to repair potential damage. He might learn to look at complaints as hidden opportunities to create positive relations with customers. At first, such a spin might seem like balderdash, as most new approaches often do. But over time such an approach can make a positive difference. Indeed, much of effective worry management amounts to creative, honest spin doctoring.

In other situations cognitive-behavioral therapy can actually encourage the patient to imagine the feared or abhorred object or event as a means of "detoxifying" it. By a system of exposing the individual, through his own controlled fantasies, to the feared, intrusive thoughts, the doctor can set up a situation in which the symptoms can be addressed systematically. What is the system? It follows common sense. The patient imagines what he fears; for example, being infected by germs coming in from everywhere. The patient is asked to tolerate the fantasy for as long as possible, and the length of time is extended in each successive session. From fantasy, the patient may then go on to reality, to actually handling "contaminated" objects, such as a dirty glove, or coins, or a dishrag. Again, the length of exposure time to the feared object gradually increases as the patient develops a tolerance for it.

In addition to bearing the tension of fantasizing or handling the contaminated objects, the patient must also try to refrain from resorting to whatever compulsions he has used to "cleanse" his mind of the germs, such as hand-washing, or some other ritual. The patient holds off as long as possible; then if he absolutely must rush to the bathroom to wash, that is OK. Next time he'll try to hold off longer, until finally he doesn't need to wash—or whatever—at all.

He can also be helped during these sessions by learning to bring to mind certain coping statements, such as "I am safe," and enact certain soothing behaviors, such as deep breathing. Taken as a package, cognitive-behavioral therapy can significantly alter the patterns of thinking in the individual with OCD.

OCD has become a highly treatable condition. As recently as fifteen years ago the prognosis was not nearly as bright as it is today. Although OCD remains a chronic condition, current treatments have made it not nearly as disabling as it once was.

13 Worry Run Amok

Panic and Social Phobia

Adrienne came to see me at the urging of her sister, after she began putting off doing the most routine errands, saying she felt too nervous to go outside. I asked her to try to describe exactly what was keeping her from going out, but instead of answering that question she told me what had happened a few weeks earlier at her bank. "I was standing in line. Suddenly, I became terrified. I felt as if I were being dragged to the edge of a cliff where someone was going to push me off. I broke out into a sweat, I started to shake, I had trouble breathing, my head started to pound, and I felt all my muscles burning and going limp, like they were melting inside me. It was totally terrifying. Here I was, just standing in line at the bank, and I felt as if I was going crazy. I'm sweating like mad, I'm panting like a dog, I'm looking around, I didn't want to do anything to embarrass myself, but I felt like I was going to explode. I could tell people were starting to notice me. I felt totally ashamed, but scared even more. Then my legs gave out and I just collapsed to the floor. One of the bank people came over and took me to a little alcove, where they sat me up and gave me a drink of water. Gradually, the world came back into focus and my heart started to slow down, but it took a while."

Panic. Everybody has felt it. It is worry intensified and taken to the ultimate—fear abruptly skyrocketing. You are wedged in the back of a slow elevator and you start to feel that you *have* to get out; you feel that if you don't escape right away you might die. Or, in an airplane, you suddenly drop a thousand feet and you feel you are going to die; you insist the airplane *must* land right away, as you cannot endure another minute. Or, in the middle of the night, you sense someone walking behind you. As you pick up your pace, your follower picks up his pace as well. Suddenly you bolt, bursting into a dead run, propelled by panic to run faster than you've ever run before.

Everyone who has felt panic knows its symptoms of overwhelming terror, of rapid breathing and a fast heartbeat, of a pulsating, burning feeling throughout the body, a desperate, physical feeling of needing to break free or get away.

Panic, when it is useful, is the nervous system's turbocharged means of escape. In states of panic people become stronger than they usually are, more durable than they usually are, faster afoot than they usually are, and generally more physically able to attack enemies, defend themselves, or flee. However, when panic strikes at the wrong time, it is like having an airplane take off in your living room!

"Do you have any idea what triggered this episode?" I asked Adrienne.

"No," she replied. "I usually have no idea when an attack will hit. It just happens. But I know I can't deal with this any longer. I can have these attacks anywhere, just out of the blue. Sometimes I have three in one week. It's crippling me. Sometimes I don't show up at work for fear of losing control, but obviously I have to go to work or I will lose my job. I'm only half-time, and my boss loves me, but how much more can he take?"

"Do you remember details about the first time this happened?" I asked.

"Oh, yes," Adrienne answered. "How could I forget? I was in my car on the Mass Pike, rushing to get home in time to meet the kids when they got back from school. Suddenly I see these blue and red flashing lights in my rearview mirror. God, it's like it was yesterday. They were right on top of me. They came out of nowhere. One minute I look in the mirror and see nothing and the next minute this bank of flashing lights look like they're in my backseat. It almost makes me sick to describe it to you now."

"Take your time," I said. "You are safe here. No one is going to hurt you. That episode is all over."

"But I can see it like it was yesterday," Adrienne went on. "It was the suddenness that got to me. And how close the lights were. Then this state trooper comes walking up to my car. I turn and smile at him, and he just stands there wearing these leather boots and reflecting sunglasses. Waves of heat come up from the pavement and make him look like he's straight out of hell. That's when it started. I could feel my vision constrict, like the whole background went blank. He said, 'License and registration,' and all I could see was the glove compartment, and I fumbled through all the maps and broken Life-Savers, and scraps of paper and receipts, and I started to feel dizzy, and it got hard to breathe, and I felt like if I didn't find that registration I'd have to go to jail, and the kids won't know what to do when they get home, and my hands started trembling sorting out all the junk in the glove compartment, when suddenly, as if it was sent by heaven, the registration just appeared in my hand, so I took it and handed it to the state trooper, but I dropped it. Then I let out a little scream. He picked up the registration and said, 'License?' and I just dumped my pocketbook out onto the seat next to me. I didn't need to do that because my license was in my wallet compartment, just like it always is, but I thought I was going to explode and dumping out my pocketbook felt like the only thing to do. I gave the trooper my license, and he went back to his car. He must have sensed something was wrong, because he came back to the car before he'd finished what he was doing to check on me. I was draped over the steering wheel, hyperventilating. The trooper asked me if I was having chest pain, and I said yes, and in minutes I was rid-

ing in an ambulance to the nearest hospital. That was my first panic attack. People sometimes say what a jerk the state trooper was, but I
think he saved my life. All he was doing was his job. It's not his fault he
has to wear a scary uniform."

"Who diagnosed panic attacks?" I asked.

"The psychiatrist they referred me to from the emergency room,
once they figured out I wasn't having a heart attack."

"And that psychiatrist, what did he do?" I asked.

"Dr. Kendall. He was a nice man. He took my history, and he talked
to me about my childhood, and he asked about anything that could be
bothering me, but he couldn't find any logical reason for me to have
had this attack, except that the state trooper scared the daylights out of
me. So Dr. Kendall prescribed Klonopin to prevent future attacks."

"What did the Klonopin do?" I asked.

"It helped. I only had a few more attacks while I was taking it.
Then, about six months later I stopped taking it and I stopped seeing
Dr. Kendall, because he moved to South Carolina."

"That was—" I started to ask.

"A year ago," Adrienne answered. "I know, why didn't I come to see
you sooner. First of all, I don't like to go out of my house. Second, I
didn't want to find yet another person to tell all this to, and I thought I
should be able to control these things on my own anyway, but obviously, I can't. I have tried for the past year to use true grit to stop these
damn things, and I'm a pretty motivated person, but true grit has not
worked. I think I must be going crazy. These attacks can be set off by
anything. And when they happen they are murder. They're terrifying.
Now I'm worried all the time. It's gotten so the worry I feel about the
attacks coming on is almost worse than the attacks themselves," Adrienne added, quite distraught.

"That's very understandable," I responded. "The attacks sound
horrible. Panic attacks produce all the same physical reactions as if you
really were about to be pushed off a cliff. Even though you are just
standing in line at the bank, you feel as if you are on the brink of destruction."

"What's going on in my brain?" Adrienne pleaded. "Am I crazy?"

"No," I answered emphatically, "you are not crazy. Not at all. You have a condition we can very likely fix. Your problem is that your alarm system is too sensitive and your imagination is too good, and you've fallen into a pattern that keeps repeating."

"What's the actual problem?" Adrienne asked. "I mean I know the name is panic disorder, but why in the world does my mind do this to me when I'm in no danger? Those poor people at the bank! I'm surprised I didn't end up in the hospital then too. The only reason I didn't is that I told them this had happened before and that I'd be OK. But what's going on with me?"

"There are many hypotheses," I replied. "The brain is so complex that we are just beginning to understand the rudiments of how it works. There is a little group of nerves deep in your brain called the locus ceruleus. Isn't that a beautiful name? It means 'blue place.' The locus ceruleus is involved in regulating the fear response, and it looks as though somehow or other the nerves in the locus ceruleus go berserk during a panic attack. Basically, they misread certain signals, sort of like a sprinkler alarm system misreading someone's cigarette smoke as a fire, then turning on all the sprinklers drenching everyone right in the middle of the grand ball. You may wonder, why does *my* alarm system do this and someone else's doesn't? It started when you were conceived," I went on. "You were born with a genetic vulnerability, an overly sensitive nervous system. This is the source of some wonderful parts of your personality, as well as your tendency to panic. For example, I'll bet you are quite attuned to the feelings of others."

Adrienne nodded.

"I would have thought so," I said. "But that same sensitivity set you up for what happened all these years later with the state trooper. Something went wrong in your brain when that state trooper stopped you. Your nervous system, which had been primed to overreact since the moment of your conception, finally found its moment to explode. You were rushing home, driving fast, feeling pressure. Then suddenly you were confronted with a scary sight. It was hot, you were in a closed space, your brain misinterpreted the data as being worse than they really were and sent you into another state—into panic. It misread the danger the state trooper represented, and it set off all your sprinklers at once. Certain centers in your brain started firing fast and furiously. Your whole body's alarm system started firing, even though it was a false alarm. But nobody knew that, including you. The next thing you knew you were in a hospital emergency room, being worked up for a heart attack."

"Why do these misfirings keep happening?" Adrienne asked.

"Because you are afraid they will. After the first panicked reaction to the state trooper, the subsequent attacks were born out of your fear that the panic would recur. It became a self-fulfilling prophecy in your own body. You became so worried that you tipped yourself over into panic again and again for no reason, other than that you were afraid of panic."

"That sounds like I'm crazy," Adrienne said.

"But it's not crazy, Adrienne," I went on, "because it's based upon real experience. If anything, you learned too well from your own experience. What we need to do now is teach you, and your body, a different way."

"What do you mean?" she asked.

"Well, the medicine Dr. Kendall gave you is excellent, but I think it might help you even more if we treated you with a process called cognitive-behavioral therapy. The medicine would be fine, but in the long term it is obviously better not to have to take medication."

"What do you mean 'teach my body'?" Adrienne asked.

"I just mean help you learn how to interpret what is going on inside you correctly. Now you misinterpret what is going on, and it makes you afraid even to go outside. This fear of going outside has a name, too, by the way. It's called agoraphobia. We have found that both panic and agoraphobia are conditions that can improve by using cognitive-behavioral therapy, through which you learn different ways of interpreting what is going on within you, specific techniques for dealing with these feelings, and new ways of directing your thoughts." *

Agoraphobia (literally, "a fear of the marketplace" or a fear of leaving home) is a condition that accompanies panic disorder about 30 to 50 percent of the time. Adrienne was developing agoraphobia, as evidenced by her fear of going to work and her postponing coming to see me. Agoraphobia is characterized by an intense fear of (and usually avoidance of) places or situations in which escape may be difficult or one imagines an attack of panic may occur. Hence the agoraphobic individual typically fears going anywhere unless accompanied by a "safe person" (i.e., someone who knows about the attacks) or a "safe object" (most commonly a bottle of medication to treat the attack if it occurs or a lucky charm).

For example, an agoraphobic individual may be willing to go to church only if he can sit in the back row, with easy access to an exit, if a safe companion accompanies him or if he can bring his bottle of medication or other talisman that makes him feel safe. The essence of agoraphobia is not real danger, of course, but perceived danger; therefore lucky charms or any other agent that acts positively on the imagination can exert a therapeutic effect.

When it comes to treatment, the options include treatments with or without medication, or a combination using both medication and nonmedication approaches. At the core of most nonmedication treatments for anxious, worried states, such as panic, post-traumatic stress disorder, obsessive-compulsive disorder, or social phobias is what is technically called "exposure." Exposure refers to a variety of methods by which you are gradually exposed to whatever makes you worried or anxious. In other words, if heights make you nervous, you might start therapy just by *imagining* you are standing at a certain height, looking

---

*Cognitive-behavioral therapy is based upon the classic principles of behavioral therapy as developed by Joseph Wolpe and others, and the now-standard principles of cognitive therapy as developed by Aaron Beck. David Barlow, Michelle Craske, and others have applied these principles ingeniously in devising the methods of cognitive-behavioral therapy and applying them in conditions like panic with and without agoraphobia.

down. Then in your imagination, and in the presence of a therapist, you'd start going up, a few floors at time. After you felt comfortable being exposed to heights in your imagination, you'd try it out in reality, using the same graduated process.

Similarly, a therapist may deliberately expose you to the physical components of your worried feelings, one at a time, to help you get more comfortable with them. For example, if your heart beats faster when you worry, part of your therapy may be to deliberately induce a fast heartbeat by doing physical exercise, then talk yourself through the feeling of having a fast heartbeat, noting how safe you are and that nothing bad happens. Then you might try breathing fast and get used to that. In this way you begin to take apart your worried state piece by piece and get comfortable with each individual piece, so that when you experience them all together, in the stew of worry, you have felt them before and you feel less afraid.

Therapies that use exposure are many and varied. Most share the component of gradually increasing the intensity of the stimulus, and also include a therapist or some other safe person to help you get used to the fearful situation. Then homework is often prescribed, as you do exercises at home to practice the new techniques you have learned.

Cognitive-behavioral therapy is one of the therapies that is based upon exposure. Using both cognition (thought) and behavior (practice) to "get used to" painful states, cognitive-behavioral therapy is a great breakthrough in that it allows for treatment of panic and many other conditions involving excessive worry without medication. At the very least it provides a potent supplement to medication, and in most instances it is even more effective than medication in treating panic, with a success rate of 60 to 80 percent!

How? A pivotal part of the panic syndrome is the fear of fear. If the fear of fear can be controlled at the start of the attack, then true panic never really sets in. This additional fear—the fear of fear—turbocharges ordinary fear into extraordinary panic. Cognitive-behavioral therapy can reduce this additional fear. Look at what I did with Adrienne as an example.

First of all I explained what the therapy would entail so that Adrienne understood what was happening and could feel in control of what was going on. "Basically," I said to her, "I am going to work with you to help you use your own body as a kind of training site. I will help you learn how to recreate the feelings of panic within yourself on a voluntary, controlled basis and then help you learn to tolerate and finally detoxify them by discovering that they are not going to overwhelm you."

"You are going to make me feel panic in here? That sounds a little bit scary," Adrienne said with a nervous laugh.

"It may be a little bit scary to imagine, but I think you'll find that you'll feel safe as we go through the exercises. If not, we can stop immediately."

Adrienne agreed. I then asked her what specific bodily sensations she associated with her panic attacks. She thought for a moment, then said, "Feeling out of breath, feeling my heart beat fast, feeling dizzy, and feeling like I'm going crazy."

"Let's look at the first three and leave the fourth aside. The fourth is really just the result of the first three anyway. What I want to do is induce feelings of breathlessness in you, as well as speed up your heart and also make you feel dizzy, but all on purpose, by design, while you are in control, OK?"

"OK," Adrienne replied, "but how?"

"Well, for a start we'll go out to the stairway together, and I'll ask you to run up and down the stairs a few times until you are out of breath, OK?"

Adrienne nodded, and we went outside my office to the stairs. She looked at me for instructions. I said, "Just walk briskly down the stairs and then run back up as fast as you can, then down and back up again and do it for a third time if you can." She did this. After her third trip up she quite was out of breath. "OK," I said, "let's go back into the office." Once inside, I asked her to sit down. She was breathing very hard. As she was catching her breath I said to her, "Now you are out of breath and your heart is beating fast, just like in your panic attacks. But there is nothing to fear. Your heart is simply beating fast and you are simply out of breath. There is nothing to fear in these sensations.

You have felt them before, playing sports or doing work. They do not mean that you are going crazy or that you are going to die. The feelings will pass in a few moments and your body will return to normal. Your heart will sense that it does not need to beat so fast any more, and it will slow down, and so will your breathing. Everything is fine."

As Adrienne's breathing slowed down, she smiled. "I get it," she said. "This is like practice."

"Exactly," I replied. "We are trying to teach your brain different ways of interpreting physical sensations that you now associate with panic. When you have a panic attack, the feeling of panic is actually brought about because you misinterpret the meaning of what your body is doing. You think everything is going out of control, which then makes everything actually go out of control. So by recreating the symptoms in here and by practicing them at home you can teach yourself new interpretations, which really amounts to rediscovering the old ones—the ones you had before you started having panic attacks. Does that make sense?" Adrienne nodded. "Do you feel ready to try feeling dizzy now?"

"If you say so. How do we do that one?" she asked.

"My swivel chair," I said, pointing to the chair behind my desk.

As I rolled the chair out from its place behind my desk to the middle of the floor, Adrienne said, "This should be fun."

She sat in the chair, and I spun her around a few times. Stopping her, I asked, "Do you feel dizzy?" She nodded. "Well, everything is OK. Soon you won't feel dizzy. This is just a passing feeling, it is not at all dangerous, and you can make it go away just by waiting a few moments and by being still. Nothing bad is going to happen. Being dizzy is just a normal feeling, a feeling that will pass." I paused. "Do you still feel dizzy?" I asked.

"No," she replied.

"Let's try these exercises one more time."

"OK," she said. "This is kind of fun."

She went up and down the stairs a few more times, and I talked her through the cooling-off period once again. It was important that she hear my words so that she could remember them and insert her own similar words when she practiced these exercises on her own. It is one thing to say, "Everything will be OK," but it is quite another to hear those words as you are experiencing their accuracy.

After she learned how to recreate the physical sensations she associated with panic, Adrienne and I worked on some relaxation techniques she could use when she felt an attack coming on. Deep, slow breathing works well. It is simple and you can do it anywhere. Also, silent meditation works well if you are sitting down and can close your eyes. Prayer can also be effective. I asked Adrienne which technique appealed to her. "Let's start with breathing," she replied.

"OK," I said. "Just take a deep, deep breath, hold it for half a second, then let it out all the way, slowly. Pause and do it again. Notice your breathing as you do this and try to focus just on that. Just on your breathing. Feel the air fill up your lungs and feel your body taking in the oxygen it needs, then feel the air your body gives up float out and away. Slow and relaxed. Just focus on your breathing, in and out."

She did exactly as I instructed and I accompanied her, both of us breathing in deeply and out slowly. We took a half-dozen breaths, then I asked her how she felt. "I liked that," she said.

"Good," I replied. "When you do it on your own, it helps to talk your way through it just as I did then, guiding your mind and soothing yourself as you do so. It's really very simple and effective."

"I can see that," she said.

"So your homework now is to practice these techniques. Do some physical exercise to get your heart rate up and your breathing, then notice that you are safe and realize that these sensations are not dangerous. Spin around and do the same for dizziness. Then, next time you come here, we'll try combining all three, fast heart, rapid breathing, and feeling dizzy. You and I will talk you through it and it will be no problem."

"OK," she said. "If you say so."

"You have doubts?" I asked.

"A few," she answered. "But I like this. It makes sense."

"And it makes sense to have doubts," I replied. "We'll just take it one step at a time."

By the next session Adrienne was able to tolerate all three sensations with no problem. She had done her homework and had practiced not only the sensations but the breathing exercises too. She was doing well.

We gradually added more imagination work into what we did in the office, imagining the scene at the bank and the scene with the state trooper. This exposure to what is feared can be controlled in the imagination in such a way that, like the physical sensations, the feared scenes can also be detoxified. This is cognitive-behavioral therapy at work.

The sufferer learns to recognize the feared physical symptoms not as harbingers of doom and death, but as normal physiological responses and learns to take steps to ease their passing in a short space of time.

Gradually he exposes his mind to more and more of the feared situations and feared responses. This is called "exposure with systematic desensitization," but all it amounts to is common sense. Get back on the horse after you fall off. If you are afraid of something, try exposing yourself to it a little bit at a time until, bit by bit, it doesn't bother you any more. If you are afraid of heights, imagine in your mind starting at the first floor, then going up one floor at a time, and looking out the window from each successive floor. Once you can do it in your imagination, go to a real building with a friend and try the same process. This is exposure with systematic desensitization.

Another way is to go whole hog and expose yourself to the fiftieth floor right off the bat. Have someone with you if you do this. Stay there until it doesn't bother you anymore. This is called implosion therapy or flooding. It works because of the biological fact that the body cannot maintain a state of peak anxiety much longer than ninety minutes, after which it runs out of the chemicals it needs to put itself on red alert. Therefore, the high anxiety has to pass, *if you can endure it long enough*. The idea is that once you have learned that the event was bearable it will no longer set off such alarms within you. Although it can be dramatically and quickly effective, it can sound frightening, so careful preparation is essential.

In treating panic disorder with cognitive-behavioral techniques, the therapist incorporates systematic desensitization by asking you to recreate the feared symptoms, a little at a time, as well as to imagine feeling the feared feeling states ("going crazy," "losing control," "spazzing out") a little at a time. Each step of the way, the therapist coaches you on how to reframe in your mind what is going on, how to see it as nontoxic and understandable, and how to offer yourself reassurance and advice. Once you have learned how to do this with a therapist present, you then begin to practice on your own, perhaps starting by having the therapist in the next room, then trying the exercise at home, perhaps with a spouse or other safe person in the next room, until finally you can do it on your own. You can experience the physical symptoms of panic without having them mushroom into a full-blown attack. What is the difference between experiencing the symptoms and having an attack? The difference is a crucial one. In an attack you add to the physical symptoms your intense fear of what is going on and what might happen next. By adding this surge of fear you prolong the physical symptoms, instead of allowing them to abate. By prolonging the physical symptoms, you only deepen your sense of fear, which further prolongs the physical symptoms, resulting in the out-of-control spiral of a panic attack. It can get so bad that people have actually committed suicide trying to put an end to the overpowering feelings of panic.

With cognitive-behavioral therapy, however, most people can get relief from their panic. Why is it that some people feel panic once but never worry about it again, while others go on to develop this painful syndrome of ongoing worry called panic disorder? Why do most people when they are stopped by a state trooper on a hot summer day, even if they are stressed out to the maximum and feel panicky at the moment, nonetheless let the episode pass without its becoming the start of years of struggle and fear, as it did for Adrienne? We do not know for sure. In all likelihood, the inherited vulnerability predisposes certain individuals to react as Adrienne did. Is there any way to identify that vulnerability before a panic disorder develops? No sure-fire way. But people who were highly reactive as children, who were sensitive or shy or inhibited, and people who are high-strung as adults or who have an elevated resting heart rate may be at higher risk.

Not only can the panic itself be disabling, but the worry that accompanies the syndrome between attacks is miserable as well. The individual carries around a constant feeling of concern over what might happen next. Some researchers have called this "anxious apprehension" or "apprehensive expectation." This apprehensive state never fully subsides, as the individual lives in a constant state of worry. The cognitive-behavioral therapy also soothes this, but not quite as well.

Sometimes the addition of medication can help, too. Indeed, some clinicians start their treatment for panic with medication, although I would recommend using nonmedication approaches first for reasons of safety as well as effectiveness. The main classes of medication used for panic disorder include the serotonin in reuptake inhibitors, such as fluoxetine (Prozac), the tricyclic antidepressants, such as imipramine (Tofranil), and the benzodiazepines, such as alprazolam (Xanax) or clonazepam (Klonopin). One of the serotonin reuptake inhibitors or one of the tricyclics are preferable owing to their low abuse potential as well as the ease of weaning an individual off the medication. Most experts would choose a serotonin reuptake inhibitor first. Some experts in the field recommend against ever using the benzodiazepines because of their side effects and the potential for their being misused. This is a decision you should make only after careful discussion with your doctor.

Social phobia is different from panic with agoraphobia in the kinds of fears involved. The most common fears of people suffering from social phobia are speaking in public, eating in public, writing in public, using public lavatories, and being the center of attention. In contrast, the most common fears of the person with panic disorder are driving or traveling, stores, crowds, restaurants, and elevators. Social phobia and panic disorder may occur together, but the individual with pure social phobia will not experience spontaneous panic attacks. Instead, he feels intense fear and anxiety around the specific feared circumstances.

I once treated a college professor who was a brilliant botanist but was afraid to give lectures. It was part of her job to give lectures, so she was severely impaired in her work by this fear. "I force myself through them," Rachel said, "but they are torture."

"Have you ever felt at ease speaking in front of other people?"

"I don't know, maybe in first grade in show-and-tell. But most of my life I haven't had to talk in front of people. But now, being junior faculty, I have to give the big lecture course. You should see me a half hour before the lecture starts. I'm like a terrified little girl. I literally tremble during the lecture. I have to hold onto the podium to steady myself, and I can't pick up my notes because I'm shaking so hard I'll drop them, and even if I don't I'm afraid everyone will see the pages fluttering in my hands. So I have to slide one page over to uncover the next, without lifting it up. Sometimes I push my notes off the podium onto the floor. I don't even bother to pick them up. Students sometimes pick them up for me, and I say, 'Thank you, just hold onto them and give them to me after the lecture.' My knees often tremble, and I worry they'll buckle underneath me. That has never happened, thank God. Sometimes I get light-headed and I feel as if I'm going to faint. That hasn't happened, either, but I wouldn't be surprised if it did."

"It probably won't," I interrupted. "You're describing the symptoms of a social phobia, and as painful as they are you'll be glad to know that people usually do not do the things they worry they might do, like collapse onto the floor or actually pass out."

"You mean all this nervousness has a name?" Rachel asked.

"Yes," I replied. "It is a type of social phobia. Does giving it a name help?"

"Yes," Rachel said, "it does. I thought it just meant I was weak-kneed, no pun intended. What is the outlook for us folks with social phobias?" Rachel asked with a slight tone of humor in her voice, the first bit of levity she had shown.

"The outlook is good," I replied. "But let me find out more. Tell me about your life." I needed to take a full history from Rachel, because sometimes social phobia is accompanied by other problems, such as depression, panic attacks, or other kinds of worried states. In addition, sometimes people try to self-medicate their phobia with alcohol or other drugs. Rachel had none of these problems. She had lived a quiet life, had always been a serious student, particularly a lover of nature. "I do think I'm too controlled as a person," she volunteered. "My husband is always urging me to loosen up. Of course, I'm always telling him to slow down."

"What kind of work does he do?" I asked.

"Medicine and music," she replied. "By day he's a hematologist and by night he's a jazz musician."

"Have you had time for children?"

"No," Rachel responded. "When we got married we both knew we wanted to spend our time pursuing the strong interests both of us had. We love children, both of us do, but we did not want to raise any. So we're everyone's favorite aunt and uncle."

"You're happy with that decision now?" I asked.

"Very," Rachel said confidently. "Happy and relieved. If we had kids, it would be impossible. We made the right decision for us."

"That's good," I said. "What is this issue of being too controlled?"

"I don't know. Maybe it is just the way I was brought up. I'm always tidying up and organizing everything."

"Do you think that has anything to do with how nervous you get in front of a large audience?"

"Oh, yes," Rachel replied. "One on one, I have some control, even in small seminars I have control. But with large audiences, I don't."

"Why don't you try just giving your lecture to the front row?"

"What do you mean?" she asked.

"You know, just block out the rest of the room and talk to the people in the front row, just as if it were a seminar."

"That might help, but in a seminar there is give and take, you know, discussion. I rely on that to keep me from getting nervous. Part of what makes the big lectures so difficult is that I know I have to keep the whole thing going by myself. Basically, I have to entertain the audience for fifty minutes."

"But you're the teacher," I said, "and the audience is made up of your students. You are the one with the power."

"It never feels that way," Rachel replied. "It feels just the opposite."

"That's the funny thing with social phobias," I said. "People lose perspective. They feel they are being judged and scrutinized in ways they really are not. In your case, if anyone is afraid of anyone it is the students who are afraid of you or at least afraid of the situation. They are sitting out there taking notes furiously, trying to comprehend what you are saying."

"I know," Rachel said. "Particularly in my course, Introductory Biology, because it is full of premed students who are all competing to get into medical school. I know they are the ones who are scared, and I want to help them. But instead I am terrified, not of them as individuals but of the entity they constitute, the audience."

"That's a great way of describing it," I added. "In most social phobias that's the way it is. Some people get scared just being in the limelight. Some people feel worried about eating in public, as if they are being watched. Even cats and dogs can be like this."

"I know," Rachel said. "Our cat hates for us to watch her eat."

"Mmm. Well, so here we are."

"And what do we do?" Rachel asked.

"Medication could help your fear of the audience. There are various different medications we can try, but I would suggest starting without medication. If we do use a drug I would suggest what is called a beta-blocker, such as Inderal, taken an hour before you lecture. How do you feel about taking medicine?"

"Fine," Rachel said. "If it will help I'll take anything. It won't interfere with my performance will it?"

"It shouldn't. At the dose I'd give you there should be basically no side effects. But before we try that, I'd like to teach you some relaxation exercises you can do before you lecture. Also, general physical exercise. Do you get any?"

"Not really."

"Is there any form of exercise you like?" I asked.

"I love to walk and run and ride bikes," Rachel replied. "I've just gotten out of the habit."

"It would really help if you started up again. Maybe with your husband or a friend, so you'll do it regularly. Exercise helps combat all kinds of worry and anxiety and is good for you in many other ways as well."

"Is that it?" Rachel asked.

"It's a start. I'd also like to refer you to a group that specializes in treating public speaking problems."

"What will happen there?" Rachel asked, a little apprehensively.

"Basically, practice. Each member of the group will have your problem, a fear of public speaking, so there'll be a natural understanding for one another. In each session, you'll give a little speech to the group. After the speech, you'll go over the negative thoughts that came into your mind as you spoke. The therapists and the other group members will give you alternate ways of looking at those negative thoughts or ways of combating them. For example, if as you talked you thought to yourself, 'these people look bored,' the group may tell you that in fact they were quite interested and that you didn't read them right. Or the therapist may suggest that you pick out a certain member of the audience and talk to that person until you see a response register. Or they may teach you a word to say to yourself, like 'RHAPSODY!' to trigger a positive response within yourself. There are all sorts of techniques, or what are called cognitive restructurings, to talk yourself out of negative thinking. Then the therapists will assign homework to the group, similar to the exercises you did in the group, such as making a toast at a party or asking a question in a public lecture or simply talking to your mirror and rehearsing the positive statements as you do so. You'll also rehearse ways of dealing with typical distractions every lecturer deals with, such as people getting up and leaving or beepers going off."

"That really sounds useful," Rachel said enthusiastically. "By the way, can you tell me now what the technique is to ignore people getting up and leaving?"

I chuckled, being a lecturer myself. "It can be awful, can't it? Basically, what you have to remember is that people leave lectures for a whole lot of reasons other than that they are tired of listening to you. They may have to go to the bathroom, get to another appointment, call home, answer their beeper, go get something they forgot, or maybe they're just constitutionally antsy—there are any number of explanations that have nothing to do with you. Many lecturers take every single leaving personally, but that simply does not jibe with reality. Sure, some people may leave out of boredom, but maybe they didn't get enough sleep the night before or maybe they aren't feeling well. The basic plan is: don't take it personally."

In Rachel's case the combination of making a diagnosis, giving her problem a name, exercise, relaxation techniques, the strategy of lecturing to the front row, and the group practice sessions worked. She found that within a month she was in much greater control during her lectures, and within three months she actually felt relaxed enough to let go of the podium, hold her notes in her hand when she wanted to, and even walk around the stage a little bit. She became a more effective teacher and much happier in her work.

In treating social phobias, some combination of medication and nonmedication approaches usually works well. The condition can be truly disabling at times, but proper treatment can help dramatically.

Among medications, in addition to the beta-blockers the monoamine oxidase inhibitors (MAOIs) have been found to be particularly effective in treating social phobia. Other medications have also been found to be helpful, including benzodiazepines and selective serotonin reuptake inhibitors.

As in the case of panic disorder, the nonmedication approaches to social phobia are the key and should always accompany or precede any medication trial. These include particularly cognitive-behavioral therapy, which may be individual or group.

It is unfortunate that the anxious apprehension between attacks of panic does not respond as well to cognitive-behavioral therapy, but it does respond to some degree. The response will in all probability be better if the sufferer does not also have some other major problem, such as depression, substance abuse, or severe social isolation.

This interpanic worry becomes in some people a learned response to life. Even if they have never had an episode of panic, they fear bad outcomes all the time and live in a state of worry every day. This is called generalized anxiety disorder, and will be discussed in the next chapter.

14   Living in Fear

Generalized Anxiety Disorder

Generalized anxiety disorder (GAD) is one of those conditions which, if you have it but don't know it, cause you to exclaim when you hear it described, "You mean there's a name for this?" When clinical depression was first being described people who were depressed had the same reaction, having believed all along that depression was simply the way life was for everyone. They were surprised and relieved to discover that there was a name and a treatment for what they were suffering from. Similarly, when attention deficit disorder was first being described in adults in the 1980s, sufferers had the astonished reaction of, "You mean there's a name for this? It isn't just life?" The starting point in therapy is understanding that the problem is nameable and treatable.

So it is with GAD. Thanks to the work of Dr. David Barlow and many others, this condition is receiving more attention, so that the general public is becoming aware of it. "You mean everyone doesn't worry all the time?" one of my patients asked me.

"Actually, they don't," I replied.

"Amazing," came the response.

We have all heard the phrases tossed around to chronic worriers:
"Can't you *ever* relax?"

"Why must you always find *something* to worry about?"

"What happened to you to make you see everything so negatively?"

"Did someone train you to look on the bad side all the time?"

"Do you think it's a *sin* to feel confident about the future?"

"Is there *any* way for you to feel that things will work out OK?"

These are the questions chronic worriers field all day long from spouses, friends, colleagues, and even from themselves. Most worriers know they worry too much. They do not like worrying too much. They know it is annoying to others. They find it painful themselves. *But they cannot stop.* They know it is irrational. They will say, "I know this sounds crazy, but could you please tell me that that boulder is not going to drop on top of us as we drive under it?"

"It's been there for thousands of years," you respond as you drive along. "Why should it drop now?"

"Because *we're* about to drive under it," comes the doleful reply.

This is the plight of the person who has GAD. Ben Miller, in chapter 1, is only one example of the many who suffer from GAD. For the individual with GAD, the world never feels safe even when it truly is.

What is ironic is that the person suffering with GAD "knows" that he's safe even as he worries. He knows, rationally, that the boulder won't fall, but he *feels* that it might. He feels that he is in danger; all his body's sensors tell him so. His bodily indicators are set at too sensitive a level. His heart races easily, he starts to perspire before others do, his hairs stand up on the back of his neck at the slightest hint of a threat, his vision narrows, and his muscles tense, even when he simply walks into another room.

He develops various recurring physical symptoms, such as restlessness or feeling "on edge," difficulty concentrating, tension in muscles and joints, difficulty falling asleep or staying asleep, irritability, and a tendency toward easy fatigability.

It is hard to talk this individual out of his worry. Spouses, friends, and professionals spend a long time trying, but the worry creeps back. It is like dust. Dusting every day helps but doesn't solve the problem. Reassurance, like dusting, cleans things up for a little while, but then wandering worry reappears.

In GAD, there is no apparent cause for the individual's anxiety as there is, for example, in post-traumatic stress disorder. It is free-floating.

But there is nothing free about how the sufferer feels. GAD colors one's view of life. It is dispiriting to "know" your life is good but not to be able to feel it because you are so worried so much of the time. Even worse, you try the patience of those around you because there is no "reason" for you to be so worried. "Why don't you save your worry," they are apt to say, "for when you really have something to worry about?" If only you could. You do not want to inflict your worry upon them any more than you want to inflict it upon yourself, but it just appears, like dust, when you look out on your life.

Like a good sport, you may try to keep it to yourself, but anyone close to you can see it as if you were wearing a red, neon sign that blinks, "I'M WORRIED." You can't not show it. It spoils your fun and can spoil the fun of those around you. It is as nasty as living in a cage of mosquitoes.

One of the troubles with GAD is that the worries can seem like mosquitoes, both to the sufferer and to others. This means they should be no big deal. Just slap them away. But if you are surrounded by them, slapping them away constantly becomes, at best, tiring. Furthermore, they leave bites that itch and must be scratched. Scratching away at your worries is no way to, say, enjoy a dinner conversation or a long drive with your spouse.

Louie Benito came to see me precisely because of a long drive with his wife. "She told me I had to get help. The whole way from Boston to New York all I did was worry about one thing after another. I knew I was doing it, but I felt like if I didn't talk about it I would go crazy. So she went crazy instead. When we got to the city, she went straight to the hotel bar." Louie worked as a driver for the MBTA. Driving a bus in the city of Boston might seem enough to make anyone a constant worrier, but Louie said he was like this long before he took that job. "If anything, I relax when I drive the bus," he said. "You know, it's so demanding I can't think about all my worries."

There was no reason I could find in Louie's past to explain why he worried so much. He was stressed out by life—as he said, "Who isn't these days?"—but he was not depressed, just worried. In fact, he was an upbeat worrier, if there is such a being. It made me smile to listen to Louie relate his worries. Hearing him talk made me feel good, not because I was pleased that he was so worried, but just the animated, friendly way he talked made me, and I would imagine most people, feel good. Indeed, it is interesting to note how many comedians specialize in making us laugh by exposing their worries: Woody Allen, Rodney Dangerfield, Bob Newhart, and Johnathan Winters come to mind among modern comics and Buster Keaton and Jack Benny from days gone by.

But it was no laughing matter for Louie himself. Lovable as he was, he didn't like living with all his worrying. We worked together in setting up a program of relaxation and stress reduction. Various techniques of relaxation are probably the oldest treatments known for GAD. Meditation and prayer have both been used for thousands of years to treat chronic worry. Indeed, the rosary beads are sometimes called "worry beads."

In Louie's case, he did not want to start praying but he was willing to try meditating. I taught him a simple technique anyone can use. "Louie, first of all you have to find a quiet room. It doesn't have to be stone silent, but someplace away from all the bustle. Then sit in a chair with your back straight and both feet on the floor. Rest your hands in your lap and close your eyes. Then focus on your body, starting with your scalp and face, and let each muscle relax and go limp. As you do this, imagine you are in a favorite place you go to relax, such as the beach or the woods. Just be there for a while, letting your mind slow down and your body fully relax. Notice your breathing and breathe slowly and regularly. Remain in this state for three minutes. Do this at least once a day and you will start to feel less anxious soon."

"Really?" Louie asked.

"In all likelihood," I replied.

"You mean, no promises?"

"No promises, but very good chances."

Relaxation helps most people with GAD. Exercise, prayer, and other kinds of meditation are excellent as well.

I also started Louie on Prozac. I chose Prozac because there was a ruminative quality to his worrying, and the antidepressants are good for ruminations. He did well on this regimen, and even his friends told him he didn't seem to be so worried all the time.

While we all worry, what separates the individual with GAD from the average person is the intensity, frequency, and duration of his worrying. The GAD sufferer worries much more often, more intensely, and over a longer period of time than the average individual. Worry becomes a way of life and a damaging way of life at that. As in the case of Ben Miller, who was forced by his worrying to retreat to Cape Cod and abandon his planned career, or Louie Benito, who drove his wife to drink after a trip to New York, the sufferer of GAD cannot control his worrying; rather, it controls him.

The worries in GAD do not focus on one or two topics. For example, an individual may be phobic about trains, so that even the idea of a train makes him nervous. This is not GAD, but rather a phobia. Or the individual who becomes anxious over only one or two specific tasks, such as public speaking or test-taking, would not qualify for the diagnosis of GAD. These problems are specific, while GAD is global and general.

Maria Toby came to see me because she was biting her nails. Of course, it wasn't just that, but that was the first symptom she mentioned. At age thirty-five, she wanted better-looking nails. But as we reviewed her life, a whole list of worries emerged. She had been called "sensitive" as a child and stayed inside most of the time. "I wanted to go out," she said, "but I was just too afraid. I kind of wish my mother had made me go out more. Maybe I would have learned how to be more social. But maybe not. Maybe I just would have hid in a corner. In college I came out of my shell, but I was still a worrier. I was the one who always worried about getting caught, whatever it was. Boys, drinking, carrying on. You name it. Don't get me wrong, I wasn't into bad stuff. I just worried all the time."

"And now?" I asked.

"Now I'm married, I have a wonderful husband who puts up with me but thinks I'm nuts and I'm still worried all the time. I do the things I'm supposed to do but I just do them with so much worry! Make dinner, get the kids ready in the morning, read the paper. Especially read the paper!"

"Has anything bad happened?" I asked.

"No. Oh, we could always use more money, I guess, and I wish I had a better job, but, no, there aren't any terrible problems in my life. Just my worries."

"What do you worry about?" I asked.

"What don't I worry about! The house burning down, my nails, my weight, my hair, the kids, their friends, their school, is my husband happy with me, am I a good enough mother, will I be on time for the next appointment, is my boss going to be nice to me today; you name it, I worry about it."

This is GAD. Many worries, no obvious cause, in an otherwise well-functioning individual. Sometimes people with GAD are also depressed, or they self-medicate with alcohol or some other drug, but in Maria's case the GAD was the only significant problem. Like Louie, she responded well to treatment, which included just cognitive and behavioral interventions.

Like what? Maria needed to learn to direct her attention away from negative thinking. This advice is as old as the hills: the power of positive thinking. But there is a lot of truth to it. Many people who suffer from GAD drift like magnets to what is negative.

So how do they demagnetize? In Maria's case we worked on learning little phrases, little cues she could use to intercept a negative pattern just as it was beginning. For example, one of her typical worries was whether she was a good enough mother. When this worry came up, I advised her to envision the smiling face of one of her children, then to say to herself, "I love you."

"How will that help?" Maria asked.

"It should change your feeling state. The image of your child coupled with the words 'I love you' make a pretty potent combination."

"But what if they just make me feel worse? What if they just rub my nose in the fact that I'm not good enough to this adorable little girl I love?"

"I don't think that will happen," I replied. "But you do talk like a worry master."

"That's because I am one," Maria replied, with ironic pride.

"You really have to consciously work on pushing away negative states of feeling instead of embracing them. Positive images, like the image of your daughter's smiling face, and positive words, like 'I love you,' can do this if you keep at it. This is work and it takes practice. You are basically learning new coping skills, new habits for your mind. It is like retraining your brain, trying to break it of the negative thinking it has learned over the years."

"Yes," Maria said. "I like that idea."

"There are other things that can help, too. Exercise. Can you get regular exercise?"

"I could, if I tried. I'd like to do aerobics at the club we joined last year."

"Well, I would advise you to make that a high priority. Exercise is great treatment for worry. Also sleep. Do you sleep regular hours?"

"Uh, no. Do you?"

I smiled. "I try to. If you can sleep more or less regular hours, that will help, too."

Maria really worked on these techniques. She came up with quite a few "positive thoughts" as she called them to replace old, negative ideas when they came to mind. "What I do," she said, "is I just use the opposite of whatever the bad one is. If I think the house is a mess, I imagine it perfectly clean. If I think I'm too fat, I see myself as thin. If I feel I'm inadequate, I imagine myself on a movie poster. I don't believe I'm really like those opposites, but you're right, just sticking them in my mind helps drive out the bad feeling I get with the negative thought."

Maria was participating in her therapy creatively, and it worked well for her. Her worrying started a steady decline.

Some people seem to think that medication alone is the cure for anxiety. It is not. Drugs of one sort or another have been used for thousands of years to treat anxiety, alcohol chief among them, but as yet none of them qualifies as a cure. Some of them, especially alcohol, can be very dangerous.

The best treatment plans are those that use medication as sparingly as possible. While the benzodiazepines, such as diazepam (Valium), clonazepam (Klonopin), and alprazolam (Xanax) can subdue acute anxiety quite effectively, one should try to avoid using them over the long term. Their negative side effects, which can include sedation, blurry thinking, and memory impairment, combined with their addictive potential make them a poor choice for long-term use. Since the GAD sufferer has, by definition, a long-term problem, we need to look beyond medication for the best help.

The various nonmedication approaches to treatment have been brought up throughout this book, and they are discussed in detail in Part Three. However, if the nonmedication approaches to treatment do not bring sufficient relief, and long-term use of medication becomes necessary, it is best not to use a benzodiazepine such as Klonopin or Valium, but instead a medication from the class called the azapirones. The azapirones are similar to the benzodiazepines in that they combat anxiety effectively and safely. However, they are preferable for long-term use because their side effects are of less potential danger. Specifically, they do not cause physical dependence, they do not interact with alcohol, and they do not slow you down physically, as the benzodiazepines can. The only azapirone currently available is buspirone. It is prescribed under the brand name, BuSpar.

It is cause to rejoice that our knowledge of the brain is beginning to help us get rid of the many moral diagnoses we have pinned onto emotional problems, "diagnoses" such as weak, loser, or simply bad. In the place of the moral diagnosis we can begin to make a medical diagnosis, which is simultaneously more accurate, more helpful, and more forgiving.

When I told Louie, Maria, and Ben they had GAD, I was not just handing them some piece of jargon for them to puzzle over. I was giving them a key to get out of the moral dungeon. GAD is a much more helpful way of looking at the problem of chronic fear and nervousness than "wimp" was for Ben or "sensitive" had been for Maria.

I explained to each the various theories we have of how GAD comes about. Most people agree it begins with a genetic vulnerability, something inherited, and then gains steam through life experience. The GAD sufferer soothes himself less effectively than others do and torments himself more readily.

This probably has a biological basis. We're not sure, but evidence that there is one is mounting all the time. About a decade ago, for example, the benzodiazepine receptor site was discovered in the brain, and about a decade before that the opiate receptor site was discovered. Both of these chemical receptor sites are involved in self-soothing. The body produces substances similar to the benzodiazepines (e.g., Valium) to soothe itself. It appears that these substances and drugs are related to an internally produced substance called GABA (gamma-amino butyric acid). The names are not important, but the idea that there is such a substance produced *within the body* is. It means that if some people do not produce enough GABA, or substances like it, they may not be as effective at soothing themselves, or shutting off anxiety, as others are.

Similarly, after the opiate receptor was discovered in the brain, the site where morphine, heroin, and other opiate derivatives bind, we then learned there are internally produced opiate-like substances, which were given the now-familiar name, endorphins. Endorphin is just shorthand for "endogenous [internally produced] morphine." We will probably soon discover other internally produced chemical self-soothers. The key point is that these substances exist.

As they exist, it is also likely that some people produce them at higher and lower rates than others, and some people have more or fewer of the receptor sites. This rate of production or difference in number of receptor sites becomes part of the basis for the hypothesized genetically transmitted vulnerability to generalized anxiety. Such anxiety can be seen simply as a relative difficulty in soothing oneself or damping down the alarm signals when they go off. The brain's inhibitory, quiet-down signal system is deficient. If you do not have enough opiate receptors or do not produce enough endorphins, you may be prone to increased anxiety. Or if you lack sufficient benzodiazepine receptors or if you produce an insufficient amount of GABA, then you also may be at risk for increased anxiety.

While this may sound complicated in its details, the general principles are simple. Some brains do not soothe themselves as well as others because they are chemically unable to do so. I want to stress the logical implications of this fact. It means that ANXIETY IS NOT YOUR FAULT. Throw off the moral diagnosis. It does not mean you are a weakling. Learn about the medical diagnosis and it can free you of unnecessary and disabling shame and guilt. You should no more feel guilty or weak because you are prone to anxiety than you should feel guilty or weak because you can't eat mushrooms. It is simply how some people, like Ben Miller, Louie Benito, Maria Toby, and millions of others, are born.

Once this insight is understood, it takes a while to believe it. Most people are taught from an early age that their feelings are moral measuring sticks. They are taught that if they can keep their feelings in check, it means that they are strong. If they cannot, they are weak. It takes a while for a person to believe that this is not true, that people can feel excess fear and worry, for example, not in proportion to how strong and brave they are, but in proportion to physical factors they cannot control, such as how many endorphin or benzodiazepine receptor sites they were born with.

15 Is There a Hidden Pleasure in Worry?

Worry as a Means of Staying Alert

Some people do *seem* to enjoy worrying. They worry all the time, every day, relentlessly. They do it with creativity and zeal. They even get annoyed if you try to reassure them or take their worry away.

I had a great aunt like that, God rest her soul. I'll call her Hannah. She was a kind and brilliant lady, a bookworm, lost in novel after novel, but when she wasn't reading she never seemed at peace a day in her life. She worried all the time. She lived alone. She was always good to me and to the other children in the family, but she was shy and nervous with most of the world. She seldom went out. As a child growing up, I once asked my mother why Auntie Hannah was so nervous all the time. I've always remembered her response. She laughed and said, "She just *likes* to worry."

When my parents dismissed Aunt Hannah's worrying as an activity she enjoyed, it reassured me because I didn't want to think of Aunt Hannah as being unhappy, but it also puzzled me. And it still puzzles me. Do some people actually like to worry? It seems that way. But how can any of us like something that hurts as much as worry?

Why do some people, if left with their own thoughts for just a few minutes, start to brood over the many possibilities of failure or doom? How is it that some people have upbeat natures while others are constitutionally down? Why do some people take great pleasure in pointing out all the bad things that can happen, and seem actually to enjoy disasters? Does the negative have some allure?

Those who seem to enjoy worrying—those who do it in their spare time—may secretly be taking pleasure in the leg-up on fate they imagine they are getting. They feel that their worrying protects them or puts them in control.

There are, however, other pleasures associated with worrying beyond the illusion of control. I have mentioned before that pain focuses attention faster than pleasure. Scary movies, horror pictures, gory photography, violent films—their unpleasant content can excite us.

Is worrying similar to watching horror movies? In a way, I think it is. Extreme worrying can actually be exciting. It focuses the mind and, more than that, it provides a kind of entertainment. The worrier can sit in his chair and settle into an hour of brooding. His mind can bear down upon one concern after another, and time will fly by. It can be like going to the movies. In really scary or gory movies, you can actually feel that you yourself are in danger, not just the people on the screen; similarly the worrier casts himself, or his loved ones, as the stars in his internal scary cinema of worry. He staggers from problem to problem in his mind, totally unaware of where he is, lost in the experience of worry.

Can we say the worrier is experiencing pleasure in the same way the horror-movie buff takes pleasure in being terrified?

The mind of the worrier returns time after time to worry just as if it were his favorite scary ride in the amusement park. You can't talk him out of it. He must get on with it. He will get angry if you try to divert him or reassure him and tell you you just don't understand.

It is tempting to say he is doing this because he likes it, but the worrier does not like his worrying the way the kid on the roller coaster likes his ride. What the worrier does get from worry, however, is stimulation. This is the pleasure in worry, to the extent that there is any pleasure. It engages the mind. It locks onto your attention and doesn't let go. Like the roller coaster ride or the horror movie, it is stimulating. But the rider or viewer knows he is experiencing controlled terror, terror that will end without disaster. The worrier doesn't know this, and so his worrying can become a torment.

When we say, "Oh, she just worries because she enjoys it," as my parents said of Aunt Hannah, I think we are wrong. Aunt Hannah was unhappy. What we really should say instead is that she, as many other people, found worry *irresistible*. She didn't enjoy worry but she couldn't stop herself from doing it. She couldn't not worry.

My Aunt Hannah was committed to worry. It seemed to be her only way of engaging with life. While no one uses worry solely as a means of enjoyment, it is interesting to consider to what extent the worriers we know may have become secretly addicted to worry, as a habit of mental stimulation, a habit they perhaps could give up if they looked at it in this light.

On the other hand, it may be that the person who seems to enjoy worry may be unable to resist it because he or she is in the grip of a biologically influenced, treatable condition, such as depression, obsessive-compulsive disorder, or post-traumatic stress disorder. What appears to be the "enjoyment" of worry in these people may instead be an irresistible urge.

In depression the mind turns as naturally to worry as leaves turn to the sun. In obsessive-compulsive disorder, worry streams in unbidden, unwanted, but unstoppable. In post-traumatic stress disorder, the sufferer is unable to rid his or her system of a memory of a horrible event or events, and so he or she lives in a state of chronic worry and fear. It is wrong to say these people "enjoy" their worry.

I think my Aunt Hannah was shy and depressed. We now know that shyness has a genetic basis to it, but Aunt Hannah was taunted growing up because she was shy. If she had had the knowledge in her day that we have in ours, perhaps she could have been helped to accept being the way she was. If she hadn't felt shame over being shy, perhaps she would have been less depressed. It is also likely that the treatments we now have for depression could have helped her worry less and feel better.

In attention deficit disorder (ADD), some people use worry to focus their minds. They do this unintentionally, of course, but the net effect of their worrying is that it becomes a means of staying focused on something, rather than drifting off into chaos. Worry is indeed an excellent focusing device. As Samuel Johnson said, "Nothing focuses the mind so wonderfully as the knowledge that one is to be *hanged* in a fortnight."

Elliot MacBain set up his life so that he was always about to be hanged. Mad rushes to meet deadlines at the last moment characterized his entire life, from grade school through his current job as a trial lawyer.

He had achieved great financial success and was sought after as a brilliant defense attorney, specializing in defending physicians in malpractice suits. His medical knowledge was impressive. Talking to him, I often learned facts I hadn't known.

"But, geez," he said, "what a way to work. I procrastinate until the very last minute, then WHAMO!, I'm up all night screaming and yelling at my legal pads as if they could talk back. It has become a regular scene around our house. 'Daddy's working late,' one of my kids will say. 'Close your doors.' It's embarrassing, because I'm always preaching to the kids about the value of being prepared. Now I just come right out and tell them to look at me as a negative example. I am what they will become if they don't learn better while they're young."

I asked him about his school history. Same story. "Everything was either late or so rushed that it wasn't anywhere near as good as it should have been. Underachiever was the label stamped on my forehead from first grade on. I knew I could do better, and I always meant to, but I just never did."

"How did you get into law school?" I asked.

"Aced the LSAT. I always could take tests. That's what added to the underachiever routine. So I went to Boston College Law School. Great school. All those Jesuits. Talk about organized. I actually hooked up with one of them as an academic tutor and he basically coached me through. I got good grades, but even then I was doing everything at the last minute. If it hadn't been for Father James I would have flunked out."

"No one wondered why you developed this pattern?" I asked. "Not even Father James?"

"I just assumed it was my character structure. You know, I like to play too much."

"But was that your problem? Were you out playing?" I asked.

"No. No, I wasn't. I just couldn't get myself interested until the last minute. It was basically too boring until the chips were down. Then, when the stakes were high, I could get turned on and really burn."

At that point I explained to Elliot the meaning of ADD. I could see his jaw drop a millimeter at a time as I talked. I told him about this genetically transmitted condition whose main symptoms are distractibility, disorganization, and procrastination, often in the face of high intelligence. I also told him that many people with ADD use danger and worry to focus their minds. "The way you describe your study habits, you seem like a classic example of such a person," I said.

"What do you mean?" he asked, not quite getting it yet.

"Well, just listen to what you said. You said you couldn't get yourself interested until the last minute, that it was too boring until the chips were down, but when the stakes were high you could get turned on and really burn. Doesn't that sound like someone who is using worry and danger to help focus his mind?"

"But I don't get it. Why would I do that *on purpose*? I mean, it really was a pain," he protested.

"You did it because it worked. It was the only way you knew. You didn't understand that you had an undiagnosed condition called ADD and that you were using worry almost as a kind of medication."

"How is worry medication?" Elliot asked.

"Well, when you worry intensely or feel afraid your body puts out adrenalin. Your adrenal glands turn on and they pump out adrenalin, which helps your brain to focus. Adrenalin is similar to the actual medications like Ritalin that we use to treat ADD. By setting up these crisis situations all the time, you were inducing your own body to pump out the 'medication' you needed to get focused."

Elliot looked at me as if I had just explained a riddle he'd been poring over his whole life. "I'm a little stunned," he said.

"Does it make sense?" I asked.

"Yes," Elliot replied, "it sure does."

From that point I worked with Elliot to help him learn more about ADD, as education is a key part of the treatment. We also needed to work on his setting up structures—lists, schedules, reminders—to help him begin to break the pattern of using crises to get him focused. In addition, I prescribed Ritalin, the medication that usually works best in treating ADD. He would not need to take it forever, just long enough for him to learn the new coping strategies and structures needed to live life without medication or self-induced crises.

Medication is not always necessary, but if you find other methods ineffective, and if your diagnosis is indeed ADD, stimulant medication like Ritalin may be a godsend not only in curbing your endless worry but in helping you focus on more important matters.

From my Aunt Hannah to someone like Elliot with ADD or some other diagnosable condition, we can see how worry can intermingle with other conditions in surprising ways. It is important to remember that the symptom of worry may be a tip-off to another diagnosis, such as depression or ADD.

16 Worry at Its Most Strange

Paranoia

Of all the states of worry, paranoia is one of the most strange, and I think it must be the most painful. This is because it so utterly alienates the individual from his surroundings and from the very people who could be of the most help. I have never experienced true paranoia in my own mind and hope I never have to, but I have treated many paranoid adults, particularly when I was a resident in psychiatry at the Massachusetts Mental Health Center, a hospital in Boston for seriously disturbed patients.

The pain of the paranoid individual is so poignant because, almost by definition, it is impossible for the paranoid person to receive comfort. Contact is not allowed. The moment you get close to someone who is paranoid, he either flees or becomes angry or even violent. He lives in a constant state of advanced fear, perceiving threats on the least bit of evidence or no evidence at all. He rarely lets his guard down and when he does, he usually becomes enraged and feels he must attack whomever he inadvertently allowed in. The paranoid person is always vigilant, watching for intruders into his precarious, jagged world. He lives in an ongoing internal spy novel, full of imagined meanings and clandestine meetings; his eye is always out for the telltale detail signifying undetected danger.

However, the mind of the paranoid person is not entertaining like a spy novel. Rather it is terrifying, often violent, and sometimes dangerous. True paranoia is worry at its worst.

Yes, we all sometimes wonder if people are out to get us. This is not true paranoia. To get a slight taste of what it feels like to be truly paranoid, all you have to do is go out for a walk at night. Almost everyone becomes suspicious in the dark, imagining possible muggers lurking in the corners or hidden behind a tree. When we don't know what's out there, most of us imagine the worst. But what separates most people from people with true paranoia is the ability to reassure themselves and to reality-test their feelings of imminent danger. The average person, when he starts sensing that people are out to get him, can step back and say to himself that he is having a bad day and that although it may feel as if the world is turning against him, that is probably not the case. Paranoid people cannot do this.

True paranoia is a psychotic state. Psychotic means crazy, divorced from reality, literally unable to tell the difference between what is imagined and what is actual. There are degrees of paranoia. The "paranoia" of everyday life isn't really paranoia at all; it is just vigilance and suspiciousness, qualities that we all need at times. However, as we move out on the spectrum, we find individuals who may function at high levels in adult life, but who are more suspicious than anyone would call normal. Have you ever had the experience in the middle of a conversation with someone you've just met at some friendly get-together of suddenly feeling an arresting sensation that the person you are talking to is living on an entirely different plane than you? You sense as clearly as if a gust of wind had suddenly blown open the windows that this fellow you're talking to has a whole different agenda than you do. You suddenly sense that *he* senses . . . well, *much more than you do.* He sees plots where you see none, malice where you don't see any, and subterfuge where you see passed hors d'oeuvres. This is the rather jolting experience of clicking onto the wavelength of a paranoid person.

In fact, many of these people make excellent businessmen, lawyers, academicians, and politicians. They never miss a trick. But theirs is a painful existence—no trust, no peace, no moments of serenity. Only vigilance and a suspicious eye, as they constantly worry who's out there doing what.

Some paranoid individuals become so consumed with their imaginings that they cannot function effectively. At the extreme, they have to be hospitalized. But most never get to the hospital. At least one, Richard Nixon, became president of the United States. Paranoid individuals are often brilliant, imaginative, and exquisitely sensitive. Some of the potentially kindest people in the world are paranoid, but they are *so* sensitive—to innuendo, tone of voice, and every *possible* meaning—they can't learn to trust anyone.

How does paranoia come about? There appears to be a biochemical basis to severe or psychotic paranoia, inasmuch as medication offers the most effective treatment. The great advances in the treatment of psychotic paranoia have been pharmacological, not psychological.

However, there is a psychology to paranoia, and an understanding of this aspect can help the much more common mild states of heightened suspicion or exaggerated vigilance we see in everyday life. The Freudian explanation of paranoia is that it results from projected rage: the paranoid individual feels angry at other people, but is afraid to acknowledge this anger, so he unconsciously projects it onto the outside world and feels his own anger directed back at him, as if it were originating on the outside. In other words, he endows other people with his own angry feelings, which makes him imagine that *they* are angry at *him,* while in fact it is really the other way around.

Most of us do this some of the time, but we rely on other people to help us snap out of it when we do, to tell us we are wrong. One reason that rich and powerful people may be more given to paranoid thinking is not just that other people are in fact out to take advantage of them, but also that they are often surrounded by people who are afraid to tell them to snap out of it, to question them or disagree with them.

Another, simpler explanation is that paranoia is a learned response to the hardships of life. Some people never get enough nurturing to develop the capacity to trust others. Like a dog who has been kicked once too many times, they live their lives on red alert. Their paranoia is the result of their conditioning. Life has taught them never to trust.

Yet another explanation is that paranoid people are simply *smart*. They are perceptive where the rest of us are not. They see through the disguises and camouflages others so skillfully put up; while most of us are taken in, the ones we call paranoid know the truth. Sometimes only the passage of time tells us who was smart and who was truly paranoid.

I remember one patient who came to me not long after I had completed my training. He sought help because he felt unsafe at work. He was in his second year at a large law firm. As we explored the dangers of the law firm, I began to sense that this man's view of life was tinged with paranoia. The average Boston law firm is not warm and welcoming to begin with, so some degree of heightened vigilance and suspicion among junior associates probably represents good judgment. However, my patient—Derek—was so tormented by his worries and fears that they seemed to me to be unrealistic.

However, I didn't know for sure. One never does in my line of work. So I did what I *could* do. I tried to sort out his fears and worries with him one by one: person by person, scene by scene, innuendo by innuendo. Was a certain man out to get him because of the way he looked at him at the end of lunch? Was a certain woman against him because of the way she seemed to turn away from him at the elevators? Was the firm sending him a message by not complimenting him on how hard he was working, even though there was a designated time of year for such comments and that time had not yet come?

Furthermore, could the senior partners tell how apprehensive Derek was, and would this count against him when they started assessing what the firm called his "comfort factor." To stay at Blank, Blank, and Blank, one requirement was that you be able to make clients feel taken care of. Could Derek convey to the senior partners the feeling that he could take care of clients, without at the same time seeming to lack the killer instinct, another prized quality at B, B, & B? "How do I let them know I can be a shark when I need to be but also be warm and fuzzy as well?"

"That is what they want you to be?" I asked, gulping a little.

"Yes. And I can tell that Peter Truesdale doesn't think I have the kill factor. That's what he calls it, *the kill factor.* He says clients want *that* in us more than anything. He says when they come to us they want us to take care of them, but they also want to feel that we can *kill* their opponents—and do it without being asked. Truesdale says for the money the clients pay us, we have to become their hired assassins or at least we have to make them feel that we are. We take the blood off their hands and put it on ours. But we have to be genteel about it. He says that's the 'art' of law these days, projecting yourself as a genteel assassin, and I can tell that he doesn't think I can project enough of the kill factor to satisfy him."

"*How* can you tell?" I asked.

"All kinds of ways. By the way his nostrils pinched in a meeting the other day after something I said. By the way he lifted his eyebrows when I said I liked the movie *Sense and Sensibility.* I know, you think I'm off the wall and paranoid, but I'm telling you, I'm right!"

The trouble is, maybe he was right. This is what makes the treatment of supposed paranoia so difficult. If I managed to talk Derek into being more trusting and less suspicious, I might talk him right out of a promotion. So I did what I do with people who I think are mildly paranoid. I tried gently to help him review the evidence, not challenge him too much, and provide some support for what must be an intensely frightening inner debate.

Our conversations went on as the year progressed, and Derek waited to hear about making partner. I learned a great deal about life at law firms in Boston these days. "They say success is all in how we're perceived," Derek said. "There are so many lawyers now, and so many law firms, all basically offering the same set of services, that the only way to distinguish yourself and get the big clients is to offer something extra. It is an *illusion* that they want us to offer, because after all we can't go out and break knees. Peter Truesdale keeps telling us to wait on them, offer not just coffee, but coffee or decaf and with how many sugars and how much cream or maybe milk, perhaps some fresh fruit as well, and offer to have the limo service on call if they need it, and any other little extra that the best of us, the most promotable of us, will naturally think up on our own. He says the clients remember that. Creature comforts. But *also* we must offer the kill factor. Make them think that you will wipe out the competition. He advises us to tell anecdotes of cases we've won where the opposition went out of business the next month or even where the CEO committed suicide. He says just mention that kind of story in passing. You get it into the client's subconscious imagination quickly without having to go into any details. But I just don't know if I can do it."

Derek presented me with a typical dilemma: whose reality was correct? Was this Truesdale fellow really giving the junior associates these kinds of orders? Was this really the state of corporate law these days? If so, how should I advise Derek? I could only continue to try to offer as sane a perspective as I thought correct. "Gee, Derek," I said, "I don't know anything about law, but I think you should be really careful about working within ethical guidelines, don't you? I mean, by the guidelines of the Massachusetts Bar, you aren't supposed to make up stories about opponents committing suicide are you?"

Suddenly Derek went white. He demanded of me, "Did the Board of Bar Overseers tell you to say that to me?"

"No," I quickly reassured him. "Absolutely not." I paused, looking at Derek to see how he was taking in my words. There was a hush to his voice that wasn't usually there. He was suddenly very scared. "Do you believe me?" I asked. "I have not been talking to anyone about you."

"The Bar hasn't been in touch with you?" he asked desperately.

"No, absolutely not," I replied.

Derek, who had been breathing fast, began to breathe more slowly. "Wow," he said. "My God, what a crazy thought. I just had this sudden idea that you were planted by the Bar to check up on me."

"You're right, that is a crazy thought. But it sure does tell me something about what it's like to work at B, B, & B." Derek was feeling so stressed, so stretched to do things he didn't feel right about that he began to imagine schemes that weren't even plausible, such as my being a secret representative of the Board of Bar Overseers. "Can I make a suggestion?" I asked. Derek nodded. "Let's try to learn something from your suddenly thinking I'm checking up on you for the Board."

"Whoa," Derek said. "This is really scary. Is this what it feels like to go crazy?" he asked.

"No," I replied. "If you were going crazy you wouldn't believe any of my reassurance. You probably would have stormed out of my office by now or totally clammed up."

"I have to get out of B, B, & B," Derek said. "That's what I'm learning from this. I'm not going to be like what Peter Truesdale wants. I can't be, and even if I could, I don't think I'd want to be."

"Don't do anything too soon," I countered. "Let's look at all the options first. You're very upset now and this is not a good time to make big decisions."

"The place is driving me crazy," Derek went on. "They're changing me in ways I hate. Can you believe they actually tell us to make up stories about opponents committing suicide? 'Just in passing,' of course. And what is really scary is that I'm sure Truesdale is the best in knowing where to steer the firm. Everyone looks up to him as knowing the most about what clients want. Many of our clients would really love the idea that we are so aggressive that when we get finished with someone they'll want to go kill themselves. Particularly if the client can pretend he didn't know that's how we work. God, this job sucks!"

That session was the first in a long series of sessions in which we tried to separate reality from fantasy. We looked at what Derek really wanted in life and at how many of his worries came from within him, from within B, B, & B, or from within the practice of law in general. What finally happened six months later is that Derek found a position in a smaller law firm outside Boston with some friends he'd made in law school. "I want to do something I can feel good about," he said.

Interestingly enough, it was his flash of paranoia—the moment when he thought I might be a spy for the Board of Bar Overseers—

that turned his life in a different direction. He hadn't gone crazy, so he still retained the mental apparatus to react appropriately to his distorted perception. But his distorted perception, his moment of paranoia, jolted him into taking corrective action.

His paranoid response set off an alarm, which he heeded. He learned from his response that his mind was in danger and that he needed to take corrective action. Usually before people get into big trouble, their minds try to alarm them.

This is the regulatory function of the observing part of yourself. When your job situation, or your marriage, or hidden parts of your life stress you so severely that worry reaches the level of paranoia, then it is time to make some adjustments. *Listen to and learn from your distorted perceptions.* Talk them over with a friend or a professional. Don't simply dismiss them out of hand. They may have an important meaning.

Most of the time the little bits of paranoia that pepper everyday life mean nothing. Many people have had the sinking feeling when they discover that they haven't been invited to a particular party that they are being excluded for some nasty reason and by a specific person or group of people. This little bit of paranoia may be an accurate perception, but more often than not it is simply hurt feelings leading to a loss of perspective. Many people have had the feeling of being stared at when they go into a meeting of strangers, even though the fact is that no one is staring at them at all. Again, this little bit of paranoia is nothing more than self-consciousness. It is a common part of normal life.

But sometimes these reactions do tell us something important. Derek had found himself in a culture he realized he hated. While he was drawn to it because of the high salary, prestige, and excitement, the day-to-day reality of the work repelled him. He liked the practice of law itself, but he hated what the high-powered law firm was asking him to do. Could he have succeeded there? Probably. Would he have gone crazy? Probably not. For most of us, fortunately, going crazy is much more a fear than a reality. Not many people actually become psychotic during their lifetimes. But we all have moments, as Derek did, of drastically misjudging reality. If we can learn from these moments, they can teach us a lot. If we can learn from extreme worry, or paranoia, we can make important changes. In Derek's case he learned simply that he was in the wrong place. He didn't want to quit law. He just wanted to quit law as it was practiced at B, B, & B.

As we continue out on the spectrum of paranoia we reach the far limits—people who are psychotically worried. They cannot function outside of a hospital because they wrestle with paranoid delusions all the time. For example, they might think that their minds are being constantly controlled by special machines at the airport, or that the city's food supply is poisoned, or that all people wearing hats are concealing loaded guns underneath.

These extremely paranoid people suffer a great deal. Unfortunately, we do not have definitive treatments for severe paranoia. Psychotherapy is usually ineffective because it is difficult to engage someone who is paranoid and also perhaps because there is such a strong biological basis to paranoia. Trying to talk someone out of a paranoid state is a bit like trying to levitate a boulder. Physical means usually work better. While we do not exactly understand the biochemistry of paranoia, we do know that medication works on it better than any other single kind of treatment. We currently have a variety of medications that can make a difference. Until recently the medications most commonly used were standard antipsychotic medications, which sometimes helped but which also caused severe side effects. Sometimes the side effects were almost worse than the paranoia—side effects such as muscle rigidity, depression, irreversible uncontrollable twitching, dangerous changes in blood pressure, and changes in the electrocardiogram.

However, the past decade has seen the introduction of a new generation of antipsychotic medications, led by the pioneer drug, clozapine. Not only is clozapine often dramatically more powerful than any of the traditional antipsychotic medications in reducing paranoid thinking and other psychotic symptoms, it does not cause the disabling side effects the other antipsychotics too frequently lead to. Clozapine can create certain hematological abnormalities, so blood must be drawn regularly and the dosage carefully monitored, but its overall effectiveness and safety take us a quantum level beyond what we have had before. Most experts agree that it represents the first major breakthrough in the treatment of psychotic illnesses since the phenothiazines (the original antipsychotic medications) were introduced some forty years ago.

As lithium revolutionized the treatment of manic-depressive illness, taking thousands of individuals out of hospitals and giving them independent lives, and as stimulant medication revolutionized the treatment of hyperactivity and attention deficit disorder in children and adults, allowing many people to participate meaningfully in school and in the workplace who had not been able to before, so this new group of antipsychotic medications has given thousands of individuals who were crippled by psychotic worries a new chance to live, love, and work on their own. None of these medications is a cure, but they all have granted sufferers of certain conditions a quality of life not thought possible before.

Clozapine has helped some patients so dramatically that they appear to have undergone an "awakening," like the awakenings described by Oliver Sacks. For example, Ms. D. was intermittently psychotic for thirty years, suffering from paranoid delusions more often than not, making suicide attempts from time to time, and never being able to function outside of a hospital for very long. Once she was started on clozapine she improved to the point she was able to live and work on her own. She now is in demand as a freelance writer and is at work on a book about her life. Of her experience being sick she said:

> Every night in the past when I went to bed I would ask God to take away my life . . . I did not want to face another day in my life. . . . Things have changed now that I am better. . . . Now I feel that there is a God. . . . there is a divine spark in all of us . . . He has His own agenda. . . . we can't analyze His will of which I have limited understanding . . . It's only tragic if I'm not on clozapine . . . My purpose in life is to do God's will. . . . He gave me a gift for language and writing . . . I have to use it to help those still suffering. . . . to write about their—our—suffering . . .

While the introduction of clozapine marks yet another dramatic gift this decade of the brain has bestowed upon us, it still is no cure nor does it help all patients. Of all the psychoses paranoia remains the most difficult to alleviate.

I remember the first truly paranoid patient I ever treated. He was a drifter, as many paranoid people are, who had hitchhiked into Boston and been picked up by the police for vagrancy. When he told the arresting officer that it was OK to arrest him because he understood the CIA had sent the officer to come to him for orders, the officer decided to take him to the mental hospital instead of jail. I had a very crazy conversation with this gentleman in which he told me that I, too, was part of the CIA, and that he understood I also had to do everything I could to conceal my identity from him.

Being inexperienced in psychiatry—it was my first year of residency—I thought I had to give reality at least a passing shot. I couldn't *not* try the most obvious intervention. So I said to the man, "Look, I'm not with the CIA. I'm a doctor here at this hospital. You are just imagining that I am with the CIA. I want to help you."

In response, the man simply sat in his chair and smiled knowingly.

"No, really," I went on. "Please believe me, I'm telling you the truth. I can't tell you how much aggravation you will save yourself if you just believe me. I am not with the CIA. There is no plot. In fact, I don't even know who the director of the CIA is. Now how could I be with the CIA and not know that?"

"I understand," the man replied, again with that knowing grin.

"You do not believe me," I said, rather disappointedly.

"Of course I believe you," the man said, with mock sincerity. "You are a doctor here at the hospital. How nice to meet you, Doctor." He looked at me as if to say our secret would always be safe.

This is how it is in extreme paranoia. There is often no way to use reality as a test or as a therapeutic tool. The best you can do, often, is to agree with the paranoid person. At least then you can join him in his view of the world and maybe build up a *little* trust so you can help him manage his life better amid his paranoid delusions. In other words, by agreeing with him that I was with the CIA, I might have built up enough trust to convince him, for example, that the food wasn't poisoned in the hospital, so he could eat.

But I didn't know enough to do that sort of thing. I was still stuck naively in my disbelief.

My paranoid patient didn't give me much time to learn from him. Instead of eating the "poisoned" hospital food, my drifter patient did what many paranoid people do. He bolted. State mental hospitals across the country provide a kind of chain of Days Inns for the severely paranoid of our population.

Now, fifteen years later, and in private practice, I see very few paranoid patients, because I no longer work at a state hospital. Usually severely paranoid people reject help for as long as they can. They do not come to someone in private practice, like me. They believe they cannot trust anyone, least of all a psychiatrist. When they finally do see a psychiatrist, it is against their wishes, in a state hospital, more often than not. The paranoid adults I do see now are much less obviously paranoid than my original fellow, because they are not psychotic. They know that their true feelings are bizarre and so they keep them to themselves. But they are tormented by them nonetheless.

17 The Ominous Core of Life

The obvious reason people worry is that there's plenty to worry about. Take death for openers. How do we get past that one every day? I was talking to a friend of mine about this book, and she said to me that she thought *all* worry derived from the fact of death. "Death is the big one," she said, "it's the one that all other worries come from." In every threat, real or imagined, we perhaps hear an echo of that final, inescapable vulnerability. Death may be the ultimate worry.

But meanwhile life itself is teeming with all manner of evil and suffering as well. Life is full of bad things that can happen and they are never very far from us. A woman named Karina, her ancestors Scandinavian, came to me for treatment of depression, or at least that was the diagnosis we put on her chart. But she was not as much depressed as she was acutely aware of what she and I came to call "the ominous core of life." Karina, a poet by inclination, could talk in beautiful phrases of what was un-beautiful in life.

"It is as if we live our lives close to a terrible, raging fire," she said, "a fire that is always consuming and destroying us and all that we produce. We almost never see the fire but we know of it; we have learned about it along the way. We feel its heat in a strange wind now and then, we see a few sparks drift overhead, we hear the cries of people who get too close to it, and we shudder. The fire is over the next hill or around the next bend; it waits for us after the lights go out or when the party is over. We feel it in a flash ourselves when a friend betrays us, or when our car crashes, or when the X ray shows a tumor, or when the hand that holds us lets us go. Although we stay away from the fire as much as we can, we always know it is there, burning and destroying. Somehow we manage to live our daily lives without paying too much attention to the fire, but we all fear it, at least once we pass a certain age. It's out there, that fire of destruction and suffering and death, and we silently agree not to talk about it too much. What else can we do? There doesn't seem to be any way to make it go out, and so we try our best to stay away from it. We try to live as long and as happily as we can before the fire burns us up, too."

"Have you always thought of life in these terms?" I asked. Karina was forty-eight when she came to see me.

"I remember in high school thinking about these things for the first time and wondering to myself how other people do it, how do they go through life smiling, all the while knowing what terrible things lie in wait for them. I remember reading that the French philosopher Blaise Pascal said we get through life by finding some favorite distraction, what he called a 'divertissement,' to take our minds off the awful conditions of life."

"And after high school?" I asked.

"I continued in my unusually morose way," Karina replied, with a small smile telling me she could laugh at herself as well.

After high school or college, most of us manage to put the kind of troubling thoughts Karina had out of our minds. We do not have time to try to solve the unsolvable and, besides, doing so isn't much fun. Even so, now and then we cannot look away. Now and then bad things happen. Now and then we are brought up smack against life at its most terrible and we feel the fire Karina spoke of.

Death, loss, disease, injustice—these are some of the bad things that can happen. None of us can avoid them forever. We all must deal with that fact somehow.

One way to try to deal with it is to avoid it, to use one of Pascal's "divertissements." "But you can't avoid it forever," Karina countered. "It is our plight as humans to know what we know. To remember and to look ahead. As far away as our minds may take us, we are all always only a heartbeat away from catastrophe. Not surprisingly, we worry. Is this pathological?" she asked, taking a long drag on her cigarette. She was the only patient who wanted to smoke in my office.

"I don't know if it's pathological," I said, "but it makes you un-happy."

"But 'it' doesn't make me unhappy," she replied. "Life does. These conditions are not fun."

It may be argued that the inveterate worrier simply is less able than other people to forget the painful facts of life, less able than others to find an effective "divertissement," and so he is doomed to bang up against the hardness of life day in and day out.

Karina was like this. She was a gloomy, brilliant woman. She came to me in part to argue, I think. She hoped I could talk her out of her position that life was pointless and miserable. But I couldn't do it. For every positive point I made, she could counter with two negatives. She could find the dark side of any bright thought. She saw all human ef-fort as purely self-delusional. There was no point in trying to do any-thing because all human production led to the same dustbin of death.

And yet she kept coming to see me. And she kept going to work. She was a librarian, and she confessed to loving books. Still, her atti-tude about life was unremittingly negative. She saw the ominous core front and center all the time.

How did Karina manage to persevere while facing this darkness? And what did she get out of coming to see me? I think the way she dealt with seeing the dark side of life, or as she put it, "seeing life as it is, without the paltry illusions most people use to dress up this mess," was by talking about it and by making contact. She made contact with the world of ideas through books, and she made human contact through the patrons of the library, through friends, and through others like me. Even though she lived alone, she was not alone in life. She connected in sustaining ways.

In one fashion or another, I think this is how most of us deal with what is hard in life. We connect to something or someone, and this connection lifts us up.

For some people, the connection takes the form of religious faith. Almost every religion addresses the fact of evil and of pain, suffering, and death. I am a practicing Christian. Does that mean I do not worry? No, I'm afraid it doesn't. I remember having a conversation with a friend who is deeply religious. I told her I worried a great deal in life. She replied that worrying too much was an insult to God and that if I truly had faith in God I would trust Him to work things out. But the fact is that I do believe in God and I do worry. The two are not mutually exclusive.

As much as I believe in God, I still do not feel safe in life. I still must deal with the ominous core somehow. I still worry for my children, and I still worry that I won't be able to make ends meet, and I still worry about getting sick and being unable to work, and I still worry that someone might sue me or try to hurt me in some way, and I still worry that I might make a stupid mistake. I pray to God to help me with these worries, but they do not go away.

I think love is our strongest weapon against these worries. Love, a passionate connection to some person, deity, cause, or ideal, holds the possibility of sustaining us no matter what.

I think you do need some framework for dealing with evil and pain, because they are so forbiddingly unavoidable. We have to have some way of responding to them and accounting for them. If it is not through religion, then in some way we need to be prepared psychologically for when bad things happen. Even my pessimistic patient, Karina, was prepared. Her preparation was a sort of "I told you so" approach. If anything bad happened to her, she would deal with it by saying, "What else can you expect from life?" Although drear, her philosophy carried a certain grim comfort, the comfort of predictability. Nothing can be too negative to be covered by this philosophy. Predictability diminishes worry by increasing our sense of power, even if the predictions are dire.

As a starting point for dealing with worry, and maybe as a finishing point, we have to acknowledge the suffering inherent in life. How you deal with it philosophically is of course an individual choice. You may deal with it through religion, or your sustaining philosophy may be a oneness with nature. It may be even a pessimistic nihilism, like Karina's, that somehow encompasses your sense of how brutal life truly is and consoles you with the stability of its truth. But inasmuch as worry derives from an increased sense of vulnerability in the presence of a diminished sense of power, then some guiding philosophy helps reduce worry both by reducing one's sense of vulnerability and by bolstering one's sense of power.

The individual must "look into himself to see what his philosophy is," William James said. "The philosophy which is important in each of us is not a technical matter; it is our more-or-less dumb sense of what life honestly and deeply means." We are stronger psychologically when we have thought things through in advance, and that is what a belief system represents: the thinking through of life. Even Karina had done this quite thoroughly.

However, even with a belief system, even armed with an honest sense of what life means, all of us become overwrought with worry at times, and to some of us this happens often. Why?

Let me allow Karina to answer.

It is because life is so hard at its center. It is terrifying, even if you have all the faith in the world. No one can look at innocent suffering and not shudder; no one can consider the possibility of the death of children and not shudder; no one can anticipate the pain of all the good-byes we have to say before we die, and the people we will miss even if we do live after we die, and not shudder. When we look at it, when we let ourselves stare into the center of life, and we see that implacable uncertainty, we feel fear. We worry. It is all we humans have left to tell us we are in danger. What we do with that fear is another matter for each one of us—you, Dr. Hallowell, and me.

18 The Example of Samuel Johnson

The misfortunes which arise from the concurrence of unhappy incidents should never be suffered to disturb us before they happen; because, if the breast be once laid open to the dread of mere possibilities of misery, life must be given a prey to dismal solicitude, and quiet must be lost forever.

Samuel Johnson, 1750

I conclude this section by offering a final "case example," only this example happens to be of a man I neither treated nor even met, at least not in person. He is one of the great geniuses in the history of English literature, a dominating figure in the eighteenth century, author of the first dictionary of the English language, essayist, critic, moralist, and psychologist. But he was also one of the greatest worriers we have on record. His struggle to contend with worry, what he called his "disease of the imagination," still comforts, surprises, and inspires all who know of it.

Samuel Johnson battled worry his whole life. While he never succeeded in beating it, he wrestled with it relentlessly. He held his ground—in that he did not let worry destroy him or his work—but he never found a cure. As he said himself, the cures for the majority of the problems in life "are palliative, not radical."

Most people who have heard of Samuel Johnson know him only from his biographer, James Boswell. Indeed, Boswell's *Life of Johnson* is perhaps the most famous biography ever written. But the picture of Johnson that Boswell gives us is not the full picture of the man. The modern scholar W.J. Bate has filled out the story, particularly in delving into the psychological pain this man knew in life. I turn here to Johnson—and Bate—to inform our discussion of guilt and worry.

Johnson's life offers a dogged account of an endless struggle to deal with the ordinary demons of everyday life. As most of us, Johnson had many reasons to worry, but, as he himself described, his imagination reflexively amplified those reasons into exaggerated waves of intense mental anguish. He fought throughout his entire life, usually with little success, to quell his fears and hidden uneasiness.

Born to older parents, Johnson's life was hard from the start. Michael, his father, was fifty-two when young Samuel was born on September 18, 1709, and his mother Sarah was forty. It was not a happy family. Michael was a melancholy man (Samuel was later to say he inherited his father's melancholy temperament), a bookseller who never made as much of himself as he might have, and Sarah was something of a social snob, who looked down upon her less well-bred husband.

Even Johnson's birth was difficult. Johnson was later to write in his diary, "I was born almost dead and could not cry for some time." George Hector, a male midwife who assisted at the delivery, held up Samuel after he had almost died being born and spoke words that could serve as Johnson's whole life story: "Here is a brave boy." He was so sickly that his parents arranged to have him christened that very night in the same room where he was born, in case he should die before morning.

Following a tradition of the time for such sickly babies, Samuel was sent off to the care of a wet nurse. Unbeknownst to anyone, the milk of the wet nurse was infected with tuberculosis. Soon the infant developed tuberculous infections in his eyes. Following medical practice of the day, an open wound or "issue" was cut into little Samuel's arm, with the idea that this would drain the infection. This wound was kept open and oozing until he was six years old.

The treatment did not help, and his condition did not improve.

Sores began to appear. His physician made the diagnosis of scrofula, or tuberculosis of the lymph glands, a condition as physically unattractive as its name. In an effort to treat this, more incisions were made into the baby's face and neck—all done, of course, without the benefit of anesthetic, which had not yet been developed. The infection got into his optic and auditory nerves, rendering him almost blind and deaf on his left side, with some compromise on his right as well.

At just ten weeks old, the baby had suffered all this. "I was taken home," he wrote in his diary years later, "a poor, diseased infant, almost blind."

But he was tenacious from the start. We have the story of his attending a school for toddlers at around age four. One day, when the person designated to pick him up did not come on time, Johnson set out to walk home by himself. Owing to his poor eyesight, he had to get down on all fours to see where the curb left off and the street began. Seeing this little four-year-old crawling out into the street, the woman who ran the school picked him up to offer help, but Samuel pounded on her chest, trying to push her away, crying out that he could do it himself.

For the rest of his life, he did it himself. Even when others helped him, he felt he was on his own. Although he was to marry and have a multitude of friends, he always felt, like the toddler on the street, that he had to find his way by himself.

Not only did he contend with severe physical limitations, but he struggled with financial insecurity most of his life, starting a school that went broke and taking on writing projects that paid little, always giving money away whenever he had a little extra. But most difficult of all, he struggled with his mind. He had two mental breakdowns, one in his early twenties and one in his fifties. Although he was not institutionalized—in those days "treatment" for mental illness amounted to imprisonment—he was immobilized by depression and vied with thoughts of suicide. Furthermore, even during his productive periods, fears and worries beset him daily, leaving him desperate for relief.

In retrospect, it is astonishing how Johnson viewed himself. For example, he worried that he was lazy. Here is a man who wrote the first dictionary of the English language, hundreds of periodical essays (many of which are now enduring monuments of the genre), a classic series of biographical essays called the *Lives of the Poets,* the best criticism of Shakespeare ever done, and an extended moral fable called *Rasselas,* as well as various poems including one that is a lasting masterpiece, "The Vanity of Human Wishes." At the same time he also carried on a career as a conversationalist that made him perhaps the greatest talker in the history of the English language, as well as, next to Shakespeare and the Bible, its most quoted source and the subject of the greatest biography ever written. Here is a man who did all this, and yet referred to himself as "a castle of indolence." Writing the dictionary alone should have excused him from that label. It took the French Academy of forty members and a multitude of support staff fifty-five years to write the French dictionary. Johnson, practically broke, doing all the important work himself, aided only by part-time secretarial assistants, wrote the first dictionary of the English language in about three years. It is one of the most prodigious feats of scholarship ever contemplated, let alone completed!

But this man thought himself lazy, "a castle of indolence." If ever a man suffered from undeserved guilt, it was Johnson. He was wracked by worry, which he described as "a desponding anticipation of misfortune, [that] fixes the mind upon scenes of gloom and melancholy, and makes fear predominate in the imagination." In reading his personal journals, diaries, and prayers, we find ongoing, painful excoriations of himself, as well as repetitive, almost desperate resolutions to do better.

Using a religious term that is now almost obsolete, he prayed to be relieved of "vain scruples": the severe and often minute objections to his conduct with which his imagination attacked him every day. The word "scruple" itself derives from the Latin *scrupulus,* which means "a small, sharp pebble." How perfect. These little thoughts embedded themselves like small, sharp pebbles into his mind and caused pain with the step of every thought. Johnson could not rid his mind of these pointed scruples for his whole life.

He could recognize how exasperating this irrationally guilty, worried turn of mind could become in others, how out of touch with common sense and lacking in reasonable perspective. For example, he told of a clerk who used to come by and chat with him now and then. One day the clerk breathlessly confessed to Johnson that he was in the habit of occasionally stealing bits of paper and packthread from his employer. The clerk felt tremendously ashamed and guilty over this "sin." Johnson advised him to tell his employer about it, feeling confident that the employer would think nothing of it. The clerk followed Johnson's advice and found that the employer not only forgave him, but told him to help himself to paper and packthread whenever he wanted to. However, the clerk still felt plagued with guilt, even though he worked well and hard for his employer, not leaving the office each day until 7 P.M., thus allowing only the five hours between 7 and his midnight bedtime to amuse himself, as he left immediately for work upon arising the next morning. Exasperated, Johnson finally gave the clerk this advice:

> I have at least learned this much [from you] . . . that five hours of the four-and-twenty unemployed are enough for a man to go mad in; so I would advise you, Sir, to study algebra. . . . your head would get less muddy, and you will leave off tormenting your neighbours about paper and packthread, while we all live in a world that is bursting with sin and sorrow.

Johnson's advice makes me wonder if we psychiatrists should add the study of algebra to our therapeutic interventions! But it is interesting that Johnson could not follow his own advice. The clerk represents a classic kind of worrier, the one who loses perspective and cannot regain it even with solid reassurance. This is exactly what Johnson did all the time. He was a man who in his writings spoke with such reason and solid common sense that troubled minds for generations since have found stability in his words. It is fair to say that Johnson, through his writings, has been an invaluable psychotherapist to a multitude of people lost in mental anguish. But in his own day-to-day life he would lose himself in meticulous ruminations over minor transgressions, such as sleeping too late or failing to exercise regularly, and then he would fall into a paralyzing funk.

This is a man who committed no crimes. There is no hidden dark deed, at least that anyone knows of, to explain the emotional pain he felt. Contrary to the lives of many great writers, in Johnson's life there are no stories of reckless irresponsibility or of his misusing other people. In fact, this was a man of unbelievable discipline and extreme generosity, who gave without others' knowing it, who provided for beggars and vagrants whenever he could, who dotingly cared for his wife out of deep gratitude to her for marrying him—he thought he was ugly and romantically repugnant—even as she sank into the oblivion of opiate addiction; this is a man who made his way on his own in life against great odds and hurt almost no one as he did so; this is a man who had no more valid reason than any person has to feel guilty, yet felt greater guilt than almost anyone could without cause. He was routinely tormented by phantasms of guilt and worry, which at times all but drove him crazy.

Why? What were his sins? They were so tame and ordinary it is hard to believe their extraordinary magnification in his mind. One of his worst sins, by his reckoning, was that he would stay in bed too late. In fact, he would sometimes lie in bed until after noon, staring at a church steeple across the street or counting drops of water as they fell from a faucet in his room, not because he was lazy but because he was in the grip of what we now recognize as depression. He was not sleeping as he lay in bed, but rather he was immobilized in a state of fear, rumination, worry, and guilt. Instead of depression, he called this state sloth.

But today we would diagnose Johnson not with a moral failing—sloth—but with a medical condition—depression. Actually, this is how he diagnosed himself. "I was born with a vile melancholy," he wrote, "and it has made me mad all my life, at least not sober." However, he could not use the diagnosis as a means of enlarging his perspective on himself or of understanding and forgiving himself because depression, or melancholy, had not yet gained enough scientific validation to emerge from the darker dominions of moral insufficiency.

There are, in fact, several other psychiatric diagnoses we could possibly apply to Johnson, including obsessive-compulsive disorder, attention deficit disorder, and manic-depressive illness, as well an array of medical afflictions, including his scrofula, which left him partially deaf, blind, and scarred around his face and neck all his life. These scars promoted his conviction that he was ugly and physically repulsive to others. Although he was not an attractive man, one has to feel that many people—women and men alike—were deeply attracted to him, as they are to this day, owing to his irresistibly engaging, sympathetic manner. He was truly a friend to man.

Still, we see in Johnson the very essence of the problem of irrational, exaggerated worry: why could this man find so little relief from his mental torment, specifically his torment over imagined sins in the past, which as far as we can tell were nonexistent, and his torment over imagined calamities in the future? Why was this man, whose literary reputation grew as strong as any man's ever has in his own lifetime, whom T.S. Eliot called "a dangerous man to disagree with," who could take on Shakespeare and Milton without blinking, why was this giant so—to use a modern term—insecure?

All the causes of worry we have alluded to in this book can be found in his life: the genetic predisposition to depression or melancholy, which often manifested as worry; the insecurity of his childhood, with an unsuccessful, older father and a social-climbing, unaffectionate mother; his illnesses and physical handicaps; his financial problems all along (he was even once arrested for debt and was helped out by the novelist Samuel Richardson); and his trouble for most of his life finding steady work. His worry fits into the pattern we have described before of worry that arises out of a sense of increased vulnerability and a diminished sense of power (even though in the eyes of others, and of posterity, he was powerful beyond compare), coupled with a genetic predisposition. The foundation for worry is there.

And yet, it still amazes us that this lion of a man could have been so terrified inside. But he was. Not of physical danger, never that. Indeed, he was extraordinarily brave, often putting himself at risk to perform physical feats. Nor was he scared of competition; indeed, he loved it. But what he *was* terrified of were the productions of his own mind, particularly his uncertainty of the future and of oblivion.

What did he do about all this? What were his "treatments"? I think there were four main ones. First, he was always on the lookout for anything that could help, anything that could, to use his phrase, "be put to use." "Every consideration," he wrote, "by which groundless terrors may be removed adds something to human happiness."

He read all he could, yearning to arrive at what he called, "the stability of truth." He was one of the last people of whom it could be said that he knew of almost all that had been written and had read most of it. He tore into books, looking for what he could use in his life. He read literature, philosophy, theology, history, science, books about food and drink and games—everything. He searched for help far and wide.

Second, he dealt with worry by working, his chief means of dealing with all of his problems. Despite his accusing himself of laziness, he was a prodigious worker. And the work he chose was hard. For this man, who could turn a critical eye on Shakespeare and Milton, writing was a bitter trial. Each sentence stood out at him, exposing its inadequacies. And yet he never stopped or gave in to the various excuses not to write that all writers can manufacture. He had to write fast to meet his deadlines, but in the process he developed a prose style that is itself one of the majesties of English literature. "A man may write at any time," he said, with a characteristic cutting to the point, 'if he will set himself doggedly to it."

Dogged, hard work. Effort. Goals, resolutions, failure to meet goals, more resolutions, more hard work. Never give up, no matter how despondent or worthless you feel. These were his bywords, his methods. And always tell the truth or as he put it, "endeavour to see things as they are . . . ," no matter how painful. He worked hard, mentally or physically, from the moment he was born every day of his life, until, fighting still, slicing open his own legs with a scissors to drain off fluid after the doctors had refused to do it any more, death finally took this fierce adversary away.

Third, not only did Johnson work hard, he also worked creatively. As I mentioned in the introduction, some of the greatest worriers are also the most creative individuals. As Johnson himself pointed out often, the imagination transforms ordinary worry into extraordinary worry. The imagination takes a mundane detail and turns it into a harbinger of doom or perceives in the future more varied disasters than most people could ever conceive. The same faculty of mind that can contrive, for example, imaginative stories or innovative architecture or stylish modes of dress can also torment the individual with intensely original visions of bad outcomes.

When Johnson turned his creativity onto a structured project, such as an essay, or a poem, or even a conversation, this engaged his imagination outwardly and constructively. However, when his imagination was left alone, without a structured activity, it feasted upon the infinite array of negative possibilities in life. His imagination was like a beast, a very hungry beast. Indeed, Johnson wrote about "the hunger of the imagination that preys incessantly upon life."

Therefore, the same faculty of mind, imagination, could be used for him or against him. When he engaged his imagination in a creative project, he subdued his worries. But when his imagination was not feeding upon an external project, it turned itself inward and tried to devour its own habitation. We might count imagination, then, as both a remedy and a cause for worry in Johnson.

In addition to amassing all the knowledge he could, applying hard work to life's problems, and using his imagination constructively, the fourth main method Johnson used to deal with worry was connecting with other people. He was, to put it mildly, great company. He went out often to his various haunts. Especially famous was The Club, a group that included, among others, Johnson, Boswell, Joshua Reynolds, Oliver Goldsmith, Edmund Burke, and the great Shakespearean actor David Garrick. Then later in his life, after his wife's death, he found something like a family with the Thrales, who took him in and loved him, as he loved them. The content of Johnson's talk is what we remember now, but what drove him at the time *to* talk was a hunger to connect and to shine and to enjoy the fellowship that eased his worried mind.

These were, I think, the four main ways in which Johnson combated his fears and worries: hard work, knowledge, imagination, and human friendship. Creative connectedness to ideas and people, sustained by effort.

He also resorted to physical exercise a great deal, primarily walking, sometimes with Boswell in tow, but other times alone, trying to walk off worry. He read a book about melancholy by George Cheyne called *The English Malady*, a well-known book in its time. Just as we still search today for methods to ease the pain of the mind, so then did experts propose remedies based upon the latest thinking. The theory Cheyne enlarged upon was the idea that it can be therapeutic to counter one negative activity with its opposite. If you are sluggish and depressed, you should exercise; this is the counteractivity for depression. After Johnson read this he started forcing himself to walk long distances every day. It might have helped, as he continued to exercise his whole life, but it was no cure.

Humor must also be ranked among his important remedies for combating worry. Johnson's wit could spring out at any time. For example, "Remarriage," he said, "represents the triumph of hope over experience." In reviewing a book, he wrote that the manuscript was, "both good and original. Unfortunately, where it is good it is not original and where it is original it is not good." Or, in conversation, he said, "Mrs. Montagu has dropped me. Now, sir, there are people whom one should very well like to *drop*, but not wish to be *dropped by.*"

In contrast to the solemn image many have of Johnson as the serious essayist, critic, and moralist, his friend Fanny Burney thought he had "more fun . . . and love of nonsense about him than almost anybody I ever saw." While others may have taken Johnson too seriously, he never so took himself. For example, there was the time Johnson was in conversation with some learned friends, one of whom had just returned from Australia, where he had seen an amazing animal, the kangaroo. In response, Johnson

> . . . volunteered an imitation of the animal. The company
> stared . . . nothing could be more ludicrous than the appearance of
> a tall, heavy, grave-looking man, like Dr. Johnson, standing up to
> mimic the shape and motions of a kangaroo. He stood erect, put
> out his hands like feelers, and, gathering up the tails of his huge

brown coat so as to resemble the pouch of the animal, made two or three vigorous bounds across the room.

In even the most potentially embarrassing moments he could laugh at himself and deflate the tension of the situation he was in. For example, on his trip with Boswell to the Hebrides, some young women sitting nearby were talking about how ugly Johnson was. Perhaps fueled by too much wine, one of them went so far as to take a bet and go sit on his knee and kiss him. How did Johnson, this august personage, respond to this indignity? "Do it again," he purred, "and let us see who will tire first."

For all his inner torment, humor never left him for long. Unfortunately, it wasn't with him often enough when he was alone.

Finally, religious faith, for many people the supreme antidote to deepest fear, was for Johnson not an easy thing. Although he was a traditional Anglican and took church doctrine as a given, his torment over the state of his future left him eager for reassurance. For example, when the prediction one Lord Lyttleton had made of the time of his own death was brought up, Johnson said, " 'I am so glad to have every evidence of the spiritual world, that I am willing to believe it.' Dr. Adams (a friend): 'You have evidence enough; good evidence, which needs not such support.' Johnson: 'I like to have more.' " Those simple five words, "I like to have more," take in a lifetime of searching for stability and reassurance, particularly from God.

But he never found it, at least not completely. He could never rest easy.

What is so moving, and I think helpful to all of us who struggle with everyday worries but are not great geniuses like Johnson, is the *ordinariness* of how he experiences these deeper concerns. Many of his worries are everyday worries, not worries reserved for minds that inhabit a higher plane. He worries, as anyone might, that he is staying in bed too late. He worries that he is not exercising regularly enough. He worries that he talked too much at the pub the night before, that he might have cut someone else off too quickly and hurt his feelings. He worries that he can't pay his bills or hasn't balanced his accounts.

He worries that he hasn't done enough work to justify his leisure time. He worries that his wife is sick and that he hasn't treated her well enough. He worries that he is not physically attractive.

Although he did not solve the problem of worry, he laid it out for us as honestly as any man ever has.

But it was not enough. For all his honesty, hard work, and knowledge, for all the support of friends, for all his humor and willingness to laugh at himself, and for all his prayer and attempts at religious faith, he never achieved peace of mind. For all he knew the folly of worry, he also knew firsthand the folly of trying to stop. This man suffered his whole life, sometimes more acutely, sometimes less, from restless insecurity and a nameless sense of guilt he neither deserved nor could control. No one ever tried harder or more courageously to wrestle peace of mind from the thicket of turmoil. It was most certainly not for want of effort nor for want of a willingness to try whatever might help that Johnson could not quell his inner torment once and for all. He made some progress but never found the ease for his troubled mind that he deserved.

At the beginning of this book I wrote that we now have more remedies available to treat worry and conditions related to worry than we have ever had before. What, then, could we offer Johnson that was not available to him back in the eighteenth century?

Putting aside the presumptuousness involved in offering help to a man as great as Johnson, we are asking an interesting question. Do we in the 1990s really have anything of value to offer Samuel Johnson?

I think we do. First of all, we could offer him knowledge. He would devour all that we have learned about the brain. He would find it marvelous and, I think, quite healing to know there were physical correlates for much of his mental anguish.

For example, he would love to learn about the firing of nerves and how the nervous system is made up of networks of nerves, or neurons, ten billion of them in the brain alone. He would be amazed by the pictures and scans we have of the brain and be impressed at how these pictures can vary depending upon an individual's emotional state. He would be intrigued by what we have learned about neurotransmitters, the chemicals that send messages from one neuron to the next, and he would be amazed to know that we have developed medications that change the concentrations of these neurotransmitters in such a way that moods can stabilize, and even "vile melancholy" can be lifted.

Johnson could not know, back in the eighteenth century, how much of what he felt emotionally depended upon how his body and brain worked. There was no knowledge back then of neurons, or neurotransmitters, or even the physiology of the fight/flight response, which was made famous by Walter Cannon in the early twentieth century.

Once he learned the physiology, I think the domain of brain science and emotional suffering would excite him greatly. Just the diagnostic categories alone would intrigue him (and give him delight in criticizing the mangled jargon the mental health field uses). I think it would also give him considerable solace to find specific names for states he felt but didn't fully understand, especially depression and the fuller physical understanding of that term we now have. I think it would relieve him to know that he was probably right in his genetic speculation about his inheriting a "vile melancholy." I think he would take comfort in knowing the symptoms he had fit into several different diagnostic patterns, from depression, to attention deficit disorder, to obsessive-compulsive disorder, to manic-depressive illness. He would chide us, rightly, at our lack of diagnostic clarity, but I know he would be pleased at the great progress we have made in the domain of diagnosing conditions of the mind. At the time of his death, mental illness was considered either a moral failing or a sort of plague—in either case there was little treatment for it and no compassion.

One of the great advances humankind has made since Johnson's death, especially in the past fifty years, is our scientific understanding of the kinds of pain the mind can suffer. Schizophrenia, manic-depressive illness, depression, attention deficit disorder, Tourette syndrome, obsessive-compulsive disorder, Asperger's syndrome, paranoia—these are all names for sets of symptoms that in Johnson's time would have been condemned as moral failings and/or the work of the devil.

Now we have lifted these conditions out of the dungeon of moral diagnosis (i.e., evil, slothful, wicked), where they had lain in rot for millennia, and placed them into the clinic of medical diagnosis, where, even though they are not completely understood, they are at least given the respect, scientific investigation, and compassion they deserve. Anyone who has suffered from mental illness or emotional distress in themselves or in a loved one knows how much it matters to find sympathy and effective treatment instead of condemnation and scorn.

Johnson would be glad to know that the doubts and worries he contended with were not his fault. They were not, as one of the great theologians of the day, William Law, had suggested, a matter of effort and resolve. Law's book, *A Serious Call to a Devout and Holy Life,* challenged Johnson as he had not been challenged before. He said he found Law "an overmatch for me." What neither Law nor Johnson could have known is what we have learned in the neurosciences of late, that many of the habits of mind Johnson exhibited were hard-wired into his brain and vexed him beyond the reach of resolve.

So the first help we could offer Johnson was help he would have loved to receive: new knowledge. With that new knowledge, I think he would have gained a more charitable view of himself. In helping him to nudge aside the great boulder of moral diagnosis that weighed him down, I think this new knowledge would have let him ease up a bit on himself. In fact, I can imagine Johnson becoming enraged at the misconceptions of the mind his century labored under and the oppressive—and cruelly inaccurate—moral diagnoses they engendered.

Beyond this fundamental recasting of how he saw himself, based upon new knowledge, many of the treatments we would recommend today Johnson used already: exercise, humor, creative work, connections to other people, keeping busy, having a daily routine, never giving up, avoiding excessive alcohol or other drugs. On the other hand, one of the great sadnesses of his life was not having a real family, but we would be in no better position to remedy that now than he was then.

Finally, there would be the question of professional treatment. What do we have today that he didn't have then? Then there was nothing. "Treatment" consisted of sermons or chains and shackles. What have we gained since then? Knowledge is the most profound addition to our armamentarium; medication is the most specific. We now have a vast array of medications that can alleviate mental suffering dramatically, often with few side effects. Although medications provide no panacea—far from it—they provide help beyond anything that Johnson knew of in his day.

The antidepressants might have changed Johnson's life. Prozac, particularly, might have helped him because it is so effective against ruminative worry. Is it heresy to propose that Samuel Johnson would have benefited from Prozac? The kind of depression Johnson suffered from often responds very well to Prozac, which usually does not blunt creativity but rather allows the individual to make better use of his mind because he is not buried under depressive feelings. I think Johnson himself would have wanted to give it a shot. Just as his heart failure would have been helped by some of the new diuretics and heart medicines we have available today, so his mental anguish could have been dramatically relieved by the antidepressants we have developed.

We can also wonder if the new treatments other than medication would have helped. It is daunting to imagine who might have stepped up to volunteer to do psychotherapy with Samuel Johnson, but if Johnson had found a good therapist it might have made a difference. He could have talked about his parents and his childhood in a way he never was able to because he never had the right forum. He could have worked on his problems with how ugly and unlovable he felt. He could have used a sounding board for his incessant self-criticisms and might have found a place where those criticisms could have been detoxified. Moreover, he might have been able to understand the vague and nameless sense of guilt he carried with him for so long.

He might also have benefited from the more cognitive and behavioral therapies we have developed to treat depression and obsessive-compulsive disorder. These treatments have a good track record.

He had the benefit of none of these, yet he endured. Indeed, he prevailed in that he did not ever completely succumb to his inner demons. I think of him at the end of his life as a battered boxer, a prizefighter who has battled every round with life and has not been knocked out even once. Although knocked down a few times, he has always gotten back up off the mat to continue the fight, never giving up, even though he has been in the ring with an ultimately unbeatable opponent. I see him still on his feet, staggering, refusing to give up, as death moves to end the fight. Who won? The one who always wins won, but neither did Johnson lose.

This man had to struggle all his life, pumping much of his mental energy into just staying emotionally afloat. It could have been less of an ordeal for him had he had the help we have today. The question of professional treatment for Samuel Johnson's mental anguish, by whatever means, from psychotherapy to medication to whatever other interventions a modern expert might select, raises the broader question of the risks versus benefits of treating the mind in general, particularly the creative mind.

If Johnson had been able to receive any of our modern treatments, what might he have lost? When mental therapies are applied, what price, if any, must be paid? Could the price include the loss of creative powers, or might it at the least involve a subtle modification of the mind resulting not in the total loss of creative power but perhaps a dulling of the sharp edge?

In a broad sense this question comes up all the time in my office and in offices around the world. If you take away the symptoms that bother me, my patients will ask, what else might you take away from me in the process? The question goes deeper than simply asking about the side effects of a given medication. The question goes right to the heart of people's ambivalence about mental therapies in general. It is one thing to give me a pill for my back pain and tell me the pill may cause nausea or a rash. It is quite another to give me a pill, or any other remedy, for my mind and tell me that the treatment may make me happier but it also may change my personality, affect my sense of humor, or diminish my ability to create. Furthermore, even if all that the treatment does is remove the symptom I want removed, let's say the inner storm that upsets me every day, how do I know that quelling that inner storm won't impair me in some way I cannot predict? How do I know, for example, that my creative powers do not flow from that inner storm?

This line of questioning is not absurd. More than a few of my patients have chosen not to take medication for depression out of a fear that they needed their depression in order to do the useful things they did. They felt that the suffering they endured from depression in some way shaped and directed their creative powers. At base, they feared that their depression could not be taken away without taking away something else that they valued very highly.

The key question becomes this: How selective can we make our mental treatments? Can we make them selective enough to remove unwanted symptoms without touching other valued mental qualities, such as creativity, spontaneity, humor, or sparkle? Furthermore, how do we know that the seeds of valued qualities are not embedded in the unwanted symptoms? When we excise a tumor, we can know that it is all cancer, but when we "excise" depression how do we know the composition of what we are throwing away? Might we be discarding hidden treasures?

History is full of creative geniuses who would have qualified for psychiatric diagnoses by today's standards. Samuel Johnson is just one of a multitude. Mozart, Dostoyevsky, van Gogh, Melville, Tchaikovsky, and Coleridge are just a few of the legion of creative geniuses who likely could have been helped by modern psychiatry. But would they, or we, have wanted the remedies?

Since we do not know exactly how medications work, or how cognitive-behavioral psychotherapy works, or how psychoanalytically oriented psychotherapy works, or how any of our mental remedies really work, it is understandable that we might fear them. All we have to guide us is experience.

Experience, however, is a reliable and powerful guide. While we do not know exactly how most of the remedies we use actually work, we do know that they usually do work and that some of them work without damaging other mental functions. On the other hand, some actually do damage other mental functions. Some of the powerful antipsychotic medications such as Thorazine, Stelazine, and Haldol take away hallucinations but they also significantly dull thinking. No one should take these medications without considerable reason to do so. Some of the antianxiety medications, such as Valium and Xanax, can dramatically reduce the painful anxieties associated with, say, generalized anxiety disorder, but at the same time induce sleepiness or cloudy thinking. Lithium, the most widely used mood stabilizer, evens out the peaks and valleys of manic-depressive illness but in the process sometimes deprives the person who takes it of certain states of mind they had enjoyed or found useful. But others of the medications we use do not have such severe side effects. Prozac, for example, and Ritalin when used properly, have few side effects.

However, even Prozac has caused some people to complain that it deprived them of a certain edge or certain indefinable qualities that they missed, even though they felt less depressed. There is no medication without side effects, nor can we predict with absolute certainty what any medication will do to a given individual, especially those medications we use to treat the mind. Medications such as Prozac do represent enormous progress, but there is still a long way to go.

The nonmedication approaches to treatment produce few side effects, but many people worry that even psychotherapy alone might take away their creative powers. While not totally beyond the realm of possibility, I have never seen it happen. To the contrary, what often does happen is that the creative individual works out problems in psychotherapy that had been getting in the way of creativity, problems such as writer's block, procrastination, or certain kinds of shame and fear. Depending upon which remedy we choose, then, we can be quite selective in which symptoms we address and which we can leave alone.

I have treated many highly creative people. None, perhaps, of the genius level of Johnson or Coleridge or Melville, but highly gifted individuals nonetheless. They came to see me because they were in pain. Some were depressed, some were extremely worried, some were blocked in their work, some were unhappy in relationships. Whatever the problem, they all felt ready to try practically anything to make the emotional pain go away.

I never saw that reducing their pain in any way hampered their creativity. Indeed, it usually promoted it, because they could waste less time immobilized by depression and invest that time in creative endeavors. The key point to emphasize here is that treatment for mental anguish does not take away all the pain of life. You remain able to feel. The treatment aims to remove unnecessary pain or disabling feelings. Psychiatric treatment does not end passion, nor does it abate the suffering that is part of normal life. Psychiatric treatment reduces the fever, so to speak, the way an aspirin does, and brings the temperature back to normal.

Is a fever required for creativity? I believe that is a romantic notion and a dangerous one. I have seen people suffer deeply, even commit suicide, in the grip of a fever of emotion. To voluntarily submit yourself to severe mental distress in the hope that it will enhance your creative powers is, I believe, a dangerous bargain and a misguided one as well. People are most creative when they feel best, not when they feel worst. The act of creation may include great pain, but it is a qualitatively different pain from the kind of emotional pain psychiatric treatment can ease.

To extend the metaphor of a fever, just as heavy exercise can raise body temperature above normal, so can heavy creative activity raise mental temperature above normal. Neither of these elevations of temperature is a fever for which the individual should seek treatment. However, pathological states of mind, such as extreme worry or depression, raise the emotional temperature in a different way, a way that should lead the sufferer to seek treatment. The fever of depression should be treated, but the fever of creativity should be left alone because it will return to normal on its own.

The pain of pathological mental states and the pain of creativity also feel different. If you are worried and depressed, it feels different than if you are working writing a story about a tragic event. In both instances you feel sad. But in the depression you are frozen, unable to use your powers productively, while in the act of composition the sadness is being put to use, in empathizing with your characters and bringing them to life. The writer whose depression gets treated usually ends up writing better.

The point is that while suffering and creativity go hand in hand, we need not strive to preserve suffering in order to preserve creativity. That makes no sense.

Johnson, now dead two centuries, still serves as a great example. An example of what? What can this man teach *us*? That even a genius like him can suffer from extreme worry and insecurity. That great achievement is possible in the midst of severe doubt, negative thinking, irrational fear. That such extraordinary anguish as he knew is *bearable,* and that the ordinary methods he used to steady himself can help over a lifetime: effort, learning, friends, exercise, humor, and a religious faith as strong as he could muster.

In all his suffering, Johnson gave us the enduring testament of a life of effort, a life of genius and great achievement, a life of pain and worry, and a life of telling the truth about it all.

Part III

Remedies That Work

19 The Basic Steps of Worry Control

Now we look specifically at what can be done to control worry in everyday life. The following eight steps outline an approach that will help everyone who worries too much. Not every person will use every step, but every step should at least be considered in order to achieve the best results. In almost all cases, no single step alone will provide optimal results. But taken as a whole, the following program can reduce unnecessary worrying for anyone:

1. Identification of your pattern of worry, or diagnosis
2. Education
3. Constructive thinking
4. Rational intervention: EPR (Evaluate, Plan, Remediate)
5. Connectedness and reassurance
6. Change of physical state
7. Medication
8. Psychotherapy

These eight steps comprise a comprehensive program for controlling worry. Each step should be considered, if not necessarily used. What follows here is a brief explanation of each step; there will be lengthier discussions in subsequent chapters. I have not included a separate chapter on psychotherapy because I have already described many of the different approaches and a wider discussion would become more detailed than is warranted here.

1. Identification of the Pattern, or Diagnosis. You begin by trying to see the forest instead of feeling lost in the trees. Is there a pattern to your worrying? Does it fit a specific diagnosis or is it more free-floating? If it fits one of the diagnostic patterns described in this book, consult with a professional to make sure you get the right diagnosis. Diagnosis, or pattern-identification, is in itself therapeutic because with it you can begin to make sense out of the chaos of worry. You can begin to organize and categorize it, which is the beginning of controlling it. Diagnosis also begins to give hope where there had mainly been a feeling of helplessness and frustration before. If your worrying is due to one of the diagnosable, toxic forms of worry already discussed, such as depression, panic attacks, generalized anxiety disorder, paranoia, attention deficit disorder, obsessive-compulsive disorder, or trauma in your past, the doctor or therapist you consult can advise you further on treatment and prescribe medication if any is indicated. If you do not know if your worrying fits one of these "diagnosable" patterns, start with your family physician or a psychologist to find out. It is well worth the time and money. The person you consult can also advise you if more extended treatment is indicated or if you can handle it on your own, with some pointers and suggestions. If you do not know whom to consult, start with your family doctor. If you do not think your worrying fits one of these patterns, but rather is more free-floating, the suggestions in this part of the book should help you manage it better.

2. Education. If your worry fits into a formal diagnosis, such as depression or generalized anxiety disorder, learn as much about it as you can. There are many books now available in any of the large bookstores addressing most of the diagnosable conditions of worry. If you are one of the millions of overworriers in this country who do not fit into any specific diagnostic category, look at the patterns of worry in your life and try to describe your worrying based upon the patterns that have been laid out in the first two sections of this book. Think of the physical and genetic bases for your worrying, as well as the psychological. Consider your worrying in terms of the "basic equation": In what ways do I feel vulnerable and in what ways do I feel a lack of power? Then, logically, remedies will suggest themselves, along the lines of how to make yourself feel less vulnerable and more powerful. As Dr. Melvin Levine, an authority in the field of learning problems, says, "The *description* should naturally lead to a *prescription* of what to do."

For example, Mary noticed that she got worried after big events. Her husband's performance appraisal at work, Christmas, her son's important hockey game, and her annual doctor's appointment were all followed by worry. It seemed she saved the worry up for afterward. To combat this she did two things. First of all the insight alone helped. If she could see worry coming, she could be psychologically prepared. Second, she deliberately planned to do something fun after such events, so that she could have a worry-antidote waiting for her.

3. Constructive Thinking. Talk to yourself in a *useful* way. Most worriers talk to themselves in half-phrases of imagined doom, little punches and jabs of negativity. Try to break this painful habit and instead learn how to talk to yourself *constructively.* Try to erase old patterns of automatic negative thinking as much as you possibly can. Everyone has a gloomy side, and life certainly has its ominous core. However, it helps to keep the negative at a certain distance. When you start down the same old route of gloom and doom, try deliberately to do something to distract yourself. Whistle or sing. Snap your fingers. Tell yourself to cut it out. Insert a positive thought that still makes sense but countervenes the stream of negativity. It may feel like too much to say, "Develop a positive view of life," but one positive thought at a time can lead to a gradual shifting of the balance from negative to positive.

4. Rational Intervention. In dealing with worry it helps to take action, rather than remaining passive as worry sweeps over you. If you want a simple guideline for such action, try using the three steps of EPR: Evaluate. Plan. Remediate. Use a structured approach. By replacing worry with constructive action, EPR begins to solve the problem. First, *evaluate* the situation you are worrying over. Then, make a *plan* to solve the problem. Finally, implement the plan and *remediate* the problem as best you can. Use structure. Use any concrete intervention you can add to your life to control or prevent worry. For example, a "To-Do" list provides structure; it reminds you of what you need to do, so you do not need to worry that you'll forget. Crossing each item off the list as you complete the task provides a feeling of satisfaction and positive reinforcement. The varieties of structural interventions are endless. The common theme in all of them is that the individual takes a specific action to fix a certain problem. Evaluate, plan, and re- mediate; don't worry. The plan may be to ask for a consultation from a professional, such as a lawyer or a doctor, or it may be something you do yourself, such as to go on a diet or a budget. In any case, try by making concrete plans to take your problem out of the domain of anx- ious apprehension and into the domain of planned remediation. Use practical preparedness to eliminate unnecessary worry *before it occurs.* Take stock of all the areas where increased structure or planning would decrease worry and then set about implementing strategies in each. A basket next to the front door for your car keys. A will. A budget. A chat with a physician and a checkup. These are the kinds of simple steps that can reduce baseline worry dramatically—and avoid the need for remediation altogether.

5. Connectedness and Reassurance. Make connections to family, friends, organizations, neighborhood, nature, church or other religious institution, your personal past—any kind of connection that will make you feel a part of something larger than yourself. You may connect through prayer or conversation, activity or letter-writing. Connected- ness extinguishes worry and insecurity. Reassurance, which depends upon having sources of connectedness, is probably the simplest remedy known for worry.

6. *Change of Physical State.* Worry is a physical state of mind as well as a psychological one. One of the best ways to deal with worry is to change your *physical* state, rather than digging deeper into the psychological content of the worry. How do you change the physical state of your brain? It is easy. There are a number of ways, most of them free of charge and entirely natural. The best are the simplest, such as exercising, listening to music, praying, getting the right amount of sleep, breathing deeply, talking to another person, writing a letter, making a list, watching a funny movie, reading a book, driving a car, meditating, making love, drinking some hot soup, or eating a snack (however, be careful of overdosing on food!). If you find you are stuck in a worried state, the chances are that one of these "state-change" maneuvers will get you out of it.

7. *Medication.* Technically, this could go into the "state-change" category, but it deserves a category and a chapter of its own. The medications we use to treat anxiety and worry can be dramatically effective. However, it is important that they be used properly, under careful medical supervision, because these medications, as all medications, can be misused. They are not a cure for worry, but they may be a potent tool in the comprehensive treatment.

8. *Psychotherapy.* This, too, could be put in the "state-change" category, but it deserves separate mention. For a long while psychotherapy was the only form of professional treatment we had for worry. When used properly, it still works well. Psychotherapy can alter brain chemistry as much as medication can. The key is to choose the right kind of psychotherapy. For most anxiety states, cognitive-behavioral therapy works best. This involves a combination of systematic exposure to whatever it is that is causing the anxiety, along with some relaxation and breathing techniques for reducing the physical symptoms. The in-

dividual also learns the cognitive process of how to talk himself through the episode of worry or anxiety, providing realistic perspective for himself when he seems to lose it, providing reassurance for himself when he seems to need it, and providing positive thoughts for himself when he seems to need them. An individual can actually *learn* how to do these things for himself. Eye movement desensitization and reprocessing, or EMDR, is a particularly helpful specialized psychotherapy technique in dealing with the worry associated with trauma, although it can be used for any kind of chronic worry.

Family and couples therapy can also help if the cause of the worry involves the family or spouse, as it so often does. Psychoanalytically oriented individual psychotherapy, long the only nonmedication treatment available for worry, remains a highly effective means of treatment for selected individuals.

20 EPR: Evaluate, Plan, Remediate

Have you had a will drawn? Have you made plans for your financial future? Do you make sure that your children see the pediatrician and dentist when they should? Have you quit smoking? Do you have a system for organizing your office or your desk? Do you have a list of important numbers next to your telephone? Do you have a place where you always put your car keys so you never start a day with a frantic search for them?

Most people would answer "no" to many if not most of those questions. The irony is that many people spend more time worrying about what can go wrong than taking positive steps to reduce the likelihood of those wrong things happening.

Instead of letting worry bore into your brain, the next time worry strikes try immediately to put the sequence of EPR into motion: evaluate, plan, remediate. If you can make this a habit, you can control many worries quickly before they control you.

For example, let's say you experience a pain in your chest while walking upstairs one day. Instead of spending the next few hours worrying what it meant, and dodging the question, you could do as follows:

1. Evaluate: This was a kind of pain I don't remember having felt before. It was sharp, in the area of my heart. It passed when I paused for breath. I do not know what this means.
2. Plan: Since I do not know what this means and since I do fear it might be serious, I will seek expert advice.
3. Remediate: You call your physician right away.

If more people followed this simple sequence, instead of worrying over the meaning of their chest pain or trying to deny it happened because it made them feel worried or helpless, then fewer people would die of heart attacks.

To give another example, let's suppose you are reading an article in *Time* magazine about the rising costs of a college education. You have two children in grade school. The article is making you tense. Instead of flipping the page to read another article, and putting off once again acting on this worry, you might instead do the following:

1. Evaluate: Yes, this is true. College costs are rising. I have two children who I hope will go to college. However, at this rate I will not be able to afford to send them both.
2. Plan: I heard an ad on TV recently about financial plans for saving for college. Who can I ask about this sort of thing? I'll call my friend Tim, who is already paying college tuitions for his kids, and ask if he has any advice. Maybe he can point me in the right direction.
3. Remediate: You call Tim.

This technique is simple. The key is to use it. To offer another example, let's say you are worried about a meeting you have with your boss in a week. You are worried that he is going to be critical of you. Instead of brooding all week you might instead try this:

1. Evaluate: I am worried that Hank is going to be critical of me. Is that realistic? He has never been critical before. I have always worried that he would be, but it has always turned out that he wasn't.
2. Plan: I think I'll review in detail all the *facts* of my performance before I meet with Hank. That way, if he is critical, I'll be up on the facts to support me. Furthermore, if, as before, he is not going to be critical, reviewing the facts should help put my mind at ease, and help me stop ruminating over what I imagine.
3. Remediate: You dig into your files and review the events since your last meeting with Hank.

What if you have done poorly and have genuine reason to be concerned? The same sequence of steps should help:

1. Evaluate: I'm in trouble. I haven't written the proposal Hank asked me to write the last time we met, and my sales figures are down since that time as well.
2. Plan: There isn't time at this late date to write the proposal, and obviously I can't generate new business overnight. I don't want to come in with excuses, but the fact is that Lizzie's illness has really been preoccupying me. I wonder if Hank knows about that. I think what I'll do is come in with a concrete timetable of when I can get the proposal on his desk, as well as some projected numbers, which are true, of how my sales should go up now that we are entering the new season. If he asks me why I've been performing poorly of late, I'll tell him about Lizzie. If he doesn't ask, maybe I'll tell him anyway. He should know.
3. Remediate: You start writing up the timetable to give Hank and putting together the projected figures.

This approach turns worry into action. It treats worry as the warning signal it should be, but prevents it from becoming a problem in its own right.

One of the keys to the success of this method is the use of structure. Structure—my generic word for lists, reminders, any organizing tools, schedules, rules—is a potent antianxiety agent. The basket next to the front door where you *always* put your car keys is worth a bushel of the Valium you might take to combat the anxiety you feel over losing your car keys over and over again!

Yet most people shy away from making structural changes in their lives. They know they "should" but their hearts aren't in it. For one reason or another they put off making the changes that could really save them a lot of time and worry.

If you are a worrier, think to yourself how many of your worries could be reduced by better structure and better planning. Make a schedule. Set up a budget. Consolidate your credit cards. Even reading these words may send a shiver up your spine because you feel guilty that you haven't done these things, even though you have been meaning to for a long time. DON'T FEEL GUILTY. IT IS OK. IT IS NOT TOO LATE. YOU HAVE LOTS OF COMPANY. GOOD RESPONSIBLE PEOPLE WHO HAVEN'T PLANNED WELL. RELAX. IT IS OK.

Having said that, let me encourage you to take a sheet of paper and give yourself three—ONLY THREE—tasks, three structural changes you want to make in your life. Make them specific and make them doable. For example, you might set for yourself the following tasks:

1. Make an appointment to make a will.
2. Make a dentist appointment.
3. Put a basket next to the phone where you'll always put your keys.

Then, next to each item, write down how and when you are going to do it. Give yourself a reasonable time frame. If each task does not get done, give yourself a new time frame. Persist until all are done. Then make a new list of three, and only three, structural changes you want to make in your life.

If you go at it systematically and slowly like this, after six months to a year, you will have dramatically changed your life for the better. You will worry less, BECAUSE YOU WILL BE SAFER. Structure reduces risk, whether it is the risk of losing something, or going broke, or dying with no will. Security alarms add structure. Datebooks add structure. Rules add structure.

Often, setting up structure is anxiety-producing. People have a lot of trouble doing it by themselves. Whenever they think of doing it, they put it off. To combat this, try setting up structure with someone else. Your spouse. A friend at work. Anyone. Just put your heads together and become partners in structure. The steps you take, one by one, will add up to make a big difference.

Structural changes will often result from using the EPR sequence as well. Basically, with the EPR method you are putting reason and action in the way of worry. You are using reason to combat fear. What happens too often is that people let fear run wild, as if they had no power over it. Reason is a potent weapon—but only if we use it.

Evaluate. Plan. Remediate. Instead of brooding.

21 Speak Well to Yourself

Learning to Think Constructively

Toxic worry almost always derives from a misreading of reality: a person makes a fundamental mistake in how he perceives his circumstances. The two most common mistakes he makes are: (1) exaggerating the danger he is in, or (2) underestimating or forgetting about the power he has to combat the danger.

For example, let's say Frank hears his company is about to finalize a merger deal that would lead to a reorganization. Instantly, almost automatically, he thinks to himself, "Oh, great, I'm dead meat. Here we go again." He assumes he will lose his job, and, furthermore, he goes on to imagine that he will be unable to find another job for a long time, at least a year, maybe two. Before you know it, he is wondering if his life insurance is paid up in case he considers suicide for the good of his family. He jumps to the worst possible conclusions and then dwells upon them immovably.

To give another example, JoAnn notes that her eighteen-year-old daughter is ten minutes late driving in from the airport. She entertains the fleeting idea that the airplane crashed, or the car crashed, or her daughter was mugged. She then puts those ideas out of her mind, appropriately deciding they are unlikely, but then, almost as if driven by some morbid, irresistible force, she goes back to those ideas and reinserts them into her consciousness, now deeming them fact. The next thing you know, she is starting to panic. She concludes her daughter is either dead or in great distress. In one fast-receding part of her mind she still knows that this is extremely unlikely, but she is increasingly losing touch with that reasonable part of her mind, as fear and worry take over, obliterating her sound judgment. She starts to catastrophize the situation totally, so when her daughter does arrive home, only twenty-five minutes late, the poor daughter doesn't even get the chance to explain that there was a big traffic jam before she must first endure her mother's shrieking explosion of anger, grief, and relief.

A third example: Alice has to give a lecture to a professional organization. Even though she is an expert in her subject, in the weeks leading up to the talk she constantly talks to herself about all the ways she might perform badly. Soon she starts to feel as though she has already given the lecture and it was dismal. She continues to worry that she does not know her material. Although she knows her material cold, she continues to doubt herself and worries herself into a frenzy before finally giving the lecture—and doing very well.

These examples are all too familiar. A suggestion gets misconstrued as an insult. A reminder is felt as a criticism. A slow week in business is interpreted as a harbinger of bankruptcy. One loss by your favorite team is taken to mean the season is over. A pat on the back is felt as a jab. A friendly smile is interpreted as a manipulation.

The worrier habitually *misinterprets* the data of everyday life in such a way that his thoughts run in a fearful direction. He can't do a reality check on his own thoughts because they run away from him too fast—toward the black hills of rumination and gloom.

This misinterpretation of the data, which culminates in worry, leads to a loss of perspective. Excess worry, by definition, means a loss of perspective. Otherwise it would not be "excess."

What is perspective? It is a sense of proportion. It is a sense of priorities. It is a sense—quite like our sense of balance, or of rhythm, or of beat. What fits where? What counts and what doesn't? What is no big deal and what is? What is the small stuff and what are the biggies? Knowing this requires perspective. Like a sense of balance, some people have it better than others. Some people can naturally *feel* that this problem is a big deal while that other one is not.

When we hear a piece of news, our sense of perspective automatically rates it and places it where it should rightfully be. A rainy day. Gee, that's too bad, but no big deal. An F on a test. Bad news, but a comeback is possible. Got fired today. Will get another job. When we lose perspective, however, our rating scale goes awry, and we start to feel danger way out of proportion to the reality of the situation. A rainy day. Oh, no, this must mean the start of a horrible week. An F on a test. Oh great, I'm going to flunk out, and my life is ruined. Got fired today. That's it for me. I might as well be dead.

Such a tendency to *catastrophize* a situation attributes more significance to each of our individual actions, and the actions of fate, than any of them has individually. It may be that for the want of a nail the kingdom was lost, but *no one* can see that far ahead.

When a person loses perspective he is forgetting that he is merely mortal. He is forgetting that he is powerless over some things, no matter what he does. For example, say you are stuck in traffic and you are worried that you will be late for an important business meeting. You are honking your horn, cursing the cars around you, trying to snake in and out of congested lanes of cars and trucks and buses as you sweat and pound your steering wheel. You are losing perspective. At the next red light, you actually honk at the light, demanding that it change. You have now lost perspective. You have lost "it." You are honking at red lights! You are behaving as if you had control over what you can't control. You are denying that you are merely mortal. You can only go as fast as you can go. You can only do as much as you can do. You cannot change red lights. You are not God.

It can help you to diminish unnecessary worry by learning to recognize when you are starting to lose perspective, when you are overreacting—when you are honking at red lights.

You can develop your innate sense of perspective in many different ways. One of the best is to talk to another person. My old teacher, Dr. Thomas Gutheil, taught me one of the most valuable methods of dealing with worry when he said, "Never worry alone." Simply by explaining a worry to another person you can begin to regain your perspective.

Worrying by yourself intensifies your worry, no matter what it is. When you worry alone you do not have the automatic reality check another person provides. Your imagination can go wild, just as it does when you are in the dark, imagining bad guys everywhere. Telling your worry to another person is like turning on a flashlight. You can see the bad guys aren't there. You regain an accurate perspective. You grow more confident as your worry subsides.

Sometimes people are too proud to tell their worries to other people, particularly if they deem them to be "silly" worries. This is a great mistake. Of course, you shouldn't tell your worries to someone you know will ridicule you; you shouldn't confide in the likes of Don Rickles or Howard Stern. But you can usually find a sympathetic ear.

Your ultimate goal is to learn how to talk to yourself. To give yourself reassurance and support.

Aaron Beck, an innovative psychiatrist and psychoanalyst, developed a technique in the 1960s called cognitive therapy. Some of the basics of cognitive therapy were discussed earlier in the chapter on panic disorder. But the methods he developed are applicable not just to panic but to all states of worry and anxiety. In cognitive therapy the therapist helps the patient *retrain* his cognitive patterns—his habits of thought—in a more realistic direction. Not a "happy" direction necessarily, just realistic. This is not a simple-minded "cheer-up" approach, but rather a systematically planned shift in how one habitually assesses the meaning of the events in everyday life. Instead of always, automatically heading down the road of negativity, the individual learns some new routes, routes that make more sense.

You can use some of the methods of cognitive therapy in your own life. In severe cases of course you should consult a professional therapist, but for many habitual worriers simply applying some of the techniques on their own can help dramatically.

How? You should take the following steps, in this order:

1. Examine your automatic thoughts.
2. Correct errors in logic you make in assessing reality and develop alternative hypotheses.
3. Revise your fundamental assumptions about yourself and life, what the cognitive therapists call your "self-schemas."

Let's look at these steps one at a time. Begin by monitoring your automatic thoughts when you get bad news or perceive danger of some sort. Examine the actual words that pop into your mind and if possible write them down. Writing them down helps you distance yourself from them and look at them more critically. Often you can see immediately how wildly exaggerated they actually are. For example, whenever Tina made a mistake she would *automatically* say, "I'm an ugly stupid idiot," and go on attacking herself instead of trying to solve the problem.

The next step is to examine these automatic thoughts for errors in logic and then think of alternative hypotheses that are more logical. It is usually pretty obvious once you look. Tina was not stupid in the least. Yet she dealt with worry by calling herself stupid. "Stupid" became her catchword for dealing with stress. Logically her catchword made no sense, as is usually the case. Instead of flailing yourself you might look for other explanations. For example, are you overgeneralizing, assuming that because you once had a bad outcome in a given situation, you will always have a bad outcome in that same situation? Might it be more logical to think that there is at least a chance that you will have a good outcome this time? Or are you using black-and-white thinking, assuming there are only two possible outcomes, one totally good and the other totally bad? Wouldn't it be more logical to anticipate an outcome that is some shade of gray, with some good and some bad? Or might you be personalizing a piece of data with no evidence to warrant it; for example, assuming a stranger's scowl was caused by you?

Isn't it more logical to think that the stranger was in a bad mood for reasons that had nothing to do with you, since he didn't even know you?

The third step is to consider how these automatic thoughts and errors in logic grow out of your own self-schema, the fundamental way you look at life and at yourself. What is your self-schema? Do you think you're stupid? In Tina's case, although she knew at one level she was smart, her self-schema, the blueprint she carried around, had stupid written all over it. Is your self-schema that you are a loser and an underachiever and that the deck of life is irretrievably stacked against you? Is your self-schema that because your father was strong and rejecting, no one in power will ever admire you? Is it that because you are overweight no woman/man will ever find you attractive? Is it that life is a bitter disappointment, with more evidence pouring in every day? Whatever your self-schema might be, you can probably change it if you try to systematically.

If you start with the first step, the automatic thoughts in the here-and-now, and then work down, you can begin to revamp your negative, worry-wart approach to life. You have to practice doing this, and overcome your initial skepticism, but if you keep at it, it will almost always help. This is because it is based upon hooking you up with the truth and disengaging you from self-created distortions. In other words, with this approach you put reality on your side instead of inventing a private "truth" that torments you.

Tina worked at revising her thinking. She first identified her tendency to say, "Stupid, stupid," to herself, sometimes even out loud, at the first hint of danger or worry. She had never really admitted to herself consciously that she did this. Once she admitted it, she could work on it, because she knew it was untrue. Instead of saying, "I'm stupid," she might say, "I better make another deposit in the bank to cover that check before it bounces," or, "It is not my fault Harry didn't call; it's Harry's problem." Gradually she consciously rejected "stupid" as the catchall explanation and started to make more accurate assessments. Not always pleasant assessments, but more pleasant than the blanket "stupid" and certainly more useful.

To give another instance, if Frank, mentioned in the example at the start of the chapter could stop and monitor what he was thinking when he heard about the potential merger, he might be able to notice how unrealistically skewed his response was. If he could examine his automatic thoughts, "Oh, great, I'm dead meat. Here we go again," he might be able to catch the exaggeration built in. He might be able to stop and ask himself, "Can I think of any other possible outcome than my being unemployed for a year?" He would have to chuckle to himself and acknowledge that of course there were other possible outcomes. Simply by stopping the rush of his negativity, a process fueled by his fearful emotions, he could begin to prevent a storm of toxic worry and replace it with some calm moments of constructive planning.

Having caught the error in logic, he could begin to ask himself what he should do to assess his situation more accurately. To whom should he talk? What might the possibilities be of his staying on after the merger? What action might he take before the merger happened to position himself well? In other words, he could begin planning instead of worrying.

Furthermore, he could realize that once again his thinking had derived from a self-schema in which he regarded himself as someone for whom life sooner or later always goes wrong. He could begin to revise this self-schema deliberately, telling himself the reasonable words, "That does not have to be the case. Life does not always have to go wrong. By thinking it will you deprive yourself of the energy you need to keep it going in a positive direction."

What Frank is now doing is using the force of thought to combat the rush of unrealistic emotion generated by a negative view of himself. Sometimes worriers behave as if they can't use their thoughts to combat their emotions. But if you try deliberately and systematically to do so, you can. It takes practice, but this approach can quell chronic worry.

One of the objections to the cognitive approach is that it is too simple. It may sound simple but it really isn't. Beck, and the many others who have written about it, provide a highly sophisticated theoretical framework for it. More importantly, it works. Cognitive therapy, combined with behavioral therapy, has been demonstrated to be effective in treating depression, panic attacks, generalized anxiety disorder, obsessive-compulsive disorder, and post-traumatic stress disorder, as well as being a useful component in the treatment of many other disorders.

But not only is cognitive therapy effective for these various disorders, the general principles and techniques are good for ordinary over-worriers as well, those millions of people who carry no diagnosis but are plagued by toxic worry nonetheless.

Such a person can benefit tremendously by learning how to talk to himself constructively: by learning how to intercept automatic negative thoughts before they build up such a head of steam that they become unstoppable; by using logic to generate alternatives to gloom and doom; and then, eventually, by chipping away at the negative self-schema that generates so much of the worry in the first place.

The automatic thoughts in themselves can be destructive. Typical responses from overworriers are phrases like: "Here we go again"; "I can't possibly deal with this"; "This spells curtains for me"; "I don't have the energy to fight this one"; "Now I'm really ruined"; "I can't believe this is happening, but I always knew it would." The negative thoughts proliferate as automatically as mosquitoes from still water.

The cognitive approach stirs the water up. Don't let the automatic thoughts settle in and lay their eggs. But the worrier must do more than simply "think positive thoughts." That alone won't work because the mind will quickly suffocate the positive thoughts unless they can draw strength from reality. Hence, as the negative thoughts pour in, you must question them realistically and logically. Instead of blandly saying, "Don't worry, be happy," you ask with a critical eye, "How much danger am I actually in? Are these catastrophic outcomes I'm imagining the only alternatives? What am I basing these conclusions on? Is there another point of view that makes any sense? What support can I find for a more favorable set of outcomes? What can I do to increase the likelihood of those occurring? To whom should I turn for a second opinion or some expert advice?"

This kind of self-questioning, as it begins to replace reflexive self-flagellation, can exterminate the automatic negative thoughts and their larvae as well. Because the negative thoughts are not based in reality, but rather in a distortion of reality, an individual can use his own cognitive capabilities to combat them. Even though his own mind conjures them up, a part of his mind can begin to put them down and keep them in perspective.

Such constructive talking to yourself takes practice. It might be helpful to visit a cognitive-behavioral therapist to learn the specific techniques and to rehearse them. This kind of therapy is brief, lasting only ten to twenty sessions. The therapist will also give you homework assignments so you can work on developing the techniques between appointments.

But if seeking professional help is not feasible, people can learn how to talk themselves out of toxic worry and into productive planning with deliberate effort on their own by following the guidelines just given or by reading other books on cognitive-behavioral therapy, such as Dr. David Burns's *Feeling Good* (Avon, 1992).

Instead of instantly honoring the negative thoughts, as if they were sent by some cosmic truth-teller, you can learn to tell yourself that your alarm system is once again going haywire, that your are once again deceiving yourself into gloom, and then you can resolve that you are not going to do it this time. You can begin to list in your mind all the various alternatives to the negative conclusions you automatically drew. Gradually, the force of reason overcomes the force of habit.

This process is sort of like a reasoned pep talk. At first you doubt it. "Give me a break," one part of your mind protests. "You can't fool me, you're just trying to make me feel better." This is because at first reason lacks the force and conviction of the negative thoughts. After all, the negative thoughts have a longer history. Also bear in mind that our brains are better wired to register fear than reassurance. But if you bear with the process, gradually the positive alternatives can gather a force of their own, not out of faith, but *because they make more sense.* Gradually what had seemed so utterly compelling about the negative thoughts begins to feel less compelling, if not downright silly or even crazy.

This kind of cognitive approach takes work. It takes work to talk yourself out of a downward spiral. It is like getting your car unstuck. You have to push. But the rewards are great. And it gets easier with time.

22 Changing Your Physical State to Change Your Mental State

We all know that worry resides in the body. It has to. If we had no body, we would have no worry—or anything else. Worry must be, at least in part, a physical condition. In other words, worry resides in living tissue, just like appendicitis, or a headache, or joint pain.

However, because worry also has imagined content (What does she think of me? Why did I do that? What if the job falls through?), most people tend to focus on the psychology of worry instead of the physiology.

However, it also makes sense to look at what most people overlook: the physical basis of worry. You do not have to learn anatomy or brain chemistry to do this. All you have to do is acknowledge that your physical state influences your mental state. If you acknowledge that, then it stands to reason that by changing your physical state you might change your mental state as well.

For example, most people felt the physical symptoms of worry the first time they had to speak in front of a group of people. Stage fright is an almost universal feeling. It includes many of the effects of the fight-or-flight response: rapid heartbeat, sweaty palms, tightness in the throat, trembling in the knees and hands, dizziness, and so forth. It is quite unpleasant and after it is felt once it keeps many people from ever volunteering to feel it again.

This unpleasant response can usually be blocked by medication. The class of drugs called the beta-blockers actually block the action of the chemicals, such as adrenalin (also called epinephrine), that the body produces that cause the feelings associated with stage fright. Drugs such as propranolol (Inderal) block the receptors in the heart, muscle, throat, and so on that cause the unpleasant feelings. By changing your physical state, in this case with the use of medication, you can change your mental state dramatically. But medication is a last resort. A multitude of simple physical steps can drastically alter your mood and reduce worry. These should be tried before medication.

For example, exercise is a terrific antidote for worry. If you feel worried, run a mile or play a game of squash or tennis. Afterward you will feel less worried. This is almost guaranteed. But how can this be? You have not changed the situation that was causing you to worry by exercising. However you have changed the vessel of your worry, the physical state of your body and brain. Exercise causes your body to put out chemicals that soothe the worried mind, such as endorphins, corticosteroids, and neurotrophins, as well as various neurotransmitters such as serotonin.

How? When you exercise your whole body responds. The bloodstream fills with chemicals responding to the body's need for more energy. This is a complex response, involving different hormones, all with different actions. Blood pressure, heart rate, and body temperature all rise, as does the rate of respiration. As these so-called vital signs rise, the body (which, of course, includes the brain) enters a whole new state, and its entire metabolism changes. Exercise induces a change in all our bodily systems. These changes soothe the brain. How? We can't say exactly, but they do. Notice how you feel after exercise: calm, focused, alert but not hyper—at ease.

A regular exercise program—exercise three or four times a week—

will almost always cut down on worry. Exercise is of course good for you in other ways, such as helping to control blood pressure and reduce the risk of heart attack. But its tonic effect upon the brain has been underestimated by most people. Exercise is good for controlling aggressive feelings, reducing anxiety, and helping the mind to focus, as well as for treating depression. As far as possible, exercise should be a part of everyone's life. It should be incorporated into any plan to reduce anxiety and control worry. Make sure you pick an exercise program that you enjoy so that you will continue it over the long term.

You can also exercise on the spot to reduce acute worry. If you are sitting in your office and find that you are having a bad day, filled with ruminative, nonproductive worry, try walking up and down a flight of stairs five to ten times. You will find that your mind is less troubled when you come back to your desk. Why? Because the change in physiology induced by the exercise "cleansed" the mind. We do not know exactly which chemicals or which physiological changes are doing what in the brain, but empirically we know that they are doing something and something very positive. Is it raising the blood pressure, is it the endorphins, is it an outpouring of GABA, is it the rise in heart rate, is it the increased oxygen intake owing to the rise in respiratory rate, is it the increased adrenalin and corticosteroids induced by exercise, is it the slight increase in body temperature, is it the flux in the serotonin system brought on by exercise, or is it some other as yet unknown factor that makes exercise, even a brief spurt of exercise, such a good tonic for the brain, a worry-reducer and a mind-focuser? We can only speculate that it is all of these and more.

Exercise works for children as well as adults. Running around outside the house or going up and down stairs can turn an anxious or a worried child into a calm one.

Other kinds of bodily motion can assuage worry too. Simply moving your body can reduce worry. If you think of "the worried look," it is usually found on a person who is at rest and immobile. Deep worry can freeze you solid so you do not move a muscle. Motion can melt the worry.

What kind of motion? Any kind of motion. However, rhythmic,

repetitive motion is especially helpful. Motions such as rocking or swaying can help. Stand up and move your upper body from side to side or back and forth or slowly rotate it on the axis of your hips. Even gently nodding or shaking your head can break a spasm of acute worry.

We do not know why this is so, but there is reason to speculate that the cerebellum, which governs repetitive, rhythmic motion, may send signals to the limbic system as a person is rocking, for example, and the limbic system may then send emotional signals that cool the heated cortex in its worrying.

Try it yourself. Next time you are really worried, try sitting in a rocking chair and rocking for a while. If you do not have a rocking chair handy, try rocking your torso forward and backward as you sit in a chair. Or you may simply try moving your arms in front of you rhythmically, as if you were doing the breaststroke in open air. You will find that your worrying subsides while you are engaged in the rhythmic motion.

In addition to exercise and rhythmic motion, there are many other physical ways to influence the state of your brain. Sleep is crucial. If you do not sleep enough, you are prone to worry. Lack of sleep makes most people irritable, edgy, and anxious. It clouds judgment, which further complicates the picture. People's sleep requirements vary greatly, but everyone should try to get the amount they need on a regular basis. The best way to determine how much *you* need is simply to notice how you feel in the morning after varying amounts of sleep. There is no one absolute norm, even for a given age group.

How does diet affect the physical state of the brain? We do not know for sure. Probably in the not-too-distant future we will have dietary advice for a range of mental conditions, from depression to anxiety to attention deficit disorder, but for now the best advice is to be empirical. If you find that certain foods, such a cup of hot soup, or certain patterns of eating, such a small snacks instead of large meals, make you feel better, then by all means use them. If you find that certain foods or certain patterns of eating make you more anxious or worried, then stay away from them.

Certain substances tend to make most people anxious. Coffee is the best example, but cola, chocolate, some kinds of tea, nicotine, and some over-the-counter cold remedies have a similar effect. If you like to get going with a cup of coffee in the morning, be careful you don't drink so much that you become wired. In the wired state the brain becomes hypervigilant, noticing every little detail, scanning the world frantically. Details that it would otherwise ignore become fodder for worry. The worrier may believe that more coffee will help, but in fact it usually makes him worry more.

The dangers of self-medicating with alcohol have already been mentioned. Alcohol and other substances may reduce worry in the short term, but in the long term they make worry much worse.

Controlled breathing can even reduce worry. For example, simply taking a deep breath and letting it out slowly can provide relief. Taking a series of deep breaths can do it even better. Indeed, one of the core components of most relaxation techniques is deep breathing. It is also a component of cognitive-behavioral therapy, which is so effective in treating many states of excess worry. Sometimes if you are worried it can help simply to *notice* your breathing. You do not have to alter it at all. Simply pay attention to it for a while—say, three minutes. If you do this you will tend to relax. You will come into the present moment and take your mind off your worries. Even if worry pops into your mind, visualize it as a bubble and say to yourself, "Ah yes, there is a worry-bubble; now watch it pop!" After it pops you can go back to focusing on your breathing.

There are advanced techniques in which people can get training in breathing exercises. Many Buddhist meditations use breathing exercises. One discipline that I have used myself to great advantage is Kundalini Yoga. This ancient technique, originally developed in India by the Sikhs, has been around for thousands of years. It is not hard to learn, and books on the subject are available in most large bookstores. However, it is a technique for which it is wise to find a teacher, as it is safer and more effective to learn these breathing and meditative exercises under supervision. It is possible to faint or become severely dizzy if the exercises are not done properly. However, when they are done right, they are extremely invigorating and mind-clearing.

Exercise, sleep, diet, and breathing. These are basic simple ways of soothing your brain. They can help reduce worry and improve mental functioning in all domains. These are the simplest and most reliable techniques, but there are many others.

Prayer and/or meditation can effectively change the state of your brain as well. If you are not religious, it is worthwhile to learn how to meditate. If you are religious, talk to God when you get worried. Remember, God is not just up there to judge people and make them worry more, but to help them solve problems in the midst of their worries. But you must first look in God's direction.

We now have brain scans that show changes in the brain during meditation and prayer, as well as EEG tracings showing electrical differences. The brain goes into a focused state during prayer and/or meditation. These changes correlate with most of our measures of improved health, such as longevity and reduced incidence of illness. Extended worry subsides with extended prayer and/or meditation.

Reading a book, watching TV or a video, or even an activity as trivial as brushing your teeth can change your brain's physical state. Instead of sinking into the quicksand of worry, next time try brushing your teeth. This may sound perfectly ridiculous, but brushing your teeth provides a distraction, some physical stimulation, a structured activity, even a tiny bit of exercise. Before you dismiss it, give it a try!

The excitement of sexual activity certainly changes the state of your brain. Obviously, this is not always possible, but if it is by all means use it. Instead of saying, "I'm in a bad mood," consider the possibility that making love might change your mood.

In addition to love-making, simple physical touch can change the brain's state: a hand on your shoulder, an arm around your waist, a pat on your back, or, more elaborate touch, such as massage. Massage is a great treatment for worry. So is dancing.

Music can magically mollify worry. Combining it with exercise, in the form of dancing, is great, but music all by itself is one of the surest and oldest remedies for worry that we have. As the playwright William Congreve wrote in 1697, "Music has charms to soothe a savage breast, to soften rocks, or bend a knotted oak." Indeed, all the fine arts can calm the worried mind, but music, perhaps above all others, does it best. When we feel tied up in knots with worry, like Congreve's knotted oak, music can sometimes set us straight.

Finally, talking to another person can change the physical state of your brain. In the survey I conducted, talking to a friend ranked number one as people's favorite remedy for worry. Not only does talking to a friend provide the reassurance and connectedness that is so helpful in combating worry, but studies have shown that talking to another person actually changes what is happening in your brain at the physical level.

All of these techniques of changing the physical state of your brain can help dramatically if you use them regularly. The choice of which to use depends upon where you are and what is available. Some—such as silent prayer or regulated breathing—are almost always available. Others—such as sleep or sexual activity—are only available intermittently. But some simple methods are always available. The main point is to keep in mind the practical importance of changing the physical state of your brain when you feel worry getting out of hand, before you get so immobilized and depressed that you can't do it.

23 Reassurance and Connectedness

Reassurance is the safest, least expensive Band-Aid for worry that we have, but it is only a Band-Aid and does not solve any underlying problems. However, if there really is no underlying problem, which is often the case with excessive worriers, reassurance can be just what is needed.

Reassurance is related to a deeper kind of help, which I call connectedness. Of all the remedies that we have for worry, connectedness is probably the best and it costs nothing. What is connectedness? It is a feeling of being a part of something larger than yourself. In this chapter we look at both reassurance and connectedness.

Reassurance is a voice that says everything will be OK. The voice may come from within yourself. In fact, one of the goals for a severe worrier should be to learn how to reassure himself. But usually the reassuring voice comes from the outside. Children look for reassurance all the time, and the need for its comfort does not end with the advent of adulthood. Grown-ups need reassurance just as much as children do.

What is the best way to get reassurance? Ask for it. Just go up to whomever it is you want reassurance from and say, "I need some reassurance," or say, "I'm a little worried about this meeting I have tomorrow; do you think things will be OK?" or say, "Tell me you think this dress looks beautiful." There is no harm in explicitly asking for the words you want, and it is most efficient. If you desperately want to hear that the dress looks beautiful, don't take a chance by asking the more open-ended question, "How does this dress look on me?" If you are looking for the truth, then ask the open-ended question. But if you are looking for reassurance, ask for reassurance.

I mean this only partially tongue-in-cheek. It is an unfortunate fact that many worried people *cannot* make the simple statement, "I need some reassurance." Instead, they set up elaborate, Rube Goldberg-like contrived conversations, hoping and praying that what will emerge from the situation are a few words of solace or reassurance.

I believe that truth is overrated and reassurance is underrated in everyday life. Psychologists, philosophers, and scientists are all in search of the truth, which they deliver to mankind. But the average person does not usually want an unrelieved diet of truth. Too much truth can't be digested in one day. But you can't get too much reassurance.

Sighs, body language, moving of legs and feet—any of these might indicate a need for reassurance. But just as most people, adults anyway, can't ask effectively for reassurance, so, too, do most people have great difficulty in giving reassurance. Even though it is free, takes no work, and requires no special knowledge, reassurance is given easily by precious few people. Sometimes it is the folks who are most in need of reassurance who become the best at giving it.

If you are a worrier or live with a worrier or are close to one or work with one, you should learn about reassurance.

To ask for reassurance, be as simple and direct as you can possibly dare to be. Don't feel you must disguise your request as something altogether different. Some people, when they ask, "What time is it?" or, "May I please borrow your pen?" are actually screaming out for reassurance, but the request has had to pass through so many revisions in their minds, being amended, edited, reworded, and disguised, that it emerges from the lips utterly unrecognizable as a request for reassurance. When they get the reply, "It is six o'clock," or, "Here's my pen," they then fall into an anxious state, having not received what they had thought they were asking for, even though they did receive precisely the object of their request.

It makes for excellent theater, these internal rewordings that emerge as something totally different. Henry James or Virginia Woolf or Harold Pinter can beautifully depict conversations in which a character's urgent need for reassurance and comfort is neither spoken nor met, but electrifies the scene nonetheless. However, as far as real life goes, it is extremely unpleasant to want reassurance but be unable to ask for it.

Most people can learn how to do it, if they try. Just speak the words. For example:

"Tell me everything will be OK."

"Of course, things will be OK, honey."

"Are you sure?"

"I'm sure."

That four-sentence, eighteen-word conversation can save a party, a day, a business deal, even a marriage. It can also save hours of indirect conversation.

"Tell me this deal will work out."

"It will work out."

"Thanks."

Three sentences, twelve words. Said between the right two people, that conversation can assuage more worry than a year of psychotherapy.

You must learn not only how to ask for reassurance, but also from whom to ask it. Do not ask for reassurance from someone you know can't give it, at least until you have taught that person how. Some people spend a lifetime looking for reassurance from someone who simply can't deliver it—a distant father, for example, or a critical friend, or an overbearing boss. It is better to look for reassurance in places where you might find it.

Learning how to give reassurance is not hard. At least the words themselves are not hard. Sometimes developing the right attitude is hard because giving reassurance goes against the grain of many people. They were brought up not getting it, and as adults they do not naturally give it. They take a sort of Calvinistic stance, feeling that all reassurance must be earned, never just given, in order to count. Some people feel that only weak people need reassurance and so it is demeaning to give it. Some people feel that they are not qualified to give reassurance because they do not have all the facts or lack special training.

What these individuals fail to understand is that we have all earned the right to some reassurance simply by taking on the task of living another day. Reassurance is not a legal opinion. It is not going to go to court. It does not have to stand up under cross-examination. It need not take into account all the facts, nor need it be absolutely accurate. Reassurance is a little gift, the kind of gift everyone can use to get through a day or a life.

Reassurance is a pat on the back, a nod from across the street, a wink from a passing car, or a wave from the back of the bus. It is a hand placed over another hand, a squeeze on the shoulder, or a little hug on the way out the door. Reassurance is often not rational or even worded at all. It is an act of good faith, a statement of hope if not of belief. The funny, if not marvelous fact is that a bit of reassurance can become a self-fulfilling prophecy. If you believe your friend will fail but you reassure him anyway, he may begin to feel confident enough to succeed.

But what about false reassurance? You wouldn't want to reassure your friend if you *knew* he would fail owing, let's say, to your having knowledge of obstacles he was disregarding. In this instance, of course, you would point the obstacles out. You should never give blind reassurance if you have concrete information that could help, however negative the information might be.

Usually, however, you are being asked for something very simple. You are being asked for the goodness of your heart, not for a factual analysis. You are being asked for an affirmative nod or an encouraging word. Don't make it too complicated. Just smile and say, "Everything will be OK."

Some excessive worriers need excessive reassurance. If you are a worrier, you need to be careful not to burden your sources of reassurance with too many requests. No one, after all, is a bottomless pit. Try to reassure yourself as often as possible. If you can't, try to imagine what the reassuring person would say to you, what that person has said in the past in similar situations. Try to envision the person giving you the reassurance, before you come right out and ask for it. Not only will this keep the other person from depleting their supplies of reassurance, it will help you develop the technique of reassuring yourself, which is a very valuable skill.

Reassurance depends upon connectedness. If you are not connected to anyone or anyplace or anything, you can neither get nor give reassurance. Connectedness is the key to emotional health. Not only does it reduce worry, it improves one's sense of well-being in many other ways.

Connectedness is the deepest form of reassurance. It is not just a Band-Aid, but a transformative bond. The connected person derives sustaining reassurance from the connection itself; he doesn't need to ask for reassurance because it is always there, like an electrical current pumping through a plugged-in wire.

In states of toxic worry, an individual loses his sense of connectedness. He disengages from his supports. In deep worry, the individual feels alone, which only intensifies the worry. Toxic worry is like an acid that burns away the cables that connect an individual, psychologically, to his sources of strength, leaving him feeling alone. Worry at its most extreme is paranoia, and the truly paranoid person cannot connect at all.

The chronic worrier, if he does nothing else to help himself, can strive to develop connectedness in his life. But how?

I break down connectedness into six domains. If you focus on developing connectedness in each of these domains, you will find that not only will you worry less, but you will start feeling better about life in general.

The first kind of connectedness is the one we are all born into: familial connectedness. "Family values" has become such a hackneyed phrase that we might overlook how important family connections really are. As Robert Frost said, "Home is the place where when you have to go there they have to take you in." Family is where we start and where we will end. Attend to your family. Spend time together. Listen to each other. Play together. Eat dinner together. Discuss issues, argue, debate. The more connected you feel to your family, the stronger you will be.

The second kind of connectedness is historical connectedness, a feeling of being a part of history and time, of belonging to a tradition. It may be your family's tradition, your region's or your country's. But it is important to know that you are a part of a larger swing of history, that you belong to a movement greater than the movement of your own, single life.

The third kind of connectedness is social connectedness. This is made up of the ties people have with friends, neighbors, colleagues, and others they meet along the way. This kind of connectedness can be sustaining in times of stress and stimulating in times of leisure. Without it, children and adults alike feel lonely and isolated. Take the time to be with friends. Make them a priority.

The fourth kind of connectedness is connectedness to information and ideas. In this day of information overload, many people feel disconnected from the world of information and ideas. They feel intimidated by it or alienated from it. They do not know how to get in, so they get out. You can combat this by reading books, learning how to use a computer, and, most of all, by getting sufficient reassurance and instruction that you no longer feel *afraid* of the world of information and ideas.

The fifth kind of connectedness is connectedness to institutions and organizations. For children, this means school. For adults, it is where they work. It also includes clubs and other organizations people join. Sad to say, adult institutions—places of work—do not inspire much of a feeling of connectedness these days. In fact, they often inspire just the opposite. From downsizing to cost-cutting, the employee can feel nervous all the time. This tends to make him less productive, more caught up in office politics than thinking creatively about how to increase his output or invent new products. The more you can feel positively connected where you work, the better job you'll do and the happier you'll be.

The sixth kind of connectedness is connectedness to whatever is beyond knowledge, call it transcendent, spiritual, or religious connectedness. This includes feelings of being connected to nature as well as to whatever created nature. Spiritual connectedness can sustain you through the worst life can offer. But even if you do not have religious faith, the feeling of being connected to the world of nature and of space and of endless time can hold you still where you are and give you strength along the way.

Connectedness activates powerful healing forces we are only beginning to understand. Dr. David Spiegel reported one of the most dramatic demonstrations of the healing power of connectedness about ten years ago when he found that group meetings prolonged the lives of women suffering from cancer. A professor of psychiatry at Stanford, Spiegel had expected to find just the opposite result. But when he studied two groups of women who were suffering from end-stage metastatic breast cancer, both groups treated medically, but one group also afforded the chance to meet with each other to talk and commiserate, he found that the women who met together regularly lived twice as long as those who did not have the group meetings! Talking honestly with each other prolonged the lives of these women. The study has been replicated, and today remains one of the landmark findings on the power of interpersonal connectedness not only to improve emotional well-being but physical health as well.

If there is one remedy I would recommend above all others in combating worry, this is it: increase connectedness in your life. In doing so you will increase your feeling of strength and power and greatly reduce your sense of vulnerability. There is strength in numbers. United we stand.

Unfortunately, today's world conspires to reduce connectedness at every turn. The family splits apart. Extended families are so extended that the individual members may never see each other. Friends are too pressed for time to see each other. History and tradition are overlooked. Institutions and organizations betray people who have given them decades of loyal service. Information comes at people like water from a fire hose and blows them away. And the world of spirituality suffers from the snickers and disdain of a highly scientific age.

What is to be done? The good news is that connectedness is free. All you have to do is make it a priority. When you get up in the morning, instead of just trying to do your job and survive, try to address connectedness as you pass through your day. Connect with people. Learn about your town's history. Eat dinner with your family. Read aloud to your children. Meet your neighbors and maybe have them over. Call your uncle in Spokane. Talk to your child's schoolteacher about something other than a problem at school. Pray or meditate. These are just a few of the scores of practical steps anyone can take— totally free of charge—to develop connectedness in his life. Over time, connectedness brings with it peace of mind, while disconnectedness brings worry and depression. Connectedness brings strength.

24   Of Golf, God, and Letting Go

How do you put aside irrational worry—worry that makes no sense, but hurts you and haunts you every day? This has been the main question of this book.

If you play golf or if you believe in God, you know that what is most important to both golf and religious belief is also what is most difficult: keeping your faith. How can you keep your faith in God in a world so riddled with injustice, evil, and uncertainty? How can you continue to play golf in the face of the many errors and bad shots you usually make? While one is a profound question and the other a trivial one, they both get at the same psychological dilemma: how can anyone believe in a good outcome in the face of past, and almost certainly future, disappointments?

I think the worrier can find a way by taking a lesson both from religious believers and from experienced golfers. I mean no disrespect in combining the sacred with the secular here; instead I offer both to sug-

gest that there is a psychology common to both believers and nonbe-
lievers.

The lesson both God and golf teach is to *let go.* To keep faith let go
of control. Both the believer and the golfer have learned that a grander
scheme will take over if they can let it.

The best golf shots are hit unconsciously. You simply step up to the
ball and let fly. Sure, you have taken lessons and practiced in order to
learn the basic swing. But after that, you do your best if you leave all
the lesson sheets at home and put all the things that can go wrong in
your swing out of your mind. There are almost as many things that can
go wrong in a golf swing as there are things that can go wrong in life.
If, as you address the ball, you try to keep all of them in mind and control each one, you will hit a bad shot for sure. If, on the other hand,
when you address the ball you put all these problems out of your mind
and instead put faith in your swing, letting the club do its work, then
you may hit a good shot, even a great one.

Similarly, if you can give up your worries to God, after you have
practiced and prepared for life, then you may do well.

In both cases I say "may," because there is no guarantee.

The people who worry the least usually have some sort of faith.
They believe in God, or in nature, or in Buddha, or in the scientific
method, or in their swing. They have learned how to let go of the need
for total control.

How? By believing in something greater than themselves. "What is
the antidote to worry?" I asked Louise Conant, associate rector at my
church.

"Hope," she replied.

"Where does hope come from?" I asked her.

"From faith," was her reply.

"What do you do if you don't have faith?" I asked.

"Pray," she answered. "It will come."

"What if it doesn't?" I asked.

Louise smiled. We were sitting on the Cambridge Common the
Sunday morning of the church picnic. This was not perhaps the time

to be asking these bald questions, especially since Louise had just given a sermon in which she told us that many church members ask her what they should do with their doubts and uncertainties regarding God and life. "How should I know?" had been her provocative reply in the sermon, and I expected her to say that to me now. But she didn't. She just smiled at me, as if to say, or so I thought, "It is OK that you have doubts, so do I. I will stay with you, but I cannot resolve your doubts for you; still I love you and so does God." This is what I read into her smile. Maybe that smile is just a rehearsed gesture she uses whenever she is backed into a tough question, but I don't think so.

This is where the rubber meets the road when it comes to assuaging worry. You will transform and contain your worries if you can put faith in what is wordless, believe in what is beyond knowledge, rely on your golf club, just swing and let go.

Easy for you to say, comes a bitter reply from a voice outside. What if you have been betrayed by life, what if you are down and out, what if you have nowhere to go? What if you have nothing left to "let go" of, except worry and fear? What if your only driving force is a wish to take revenge?

The wish for vengeance can become a lifelong worry. If a person has been wronged, and deeply so, he may turn his hurt into an active desire for retribution. He may find himself fantasizing scenes of revenge, imagining exactly how he will take out his fury upon whomever hurt him.

In trivial ways this happens every day. Someone cuts us off in traffic and we drive the next ten miles steaming at the driver of the other car, imagining how we would like to ram into him with an armored truck, or cut up his tires while he's parked, or drive him off the road into a ditch. On the other hand, if we are not given to violent fantasies, we rage inside against rudeness and protest most vehemently—to some judge we have conjured up—against the rank injustice of the other driver's behavior, how he deserves to be punished, suspended from the road, fined, and made to feel ashamed of what he did. We argue our case in our minds with the full flourish of a trial lawyer pleading the case of his lifetime. Then, gradually, our anger abates, and we drive on, thinking about some more serene topic, until the next rude driver intercepts our path.

In these trivial scenes, the wish for revenge is fleeting and self-contained. Once in a while traffic vengeance does indeed explode in crazy dimensions, but most of the time it is contained within drivers' minds and sealed within their cars. Traffic makes for one of the most common battlefields of everyday life, and the wish among drivers to get back at tormentors on the highway is almost universal. This common wish, of course, does not turn into a lifetime of worry, but deeper hurt can make you spend your whole life wanting to get even.

It is painful to live with an active wish for revenge. Once you take that desire to heart for any length of time, once you let the desire for revenge take root, you find that you cannot let it go. You may want to forgive, or at least to forget, but you find that you can't. The wish for vengeance becomes like a note that has to be played to complete the chord; your mind cannot rest until you hear its sound.

Such a rooted wish for vengeance can become an abiding worry, a preoccupation like any other worry. It will interrupt your good times; it will keep you awake at night; it will prevent you from ever relaxing completely. Until vengeance is taken, you feel cannot rest easy. Unless you find a better way. Unless you trust in your swing. Unless you can find faith—in something greater than yourself.

Medical literature and popular magazines are replete with studies of the formative, healing power of faith. A 1995 study at Dartmouth showed that patients who drew strength from religious faith survived open-heart surgery at three times the rate of those who did not. A review of thirty years of research on blood pressure shows that church-goers have lower blood pressure, by 5 mm/Hg, than nonchurchgoers. Many studies have found lower rates of depression and illnesses related to anxiety among those who have a belief in God. There have been studies that show that people who attend church regularly die from coronary-artery disease at half the rate of those who never attend, even taking into account smoking and socioeconomic factors. These statistics are quoted from *Time* magazine's cover story on faith and healing of June 24, 1996.

In that same issue of *Time* I found a short essay that took my breath away. By Martin Kaplan, a former speechwriter for Walter Mondale and currently a Hollywood executive as well as a screenwriter and producer, the essay was about his discovering God. "The God I have found," he wrote, "is common to Moses and Muhammad, to Buddha and Jesus. It is known to every mystic tradition. . . . I used to think the soul was a metaphor. Now I know there is a God. . . ."

He did not offer any evidence, as I would have thought he would have to. He simply implied that faith came to him as revealed truth. What took my breath away was that I had known Martin Kaplan—from a distance—when he was a year ahead of me as an undergraduate at Harvard. He was, as they say, *a brain*. He was THE brain in his class, and since he lived in my dorm or what was called house, his reputation cast a shadow, or a light, onto my life. Since at Harvard the intellect was tantamount to God, Marty Kaplan was a god. Not only was he a *summa* in molecular biology, he was also as quick as greased lightning with a put-down or a witty remark. When it came to brains, this guy had it all. But he seemed to use his brains not in the service of God but in the service of skepticism, wit, and scientific proof. That was the Harvard way; indeed it is the modern way. As he said in his *Time* essay, "I'm the last guy you'd figure would go spiritual on you."

But here he was going spiritual! More and more these days the previously skeptical are discovering the power of faith. Just in terms of numbers, most people believe in the power of prayer and most people believe in God. However, in my own circle, in the Boston area, and in many other circles nationwide, faith in God is still a little dicey to own up to. Maybe it shouldn't be.

However, the point of this chapter is not to promote God, or golf, but to point out that the worried mind may find strength in faith, not as an opiate or a duller of the senses, but as a potent stabilizer, a practical solution that works beyond human knowledge and control.

How does faith work in life? There are as many answers to this question as there are people of faith. I am going to choose one person, Janet Ardoyno, to use as an example here. I met Janet in Texas, when I was giving a lecture there in 1993. She sat down next to me during a break and told me about one of her children. That conversation began a relationship that has lasted to this day. The way she has dealt with the extraordinary burdens of her life is through her faith in God. Her faith provides her with a matrix of principles and prescriptions through which she passes all that happens to her.

Janet thinks of herself as pretty ordinary, certainly no big shakes. But she is a big deal to the people who know her. This woman has lived with pain and danger her whole life, but she laughs it off, never considering her plight as anything special.

Now in her mid-forties, Janet started her life by almost dying. She had open-heart surgery at thirteen months, which at the time was a brand-new procedure. In second grade she had to have open-heart surgery again, and throughout high school she was in and out of the hospital due to episodes of heart failure related to abnormal heartbeats. She had intended to go to medical school, and she was getting good enough grades for this to be a possibility, but her heart condition made this impossible. So she became a social worker instead. During those high school years she developed a strong faith in God.

At age twenty-five she married David Ardoyno. David works for UPS, while Janet works for, well, just about everybody else. She is active in her home town of Abilene, setting up the "Make a Difference Day" so successfully that she had 40,000 people participate last time around and was invited to the White House for special recognition, and she is active throughout the state of Texas promoting knowledge about physical disabilities as well as learning disabilities.

But her children come first. She has three, two boys and a girl. Despite her bad heart she was able to have her two boys on her own. Then, although Janet had to have open-heart surgery for a third time to replace her mitral valve, she adopted her third child, Emily. Emily and Justin, the older boy, have ADD (attention deficit disorder). And Jonathan, the middle child, has cerebral palsy as well as cortical blindness, but he is able still to get around in a wheelchair he operates himself. He and his mom travel around the state giving talks to parents and children about how to cope. They laugh a lot in the talks they give, and they make other people laugh and cry and, most of all, take heart.

During the writing of this book Janet suffered a heart attack, but she recovered soon enough to organize still another Make a Difference Day in Abilene. I asked her how she did it. She answered, as she always has, "The main reason I have been able to get through my life is that I have a strong faith in God and prayer."

If you don't believe in God, Janet's faith may seem of little use to you. But I think we all can learn from Janet, and from the others like her who have such strong faith. We can learn that belief itself, belief of any kind, can stabilize the worried mind. Janet's faith did not stop her from worrying, but it kept her from capsizing.

She was able to let go of control. "One of the things that has helped me through the years," she said to me, "is understanding that God's timing is not always what mine is, and when I had that belief, then I didn't fret as much about why something was or wasn't happening when I wanted it to. That's not to say that I didn't ever worry or fret. But my belief really did help to put things into perspective."

Most people believe in something, whether they know it or not. Nature. Their families. The scientific method. The cause of freedom and equality. Whatever your belief might be, invoking that belief can strengthen you in times of worry. The stronger your belief, the more it can strengthen you when you need it.

How can a belief in the scientific method give you strength? By providing some solid ground. As Samuel Johnson wrote, "The pleasures of sudden wonder are soon exhausted, and the mind can only repose upon the stability of truth." The stability of truth provides a certain kind of comfort.

These are big words, but we need big words for these highest of stakes. When life is at its worst, and we're hanging by a thread, where do we turn? To a friend, our families, God, or where?

If you have a belief system, it provides a matrix for you through which you can pass the unexplainable. It does not provide answers always, but it provides a method, a means of making some sense of the ordeal.

Coming back to the secular analogy of the golf swing, even if you hit bad shot after bad shot, you come back to your swing as your basic belief. You may tinker with your swing, practice it over and over, to get in shape for the big match. But when that day comes, you put aside your preparation and just swing. The more you let go, the better you do.

What is the best swing? Who knows? But at least you can ask, seek, maybe even find. If you ask yourself that question in advance, you can prepare for the matches to come. Whether we know it or not, we are preparing all the time. Each time we say goodbye, we are practicing how to die.

25 Medication

*What to Use, When to Use It, and When
Not to Use It at All*

I once treated a woman, let's call her Jane, who came to see me because she was feeling depressed and worried. She was a lovely woman,
tall, elegant, olive-skinned, and trim. But she also exuded an unmis-
takable quality of vulnerability from the moment she sat down, even in
the way she shook my hand at the door. She had dealt with worry for
most of her life, but recently it had become too much for her.

We talked about her life, her past, and what was going on right
now. We explored the options and made a plan. She improved much
more dramatically than she had thought possible. The results she got
were so favorable that she wanted others to know. She asked me if she
could write a brief account of what happened to her so others could
benefit from it. Here is her story in her own words:

> I experienced a sudden and prolonged separation from my mother
> when I was a young child. Although I was eventually reunited with
> her, I could no longer trust that the world was a safe, secure, and

predictable place. I thought that I somehow must have caused the problems which led to my mother being separated from the family. In a strange way this thought was comforting because it allowed me to think that I had some control at a time when I must have felt completely helpless and powerless as my world was falling apart.

I began to worry. My worries were relatively mild and unintrusive at first. Good times and good feelings were tempered by fears of enjoying myself too much. If I enjoyed myself too much I risked setting myself up to be even more devastated when disaster would inevitably strike again. My worries did not stop me from pursuing and attaining my goals of earning college degrees, having a career, marrying, and having children, but they kept me from feeling truly happy and from ever enjoying a sustained sense of well-being.

I worried more when I became a parent. I worried that I would inadvertently do something which could hurt my children or which could result in me losing them, or in them losing me. I did not worry that I would intentionally harm them; rather I worried that the pesticides in the food I fed them or the radiation in the X-rays which I gave permission to the doctors to give them would contaminate them and later result in the development of some dread disease. I became increasingly afraid to fly in airplanes, and I eventually stopped flying altogether. I worried that flying for happy occasions such as vacations or visits to loved ones made me and my family particularly vulnerable and at risk of being harmed.

Aside from experiencing anxiety mentally and emotionally, anxiety and worry have at times affected me physically as well. I have never had a full-blown panic attack but when I have been especially worried my heart has beaten faster and I have felt jittery and light-headed. Luckily I have experienced this physical distress infrequently and for very brief periods of time.

Being organized and neat helped to mitigate my worries and calm myself down somewhat. I distracted myself from worries by becoming engrossed in projects and activities. I also tried to alleviate my worry by mulling thoughts around in my head. I was hoping at least to achieve an illusion of having control over events in life which are not controlled easily if at all.

As my family's dependence on me for emotional and financial security increased, my worries intensified. I was especially concerned about suddenly losing the security which I had so painstakingly established in my family over the years. Around issues which triggered my anxiety, I exaggerated the significance of insignificant problems. In my mind, hypothetical problems became real problems which were—no doubt—destined to materialize. I expended and wasted a great deal of my precious energy worrying about bad events which never happened.

The trouble came when I began to have real problems to worry about. My worst fear was becoming a reality. Bad things were in fact happening in my life and I was losing ground trying to control and cope with the problems. I ran out of fingers—and toes for that matter—to plug up the holes in the dike where the water was bursting through. I worried so much that I became depressed. I felt an overwhelming sense of horror and powerlessness as my world again seemed to be crumbling before my eyes. No matter how hard I tried I was not able to solve my problems in the ways that had always worked well enough for me in the past. I knew that I could not give up. My family depended on me to be there for them, and so I realized that I *had* to find a way of stopping myself from sinking further into the abyss of despair.

I knew that I had to get professional help. I was not separated from my mother as a child because of medical illness or divorce, but because she became extremely depressed and was unable to live at home or take care of her children. I did not want the same thing to happen to me that happened to my mother. I acted quickly. I consulted with Dr. Hallowell, who prescribed Prozac. At his suggestion, I also began to see a psychotherapist and to exercise daily. I felt good about myself for having the courage to know what I needed to do and to do it.

My response to Prozac was dramatic. Within several weeks I stopped feeling depressed. I expected this to happen. I did not, however, expect that I would also stop worrying, but I did. Prozac did not change my personality, it did not alter my state of consciousness, and it did not solve the problems I was contending with in my life. Prozac simply enabled me to be myself without being burdened by excessive worry. I began to expect that problems could be resolved, and I resolved them. I became stronger each time I remained calm and maintained a positive attitude while dealing with stressful situations. My outlook on life in general became more optimistic. Because I was no longer wasting time and energy worrying unnecessarily, I became more energetic. I spent more time doing fun things with my family and enjoying life. I am now better able to face life's challenges with enthusiasm and confidence.

Psychotherapy is helping me to understand and to work on important issues. Exercise helps me achieve a sense of mastery and well-being through physical rather than only mental means. I find that exercising outdoors, where the beauty of nature can be experienced and appreciated, provides me with an atmosphere which is exceptionally conducive to maintaining a balanced perspective.

As Jane points out, medication is not the whole answer to worry, but it can be a dramatically effective part of the treatment. The advances we have made over the past fifty years in developing medications to treat toxic forms of worry mark a major breakthrough in the treatment of human distress.

While many people are rightly concerned that we must take care not to overuse medications in the treatment of worry or any other emotional distress, still we should be glad that we have the option of using them when they should be used. Jane's story is just one of millions of examples of people whose lives have improved dramatically, without significant negative side effects, thanks to the availability of the right medication.

In the chapter on Samuel Johnson, I commented that one form of treatment we have now that Johnson did not have back in the eighteenth century that might have helped him more than anything else was medication. None of the medications we use to treat emotional problems is a panacea or cure-all, and they all can be dangerous if they are misused. But when used properly they can ease human suffering safely and effectively.

Unfortunately, these medications are widely misunderstood. Sometimes people talk about medication as if it were a political or religious tenet, instead of a medical tool. People sometimes ask me if I am in favor of or opposed to medication, as if medication were a candidate up for election. My answer is that I am neither in favor nor opposed. Instead, I emphatically endorse the *proper* use of medication. I am a radical moderate; I believe radically in preserving a balanced perspective. Medications should be used when they are indicated, and they should not be used when they are not indicated. It is that simple. In the case of most medications the average citizen needs professional guidance to know when a given medication is indicated and when it is not. The key, therefore, to the proper use of medication is not political rhetoric but scientific knowledge and competent advice.

What are the facts about the various medications we use to treat worry?

For centuries the main "medication" readily available to treat worry was alcohol. In fact, alcohol is an excellent antianxiety agent—over the short term. But over the long term, its toxic side effects are horrendous. Happily, we now have many safe medications to treat worry, and they are quite effective. However, they cannot be used indefinitely, and they do not cure the problem.

The most common group of medications currently used to treat worry and anxiety are the benzodiazepines. Introduced in the 1960s as muscle relaxants, the benzodiazepines soon became the mainstay of the medication management of anxiety. Most people have heard of Valium (generic name, diazepam), but there are now many other benzodiazepines as well.

Recently, medical scientists discovered chemical receptor sites for benzodiazepines in the brain, which are linked to the receptor sites for a certain neurotransmitter that occurs naturally in the body called GABA (gamma-amino butyric acid). GABA is a neurotransmitter for inhibitory neurons. There are two kinds of neurons in the brain, excitatory and inhibitory. The inhibitory neurons help damp down excess activity in the brain, activity that an individual subjectively can perceive as anxiety or worry. It makes sense that inhibitory neurons would play a role in reducing anxiety, as anxiety is a form of overstimulation. The anxious, worried brain needs to put on the brakes. Substances such as the benzodiazepines that bolster the work of GABA reduce anxiety by promoting the inhibitory circuits to damp down excessive stimulation. (Incidentally, alcohol does this too.) The key action is the damping down of excessive excitatory activity in the brain.

If the benzodiazepines work so well to reduce worry and anxiety by shutting down an alarm system in the brain that is going off too quickly, why do they not constitute a cure for excessive worry? First, because there are side effects; second, because their action is not permanent; and third, because medications alone do not do the whole job.

As to side effects, some of the benzodiazepines can be habit-forming, even addictive, and can be associated with severe symptoms of withdrawal even after just a month's use. Some interact dangerously with alcohol. Some are sedating. Some cause loss of coordination and dexterity. Some impair memory and concentration. At higher doses some can be fatal by suppressing respiration. When they are discontinued they must be carefully tapered to avoid dangerous withdrawal effects. These are not trivial drugs and must be monitored closely by a physician.

The benzodiazepines are used best as part of a short-term intervention, to help an individual get stabilized, as he is learning new methods of dealing with worry and anxiety that do not involve medication. I have stressed the importance of these nonmedication approaches to worry—methods such as reassurance and connectedness, exercise, increased structure, organization and rational intervention, proper diet and sleep, meditation and/or prayer, cognitive-behavioral therapy, psychoanalytically oriented psychotherapy, and other forms of counseling.

But as the individual is learning these nonmedication approaches, medications can provide immediate help. As long as you do not turn to them as the total solution, they are potent allies. The benzodiazepines are fast-acting and are easily tolerated by most people. They *can* be used long-term (i.e., six months and longer) to treat chronic states of worry and anxiety, but this use is controversial and must be carefully monitored and evaluated regularly for risks and benefits. Benzodiazepines should never be prescribed without also providing education, support, and advice on how to learn and master the nonmedication approaches to treatment.

If given properly, a benzodiazepine can break a spasm of anxiety in a short period of time. It can open the way for other, nonmedication methods to be mastered. We now have some thirty years of clinical experience with these medications, as well as the knowledge gained from a great deal of formal research. There is a wide range of benzodiazepines for a physician to choose from, some shorter-acting than others, some more sedating than others, but they all share the common benefit of prompt anxiety reduction.

There are other antianxiety agents besides the benzodiazepines. The barbiturates, for example, were the mainstay of the pharmacological treatment of anxiety before the benzodiazepines were introduced. This class of drugs includes medications such as secobarbital (Seconal) and phenobarbital. Now these medications are largely reserved for surgical anesthesia and for the treatment of seizures.

There is now in addition another, new antianxiety agent called buspirone (BuSpar) that has been found to be helpful in anxiety reduction. It appears to work well, although not as well as the benzodiazepines, but it has fewer side effects. Especially advantageous is that it is not particularly sedating, nor has it any abuse or addictive potential to speak of. However, many clinicians have been disappointed by its general lack of potency.

The antidepressants also play an important role in the treatment of worry. The antidepressants are divided into different groups: the tricyclic antidepressants, such as imipramine (Tofranil); the selective serotonin reuptake inhibitors or SSRIs, such as fluoxetine (Prozac); the atypical antidepressants, such as bupropion (Wellbutrin); and the monoamine oxidase inhibitors (MAOIs), such as phenelzine (Nardil).

The introduction of the tricyclic antidepressant, imipramine, by Donald Klein in 1962 to treat panic attacks marked a major advance in medicine. It opened the doors for the ensuing decades of spectacular progress in the field of psychopharmacology—the study of how medications affect the brain—and Klein remains a major contributor to the field as well as one of its pioneers.

When they were first introduced, the tricyclics were regarded with great skepticism, and Klein was dismissed as a heretic by more psychoanalytically oriented colleagues. How could you treat an emotional problem with a drug? people asked. A common assumption at the time was that panic, worry, and anxiety were the result of unconscious conflict that needed to be talked out. Medication might simply cover the conflict over, leaving the unconscious still armed to attack again once the medication wore off. Medication was viewed as a means of evading the "real" problem.

However, Klein cogently argued against the ruling orthodoxy of the day. He argued that sometimes the "real" problem is biochemical, not just psychological. Therefore, it makes sense to treat the problem physiologically, i.e., with a drug. The debate raged for a while, but as doctors and patients alike began to see the remarkable benefits of medications, the tricyclic antidepressants took their place as one of the most effective tools available in the treatment of panic attacks, as well as in the treatment of depression. Now the tricyclics are used to treat a number of other conditions as well, such as refractory headaches, bedwetting, and attention deficit disorder. How can one kind of drug be effective in so many different conditions? We don't know for sure, but it is probably because these conditions are all influenced by the same neurotransmitters and these are the ones that the tricyclics act upon.

This debate of whether it is proper to use medication to treat emotional problems still rages. Dr. Peter Kramer wrote about it eloquently in his book, *Listening to Prozac* (Viking Penguin, 1994). He pointed out that many people feel a kind of gut-level reluctance to resort to medication as a means of treating their mental state. They think of it almost as a form of cheating, as if it were immoral, or at least against nature's way. Kramer dubbed this attitude "psychopharmacological Calvinism," aptly capturing the internal conflict medication can spawn in many individuals.

To my way of thinking, the most sensible approach is to regard medication as one possible component of therapy, neither a cure-all nor a forbidden fruit.

Beyond the tricyclics, many other antidepressants have been developed since Klein offered his first report. By far the most famous now are the SSRIs, such as Prozac and Zoloft. These medications, which increase the amount of serotonin available in the brain, have been so widely used that my own personal physician speculated one day,

"Maybe the whole country has some kind of genetic serotonin deficiency!"

The fact is that the SSRIs are very good medications for dealing with ruminative worry. For people who brood and fret needlessly and endlessly, an SSRI can break the cycle. As the ruminating subsides, usually the individual feels less depressed and becomes more effective in his life. This is why these medications can seem to change a person in as fundamental way as Prozac changed Jane, the woman whose story was given at the start of this chapter. However, this change is not mind-altering so much as it is mind-healing. Ruminations are like severe headaches. If they go away, you can feel like a new person, although you are not in fact a different person at all. You are just the healthy version of yourself.

An SSRI can sometimes restore a ruminative worrier to health. However, the worrier should not stop there, but should go on to master the nonmedication approaches to worry we have already spoken of.

The SSRIs have become the first choice in panic disorder. The SSRIs have also been found to be helpful in obsessive-compulsive disorder (OCD), although most people still consider the tricyclic clomipramine (Anafranil) to be the medication of first choice for OCD. Interestingly enough, clomipramine is a tricyclic that also acts on the serotonin system, as do the SSRIs—so it makes sense that both clomipramine and the SSRIs would be useful in OCD. How do you decide which one to use? The track record for clomipramine is better than the SSRIs, but its side effects are worse. Therefore it makes sense to start with clomipramine, but if the side effects are intolerable to switch to an SSRI.

The atypical antidepressant Wellbutrin is a good second-choice medication for both depression and attention deficit disorder, but it is not particularly helpful in treating panic disorder. The side effects of Wellbutrin are few, except for the dire, rare side effect of seizures. If an individual has a history of seizures, Wellbutrin should be avoided; otherwise most doctors feel it is safe to use.

The monoamine oxidase inhibitors (MAOIs, such as Nardil) are a class of antidepressants unto themselves. More widely used in Great Britain than in the United States, the MAOIs are gaining in popularity here, particularly in the treatment of social phobia, refractory depression, and other states in which fear of rejection plays a prominent part, such as post-traumatic stress disorder. For example, some people have the symptom of insecurity so severely that they cannot function day in and day out without constantly worrying about who likes them and who doesn't, who is rejecting them and who isn't. This is called "rejection sensitivity." For people who are highly rejection-sensitive, an MAOI can make a big difference. It is intriguing that a symptom that sounds as purely "psychological" as sensitivity to rejection should respond well to a chemical intervention—but it does.

The reason the MAOIs haven't been used as widely in the United States as in Britain may be because of the potential side effects. If you are taking an MAOI, you have to comply with a diet that restricts you from eating all foods high in the amino acid tyramine, such as aged cheese, red wine, and a number of other less common foods. The diet is not exceedingly difficult to follow, but if you forget and eat one of the forbidden foods, your blood pressure may shoot up. This can result in having a stroke, or even dying. Obviously, death is the worst of all "side effects." However, it can easily be avoided simply by following the prescribed diet.

A final class of medications that are useful in treating various states of worry are the beta-blockers. These medications were originally introduced to treat high blood pressure and heart disease. However, it was soon discovered that they effectively blocked certain physical symptoms of anxiety, such as tremor, palpitations, sweating, and the feeling of nervousness. The beta-blockers, such as propranolol (Inderal), have become popular among people who fear public speaking. Taking a low dose of Inderal an hour or so before giving a speech can curtail many of the anxious symptoms public speaking so often induces. Beta-blockers can also be helpful in combating other kinds of performance anxiety, such as stage fright or the anxiety that may accompany giving a recital, or even bowling competitively.

Beta-blockers, as all medications, have some side effects. They cannot be used in people who have asthma, as they can cause bronchospasm, a tightening of the lungs. They can also lead to a lowering of heart rate and blood pressure so, especially at higher doses, they must be carefully monitored. Beta-blockers may also precipitate depression, so they should only be used under medical supervision.

Although not antianxiety agents, the stimulant medications, such as methylphenidate (Ritalin), can greatly diminish the excessive worry that often accompanies attention deficit disorder (ADD). If excessive worry is a chief symptom of an individual's ADD, a trial of Ritalin may significantly reduce the unnecessary worrying. If it does not, an SSRI would make a good second choice.

The following table summarizes the more common kinds of worry for which medications may be helpful. Bear in mind that these medications are never a cure, but only a potentially useful component of therapy. The abbreviations used in the table are as follows:

BZ = benzodiazepines, such as diazepam (Valium)

BP = buspirone (Bu Spar)

TCA = tricyclic antidepressant, such as imipramine (Tofranil)

MAOI = monoamine oxidase inhibitor, such as phenelzine (Nardil)

SSRI = selective serotonin reuptake inhibitor, such as fluoxetine (Prozac), sertraline (Zoloft), or fluvoxamine (Luvox)

Beta = beta-blocker, such as propranolol (Inderal)

Clom = clomipramine (Anafranil)

Stim = stimulant medication such as methylphenidate (Ritalin)

KIND OF WORRY	RECOMMENDED MEDICATIONS
Panic disorder	SSRI or TCA, particularly imipramine; MAOI, particularly phenelzine
Social phobia	MAOI
Generalized anxiety disorder	BZ or TCA; BP
Obsessive-compulsive disorder	Clom or SSRI, i.e., Prozac or Luvox

Post-traumatic stress disorder	immediate: BZ; later on: TCA or SSRI or MAOI
Depression	SSRI or TCA or MAOI
Excessive ruminations	SSRI
Rejection-sensitivity	MAOI
Attention deficit disorder	Stim or TCA
Performance anxiety	Beta

This table does not mention all the classes of medications that have been tried for each condition, just the most commonly used. The fact is that all of the medications mentioned have been tried at one time or another for all of the different anxiety syndromes described! The whole field of psychopharmacology is still at the trial-and-error stage. This makes treatment frustrating at times, as we do not have enough data to predict accurately which medication will produce what result for which patient. We have learned a great deal, enough to have determined what are called the drugs of "first choice" for most of the syndromes described. However, when the first choices don't work, an individual may find unexpected relief from another medication. We simply do not understand the brain well enough to be able to predict with certainty which medication will work when and which will not.

So don't give up too soon! You may be just one medication away from finding what you need. On the other hand, don't think there necessarily will be a medication that will help you. Sometimes there is not. Let your physician be your guide.

26 Fifty Tips on the Management of Worry Without Using Medication

Thereare probably as many tips in common folklore for dealing with worry as there are for treating hiccups. However, as with proofs of the existence of God, one can never have enough. Many of the tips below will have been presented already in connection with one of the case examples or in discussion of a particular syndrome.

These tips are intended to be practical. They should work. If, as the warning labels on the medication bottles say, your symptoms persist, you should consult your physician. However, most of the time a physician's assistance will not be needed. If you take the task of "brain management" seriously, you'll be surprised how much tips like these that follow can help.

1. Separate out toxic worry from good worry. Remember that good worry amounts to planning. You need to plan. Don't get so extreme in trying to wipe out worry that you wipe out the worrying you really must do. Toxic worry is the enemy, not good worry. Toxic worry is unnecessary, repetitive, unproductive, paralyzing, frightening, and in general life-defeating worry.

2. Get the facts. Base worry on reality, rather than on a terrifying fantasy your imagination has concocted. As Samuel Johnson said, "Shun fancied ills." Do you remember how many of your worries as a child were based on misinformation? The same is true for an adult! The problems that reality provides are serious enough without adding to them in your imagination.

3. Exercise at least every other day. Exercise helps prevent toxic worry. It reduces the background noise or anxiety the brain accumulates during the average day. Exercise is one of the best treatments for worry we have.

4. Develop connectedness in as many different ways as you can. Connectedness refers to a feeling of being a part of something larger than yourself. It prevents worry. I think of connectedness in terms of six different domains. First, there is familial connectedness, the kind we are born into. Second, there is historical connectedness, the connection between the individual and the past. Third, there is social connectedness, or the connections to one's friends, neighbors, and colleagues. Fourth, there is connectedness to information and ideas, the feeling of being at home with the very wide and complex world of what is known and thought. Fifth, there is connectedness to institutions and organizations, one's feeling of belonging to where one works, plays, or learns. Finally, sixth, there is connectedness to what is beyond knowledge, call it religious or transcendent connectedness, a sense of being a part of nature, or held in the hands of God. The more you develop and increase your feelings of connectedness in all these six domains, the less you will suffer from toxic kinds of worry, and the happier and healthier you will be.

5. Get reassurance. Have a network of people on whom you can depend to give you reassurance. Don't ask for reassurance from someone you know won't give it. Don't show your poems to someone who hates poetry. The only reason for even mentioning this obvious advice is that many people are oblivious to this simple piece of good sense and spend their whole lives trying to get reassurance from precisely the wrong people. Many other people never dare to ask for reassurance. But if you don't ask for it, you may not find it when you need it.

6. Analyze the problem and take corrective action. This is what non-worriers do all the time. They can't understand why worriers don't do it also. The nonworrier will simply say, "I fix what I can, then I put the rest out of my mind." It is awfully hard for worriers to put anything out of their minds. However, one good way to start is by taking whatever corrective action you can think of. Sit down with a spouse or friend and ask, "Now, what concrete corrective action can I take to reduce my worries on this matter?" It is better to do this with someone because alone you'll be more likely to become anxious and quit.

7. Attack your worry; don't let it attack you. There is a maxim from baseball which says, Play the ground ball; don't let the ground ball play you. This piece of advice may be lost on people who are not athletically inclined or who have never played baseball or softball, but the proper fielding of a ground ball is a wonderfully instructive skill all people can learn from. A ground ball is a baseball hit by a batter that bounces very fast along the ground. The fielder's job is to stop the ball so that he can throw it to first base before the batter can reach there. In order to make the throw in time, the fielder needs to field the ball "cleanly," that is without bobbling it or letting it bounce of his chest. The novice fielder's first instinct in fielding a ground ball is to back up on the ball and try to predict the bounces as the ball skips toward him. This is called letting the ball play you. You are at the mercy of the unpredictable hops the ball can take. You naturally tense up and worry, *Can I field this ball or is it going to get past me?* This is a disastrous attitude to have in fielding a ground ball. You will likely kick the ball or miss it altogether. Instead, what you should do is play the ball, rather than letting it play you. You should charge toward the ball as it speeds toward you. Then you will not overthink the problem of how to field it; you will simply act. You will grab the ball before you give your worry-center a chance to think too much and inhibit you from successfully fielding it. This principle is, in my opinion, a great key to the successful management of worry and of decision-making in general. You do better if you attack a problem, rather than letting it attack you.

8. Ask for advice. Part of attacking a problem is being able to ask for help and advice. We need more than just reassurance in dealing with our worries. We need solutions and often we do not have sufficient information to come up with the best solutions. Therefore, it is good to know whom to ask or where to look.

9. Do what is right. This is obvious advice but it is worth mentioning because so many of us behave as if it were not important. The fact is, thank goodness, that most of us are equipped with consciences. If we do wrong, our consciences will give us a hard time. Some people have no consciences and are very dangerous, but they are not common. Some people have hypertrophied consciences, and they become paralyzed with guilt over even the slightest misdeed. But most of us are in the middle. And the simple but hard fact is that if we do wrong over and over again we will not be happy. We will worry and suffer inside, no matter how happy we may pretend to be.

10. Pray or meditate. If you are religious, pray every day, even several times a day. You can pray anywhere—in the shower, as you drive, in a boring meeting, on an airplane, or standing in a line. Talk to God. This is good for your soul and it can make you worry less. If you are not religious, meditate. You can meditate anywhere, too. If you don't know how, read Dr. Herbert Benson's classic book, *The Relaxation Response* (William Morrow, 1975), or some other book on meditation. Prayer and meditation help us keep things in perspective. They calm our minds.

11. Sleep properly. Shakespeare wrote that sleep "knits up the raveled sleeve of care." Lack of sleep can make you irritable, distracted, and prone to useless and destructive worrying. What is the right amount to sleep to avoid toxic worry? There is no one schedule to fit everyone. Pay attention to what your body tells you. You'll know it if you need more or even less sleep.

12. Eat properly. Is there a right diet to avoid worry? No. As in the case of sleep, there is no one right diet for everyone. In general, eat a balanced diet, take care not to overeat or undereat too often, take time when you eat so you will make good use of your food, and watch your weight, keeping in mind that some people are heavier than others simply because they are programmed to be. Don't become a fanatical worrier about your weight! Also take care not to use food as an antiworry agent, i.e., don't eat to try to make your worries go away.

13. Add structure to your life where you need it. Many everyday worries are directly related to disorganization: What have I forgotten? Will I get there in time? Why didn't I bring that brochure with me? Lists, reminders, a daily schedule, a basket next to the front door where you always put your car keys so you don't start off your day with a frantic search for your keys—these concrete bits of structure can dramatically reduce the amount of time you spend each day in useless or destructive worry. People put off setting up these structures because setting them up seems like such an onerous task; however, worrying or flubbing up are more onerous still!

14. Try doing something you like if you can't stop worrying. It is almost impossible to worry destructively if you are engaged in a task you enjoy. You may worry constructively—e.g., Am I turning this screw properly?—but you will not ruminate if you are doing something you like.

15. Try to turn off your gloom-and-doom generator. Many people who are problem-worriers have a tendency to "catastrophize" ordinary concerns. They can turn a minor problem into a potential disaster. By pumping up everyday worries into possible catastrophes, the worrier inflicts great pain upon himself. Why does anyone do this? There are many reasons but they all converge upon the inability to keep a realistic perspective when under even mild stress. The best way to counter this tendency to catastrophize small worries into huge ones is to "reality test" the severity of the situation by talking it over with a trusted ally or friend.

16. Don't watch too much TV or read too many newspapers and magazines. The media love bad news. Next to sex, bad news sells best. From the moment we turn on the TV or open the newspaper in the morning to the time we go to sleep at night watching the local news, the mass media lacerate us with upsetting stories. While it is true that we live in a world full of bad news, it is also true that good things happen every day. The media present life in a hideously unbalanced fashion. If you do not consciously limit the amount of media news you consume, you will become toxic with it. You will overdose on worry.

17. Keep a pad by your bed so you can write things down that you think of in the middle of the night. That way it is easier for you to let yourself go back to sleep since you know you have written down your concern and you won't forget it in the morning. When the light of day does come, you will likely be better equipped to deal with the problem, as all worries appear more severe in the middle of the night.

18. Don't drink excessively or use other drugs as a means of making your worries go away. Alcohol and other drugs provide short-term solace, but they create long-term problems. Alcohol and other drugs in fact render you much less capable of dealing with worry; they can make you depressed and can cause you to do things that will give you a lot to worry about later on.

19. Never worry alone. This maxim was taught to me when I was in my psychiatric training. When you share a worry, the worry almost always diminishes. You often find solutions to a problem when you talk it out, and the mere fact of putting it into words takes it out of the threatening realm of the imagination and into some concrete, manageable form.

20. Hire experts to guide you. For example, a financial consultant can turn your toxic worrying about money into constructive worrying, i.e., planning.

21. Use humor. One of the best ways of dealing with worry, or any stress in life, is to use humor. Make friends with amusing people. Laugh as much as you can. Keep in mind that it's OK to laugh, even when times are tough. Make jokes out of bad times. Not only is it OK, it's an excellent idea. Toxic worry almost always entails a loss of perspective; humor almost always restores it.

22. Maintain a reserve cash fund. This is a specific example of a general technique I call practical preparedness. Instead of waiting for a disaster and fretting over it, take action to prevent it. It will take no more time, probably less, than worrying about it.

23. Look for what is good in life. We are reminded so often of what is bad, we have to look for what is good. Take an inventory every day of what is good. Big things—children, friends, health, a mate—and little things—a pair of shoes you like, a door that closes without squeaking, a tuna fish sandwich that tastes good.

24. Try to reduce your exaggerations of risk. Remember that statistically speaking, you are much safer than you think. Although when you read about someone being struck by lightning it is a fallacy to say, "It can't happen to me," it is true that it probably won't.

25. Buy insurance. This will help take care of those times when disaster does strike.

26. Use teamwork. A mother wrote in a letter to her worried son, "There is nothing that as a team we can't take care of." This is great advice. When you are worried, bring your worry back to your team and talk it over with them.

27. Get enough light. People who live in the north do not get enough sunlight during the winter. They tend to become worried, gloomy, and depressed. A simple way to combat this is to make a deliberate effort on sunny days in winter to go outside as much as you can. Even if it's cold outside, the sunlight is good for your mood and will make you worry less.

28. Touch and be touched. Get plenty of physical contact. People do better if they are touched and hugged regularly. We are a social species. We do not do well in isolation. Find someone, or someones, you like a lot and hug them often. Stroking and massaging are good, too. Your children are particularly wonderful people to hug because they tend to love hugs un-self-consciously, at least while they are young.

29. Make a will. What happens to your estate (even if you do not think you have one, you do) after you die should be your decision, not the state's. This is one worry very easily taken care of by making a will. Don't put it off. Do it now.

30. Listen to music. In ways that we don't yet understand, music reduces tension and anxiety while often also improving performance. Music harmonizes the brain. Let music into your home and workplace.

31. Complain. One of my favorite responses in the survey of worry I conducted for this book was from the lady who said in reply to the question how she dealt with worry, "I bitch." It's good to let it out.

32. Try yoga, particularly Kundalini Yoga. Kundalini Yoga is an active form of yoga involving breathing exercises as well as movements of the body. There is a good how-to book about it, entitled, *Kundalini Yoga: Guidelines for Sadhana (Daily Practice),* published by Arcline Publications, Los Angeles, CA (ISBN # 0-89509-004-X).

33. Learn how to "give up" a worry. When you are in limbo, not knowing what will happen, perhaps in extreme straits waiting for a loved one to get better or to die or, at a less dire level, waiting to see if you'll pass the exam or get into the medical school, try to ask for help from God or from whatever is beyond human power, to help you give up your constant worrying. You do not have control in these situations. You might as well give it up to God. If you do not believe in God, give it up to fate. Try to develop in yourself the ability to give up a worry, instead of gnawing on it incessantly and having it gnaw on you. How? The methods vary from person to person, and from tradition to tradition. Most people grew up with certain methods of appealing to a higher power, whether it be prayer or song or group meditation or solitary thought. Many people also develop their own personal methods for giving up a worry, such as the woman in my survey who would imagine putting her worry in the palm of her hand, then blowing it away, or a patient of mine who deals with worry by buying someone else a present. See what works for you. Perhaps a talisman or good luck charm can help you give up your worry, perhaps sitting in a certain chair and envisioning a certain scene, perhaps driving to a specific place, or taking a walk down a certain street. Perhaps listening to a certain old song will do it for you, perhaps calling an old teacher, or reading a certain book. Whatever your methods are for giving up a worry, keep them in the back of your mind for when you need them most. One of the awful things about deep worry is that it can make you forget what you know, such as the best methods of making the worry go away.

34. Take a vacation. Obviously, this is not always possible. But if you find you are worrying more than ever, what you might need is some time off. Try to take this time away if you possibly can.

35. Reality-test your worry. Regain perspective. Ask someone who should know if what you're worrying about makes sense or if you may have exaggerated it. Remember Freud's advice: if you're worried about lions in Africa, that's OK. But if you're worried about lions in Venice, probably you should talk to someone.

36. Make friends with angels. Even if you do not believe in angels, make up fictional angels in your imagination and allow yourself to become friends with them. This is not psychotic; it is helpful management of worry. If you want a theoretical justification, you can think of it as a means of concretizing your positive introjects. But you really don't need justification. Just make friends with some angels. They come in handy on long drives alone.

37. Learn how to talk to yourself in a calming, reassuring way. Most worriers do just the opposite. They are forever yelling, "FIRE!" within their minds. Learn phrases you can repeat to yourself, such as "It's never as bad as you think," or "You're making a mountain out of a molehill," or "Remember last time? It all worked out OK." Watch out for what the cognitive therapists call your "automatic thoughts," the thoughts that pop into your head as you're dealing with a problem. If they tend to be negative, "Here we go again," or "I'm going to get screwed," or "I'll bet she meant that as a put-down," consider the possibility that you are wrong, that these negative conclusions are self-inflicted. Try reexamining the evidence and saying something more positive to yourself.

38. Don't be your own worst enemy. Don't undermine your own confidence and sense of personal power. Don't do to yourself what the competition can't do! Don't fall under the superstitious belief that you are obliged to torment yourself with worry.

39. Try not to invoke the "moral diagnosis." Labeling yourself a loser or a worry-wart won't help. Mental anguish is not a state to be despised. Rather it is a state to be understood and better managed. Think of your worrying as a subject of curiosity. Why am I doing this to myself? There is usually an answer. If you can't find it ask someone close to you or consult a professional.

40. Make sure you have the correct and complete diagnosis. As we have pointed out in this book, excessive worry often heralds a medical or psychiatric diagnosis. Check it out with your doctor. Make sure the diagnosis is complete as well as accurate. For example, people with panic disorder often suffer from another condition as well, such as depression. To give another example, ADD rarely occurs by itself. People with ADD usually contend with other problems as well, such as substance abuse, an associated learning disability, or depression.

41. Look back in your family tree for other worriers. One good way to understand yourself better is to look at the people who came before you. Not only your parents, but your whole extended family tree, as much of it as you can learn about.

42. Disengage from toxic worry the minute you feel it wrapping itself around you. You must do this deliberately, sometimes with great force. Get up out of your chair, walk around, pick up the telephone, turn on the TV, walk up and down stairs, take a shower, write a letter, talk to a friend. Do not settle into worry. The longer you let worry last, the harder it becomes to escape it.

43. Have faith. In what, of course, is up to you. If you believe in God, practice your belief. As the saying goes, "Let go, let God." Give over to the Lord the power that is the Lord's. Let go of your impossible need for control.

44. Remember that sometimes extreme worry is warranted. Sometimes you are right to worry. Your mind may be telling you that you are in a dangerous place and you should get out.

45. Sing. It is hard to worry and sing at the same time. If you want to sing a particular song, try this old one:

> What's the use of worrying?
> It never was worthwhile.
> So pack up your troubles in your old kit-bag,
> And smile, smile, smile.

46. Read. Have a stash of books you can get into easily. Maybe a mystery novel, or maybe a gardening book, or maybe a historical novel— some books you can read easily and you know will take you away.

47. Watch a video. Same idea as reading. If you own a VCR, keep a few videos on hand that you know will make you laugh. The Marx brothers, for example, are a pretty good antidote to anxiety.

48. Cry. Many adults cannot cry. They feel ashamed, embarrassed, or afraid. They fear that if they start to cry they will not be able to stop, or they fear losing control. But crying can be as essential a part of life as sneezing. Sometimes worry is a form of pent-up sadness. Sometimes what you really need and want to do is let it go in a torrent of tears. Crying eases the mind. A good cry can wash away bad worry.

49. Don't sweat the small stuff. And remember, from the widest perspective, it's all small stuff.

50. Remember that nothing lasts forever, not even worry.

Appendix
Where to Go for Help

If you found yourself, or someone you know, described in the pages of this book, that is good news, because there is help available for you. Probably the best place to start is your family physician. He or she can talk over your concerns with you and make a referral to a specialist if it seems appropriate.

The treatments for the various kinds of worry described in this book do not necessarily have to be supervised by a physician. Such remedies as exercise, meditation and/or prayer, reassurance, and connectedness are entirely safe and do not need the involvement of outside professionals. However, the initial phase of treatment is the identification of what is to be treated, or diagnosis, which should involve consultation with a medical professional. There are a number of medical conditions—such as hyperthyroidism or pancreatic cancer—which can cause symptoms of fear and anxiety as their initial manifestation. Only a physician will be able to diagnose such potentially severe underlying medical problems. Therefore, you should consult your doctor at the outset of any sort of treatment regimen, just to make sure you aren't missing something important. One of the great lessons we have learned is that worry isn't just in your mind. Like a dog barking, worry may be trying to tell you that there's trouble brewing in some other part of your body.

In addition to your family doctor, be sure to consult with experts in other fields when necessary, such as a financial advisor or a lawyer. Although such consultation does cost money, it can save you a lot more money—and worry—in the long run. One of the most important principles of successful worry management is, "Never worry alone." The corollary to that principle is, "Choose the best person to worry with for each specific problem." Sometimes the best person is a hired expert.

In addition to help from consultants of various kinds, a great deal of information is free and only a telephone call away. There are a number of organizations, both public and private, publishing the latest information on the various disorders of worry mentioned in this book.

For general information on anxiety, call:

1-888-8-ANXIETY (1-888-8-269438; you don't have to dial the "y" to get through). Operated by the National Institute of Mental Health, this line provides information in both English and Spanish. You can request pamphlets on phobias, post-traumatic stress disorder, obsessive-compulsive disorder, panic disorder, generalized anxiety disorder, and depression, as well as a listing of resources around the country where you can go for further assistance. The line is open all the time, and the service is free.

The following organizations also provide useful information:

Anxiety Disorders Association of America, Dept. A, 6000 Executive Blvd., Suite 513, Rockville, MD 20852. Tel.: 301-231-9350.

Freedom from Fear, 308 Seaview Ave., Staten Island, NY 10305. Tel.: 718-351-1717.

National Anxiety Foundation, 3135 Custer Drive, Lexington, KY 40517-4001. Tel.: 606-272-7166.

Obsessive-Compulsive (OC) Foundation, Inc., P.O. Box 70, Milford, CT 06460. Tel.: 203-878-5669.

American Psychiatric Association, 1400 K St. NW, Washington, DC 20006. Tel.: 202-682-6220.

American Psychological Association, 750 First St. NE, Washington, DC 20002-4242. Tel.: 202-336-5500.

Association for Advancement of Behavior Therapy, 305 Seventh Ave., New York, NY 10001. Tel.: 212-647-1890.

National Alliance for the Mentally Ill, 200 N. Glebe Rd., Suite 1015, Arlington, VA 22203-3754. Tel.: 800-950-NAMI (950-6264).

National Institute of Mental Health, toll-free information services: Depression: 1-800-421-4211. Panic and other anxiety disorders: 1-800-647-2642.

National Mental Health Association, 1201 Prince St., Alexandria, VA 22314-2971. Tel.: 703-684-7722.

National Mental Health Consumers' Self-Help Clearinghouse, 1211 Chestnut St., Philadelphia, PA 19107. Tel.: 800-553-4539.

Phobics Anonymous, P.O. Box 1180, Palm Springs, CA 92263. Tel.: 619-322-COPE (322-2673).

Society for Traumatic Stress Studies, 60 Revere Dr., Suite 500, Northbrook, IL 60062. Tel.: 847-480-9080.

In addition to these organizations and institutions, there are many books that provide useful information on worry in its various forms. Some of the best are:

GENERAL

Anxiety and Its Disorders, by David Barlow, Ph.D., Guilford Press, New York, 1988.

It's Not All in Your Head, by Susan Swedo and H. L. Leonard, Harper-Collins, New York, 1996.

Mastery of Your Anxiety and Panic II, by David Barlow and Michael Craske, Graywind Publications, Albany, NY, 1994.

Triumph Over Fear: A Book of Help and Hope for People with Anxiety, Panic Attacks, and Phobias, by J. Ross, Bantam, New York, 1994.

POST-TRAUMATIC STRESS DISORDER

Trauma and Recovery, by Judith Herman, Basic Books, New York, 1992.

Traumatic Stress, ed. by Bessel A. van der Kolk, M.D., et al., Guilford Press, New York, 1996.

OBSESSIVE-COMPULSIVE DISORDER

The Boy Who Couldn't Stop Washing: The Experience and Treatment of Obsessive-Compulsive Disorder, by Judith Rapoport, M.D., Dutton, New York, 1989.

Learning to Live With Obsessive Compulsive Disorder, by B. Livingston, OCD Foundation, Milford, CT, 1989. (Written for the families of those with OCD.)

ATTENTION DEFICIT HYPERACTIVITY DISORDER

Attention Deficit Hyperactivity Disorder: A Handbook for Diagnosis and Treatment, by Russell Barkley, Ph.D., Guilford Press, New York, 1990.

Driven to Distraction, by Edward M. Hallowell, M.D., and John J. Ratey, M.D., Pantheon, New York, 1994.

Answers to Distraction, by Edward M. Hallowell, M.D., and John J. Ratey, M.D., Pantheon, New York, 1995.

The Hyperactive Child, Adolescent, and Adult, by Paul Wender, Oxford University Press, New York, 1987.

SOCIAL FEARS
Dying of Embarrassment: Help for Social Anxiety and Phobias, by B.G. Markway et al., New Harbinger Publications, Oakland, CA, 1992.

WORRY IN CHILDREN
When You Worry About the Child You Love, by Edward M. Hallowell, M.D., Simon and Schuster, New York, 1996.
The Emotional Problems of Normal Children, by Stanley Turecki, M.D., Bantam, New York, 1994.
It's Nobody's Fault, by Harold Koplewicz, M.D., Times Books, New York, 1996.

WITH THANKS TO

My family heads the list. My wife, Sue, and my three children, Lucy, Jack, and Tucker, have put up with my typing away endlessly in my office on the third floor of our home. They resisted the temptation to interrupt me many, many times. I'll welcome the chance to be interrupted now! There is no one in the world I worry over more than you four, so you take care, you hear?

Linda Healey, my editor at Pantheon on this and two previous books, makes everything I write better. She has a knack for knowing what I need to do. She is a magically skillful editor, and I am very lucky to have found her.

My agent, Jill Kneerim, shepherded me through this book, and, once again, was always there when I needed her. She is the best.

I have consulted many experts in the field of worry, some in person, some by reading their books, some in correspondence. Dr. Tom Gutheil, my old teacher at Mass Mental, got me thinking about *managing* worry, instead of just suffering it, when he told tell me, "Never worry alone." That was excellent advice. Dr. David Barlow's authoritative text, *Anxiety and Its Disorders,* was my most valuable reference source. The great Walter Jackson Bate, Samuel Johnson scholar at Harvard, not only helped me with his definitive biography of Johnson, but also read and offered suggestions on the Johnson chapter in this book. Dr. Jeff Sutton, both a neuroscientist and a psychiatrist, aided me in understanding some of the biological basis of worry. Dr. Bart Herskovitz helped me to define the basic equation of worry. Dr. John Ratey, my erstwhile co-author, gave me ongoing encouragement as well as specific suggestions. John has been an inspiration to me ever since he demonstrated the importance of connectedness to me when he was my chief resident at Mass Mental.

I consulted other experts along the way. Dr. Joseph Coyle stressed the physical nature of worry. Dr. Leston Havens gave me advice about the psychology of worry. Both Drs. Coyle and Havens and most of my mentors in psychiatry counseled me always to balance the psychological and the physiological explanations of human nature. For this I am deeply grateful. It is essential that we use *both* biology and psychology to understand ourselves, not one or the other.

Drs. Edward Khantzian and Charles Magraw, the people I consulted most regularly, gave me sane guidance when I needed it and always had an encouraging word.

The most valuable experts, of course, and also my most generous teachers, have been my patients. Some of them contributed material to this book directly, but they all inform its every page. Thank you, all of you, for teaching me, from your hearts, about worry, and about life.

Sharon Wohlmuth, the gifted photographer/creator of *Sisters* and *Mothers and Daughters,* took my photograph for this book. She has become a dear friend and I thank her for her help.

Many other friends helped me out. Peter Metz told me not to worry, the book would be good. Susan Grace Galassi, and her husband, Jonathan, read early drafts and made shrewd suggestions, while also giving warm encouragement. Michael Thompson played tennis with me when I was full of writer's cobwebs, and always had warmheart words. To all my friends I owe a huge debt; thank you a million times over!

My colleagues at my center in Concord helped me in many different ways. Dr. Paul Sorgi, Christine DeCamillis, and Colleen Keaney kept me on track week after week. Many thanks!

In addition to Sue and my kids, my extended family has helped me in this project, as in all others. The book is dedicated to my cousin, Josselyn Bliss, for she has done more to prevent worry in my life over the past forty-seven years than any other person. The other members of her family, and my cousin Jamie, as well as my brothers, John and Ben, have helped me enormously over the years as well.

Thanks to you all, and to the many others whom I didn't mention by name. There is a key to how I manage worry: it is you.

INDEX